ADVENTURE STORIES FOR GIRLS

ADVENTURE STORIES FOR GIRLS

OCTOPUS BOOKS

First published in 1978
This revised edition first published in 1988 by
Octopus Books Limited
Michelin House
81 Fulham Road
London
SW3 6RB

ISBN 0 7064 3275 4

Line illustrations by David Godfrey (207, 160, 179); Lee Noel (99, 255) (both represented by David Lewis); José María Miralles (243); Phil Stevenson (62, 69, 266)
Colour illustrations by Susan Hunter
Cover artwork by Andrew Walker

Printed in Czechoslovakia
52164

Contents

Contents *(contd.)*

Colour Illustrations

THE LEFT-HANDED SWORD

E. Nesbit

His name was Hugh de Vere Coningsby Drelincourt, and he lived with his mother in a queer red-roofed house incoherently built up against the corner of the old castle that stands on the edge of the hill looking out over the marshes. Once the castle and the broad lands about it had all belonged to the Drelincourts, and they had kept great state there. But they had been loyal to King Charles, and much went then. Later Hugh's father had spent what was left on lawyers, gaining nothing. And now only the castle itself was left, and some few poor fields. His mother was Lady Drelincourt by rights, and he himself, since his father was dead, was Sir Hugh, but there was no money to keep up the title, so she called herself plain Mrs Drelincourt, and he was just Hugh.

They lived very simply and kept cows and pigs, and Hugh did lessons with his mother and was very happy. There was no money to send him to school, but he minded that less than his mother did. It was a pleasant little house, and all the furniture in it was old and very beautiful, carved oak and polished apple-wood, and delicate lovely glass and china. But there was often only bread and cheese to put on the china plates, and cold water from the well in the castle courtyard to fill the Venice glasses.

There were relics too—an old silver bowl with raised roses round the brim, and a miniature or two, and a little sword that some boy Drelincourt had worn many many years ago. This sword Hugh had for his very own, and it hung over the mantelpiece in his bedroom. And the sword had been made for a left-handed little boy, because all the Drelincourts are left-handed.

Hugh used to wander about the old place, climb the old walls, and explore the old passages, always dreaming of the days when the castle was noisy with men-at-arms, and gay with knights and ladies.

Now the wild grasses and wallflowers grew in the rugged tops of the walls, and the ways to the dungeons were choked with fern and bramble. And there was no sound but the cooing of pigeons and the hum of wild bees in the thyme that grew over the mounds beyond the moat.

'You spend all your time dreaming,' his mother used to say, as she sat darning his stockings or mending his jackets, 'and the castle comes through all your clothes.'

'It comes through all everything,' Hugh would say. 'I wish I could see it as it was in the old days.'

'You never will,' said his mother, 'and isn't it beautiful enough as it is? We've got a lovely home, my son, and we've got each other.'

Then he would hug her and she would hug him, and he would try to pay more attention to his lessons, and not so much to the castle.

He loved his mother very much, and did many things to please her—lessons and errands and work about the house; and once when she was ill, and a silly woman from the village came in to do the housework, he mounted guard on the stairs all day, so that the woman should not disturb his mother with silly questions about where the soda was kept, and what dusters she was to use.

So now he tried to think less of the castle; but for all his trying the castle filled his life with dreams. He explored it and explored, till he thought he knew every inch of it.

One wall of Hugh's bedroom was just the thick, uneven stones of the old castle wall, against which the house was built. They were grey with time, and the mortar was crumbling from between them; the fires he had in the room in the winter, when he had colds, dried the mortar and made it crumble more than ever. There was an arch in this wall that had been filled up, in forgotten days, with heavy masonry. Hugh used to watch that arch, and wish it was a door that he could get through. He could not find the other side, though he had searched long and well.

'I expect it was only a cupboard,' his mother said, as she peeled the potatoes or made the puddings; 'I wouldn't worry about if it I were you.'

Hugh did not worry about it, but he never forgot it. And when the next winter he had one of those bad colds that made his mother so anxious, and caused him to be tormented with linseed poultices and water-gruel and cough-mixture and elder-flower tea, he had plenty of time to think, and he thought of the arch, and of nothing else.

And one night, when his mother had gone to bed, tired out with taking all sorts of care of him, he could not sleep, and he got out of bed and fingered the stones inside the arch as he had so often done before, to see if any one of them was loose. Before, none ever had been—but now . . . oh, joy! one was loose. The fire had dried the old mortar to mere dust that fell away as Hugh's fingers pulled at the stone—weakly, because his cold had really been a very severe one. He put out all the strength he could, however, and pulled and tugged and twisted, and shifted the stone, till it was quite loose in its place, and with the help of the poker he prised it out, and with difficulty put it on the floor.

He expected to seek a dark hole, through which a cold wind would blow; but no cold wind blew, and curiously enough, the hole was not dark. There was a faint grey light, like the light of daylight in a room with a small window.

Breathless and eager, he pulled out another stone. Then his heart gave a jump and stood still. For he heard something moving on the other side of the arch—not the wind or rustling leaves or creaking tree-boughs, but something *alive*. He was quite as brave as most boys, and, though his heart was going like a clock when you have wound it up, and forgotten to put on the pendulum, had the courage to call out:

'Hullo! who's there?'

'Me,' said a voice on the other side of the arch. 'Who are you?'

'Who are you, if it comes to that?' Hugh asked cautiously.

'Sir Hugh de Drelincourt,' said the voice from the hole in the wall.

'Bud thad's *by* dabe,' said Hugh with the cold in his head; and as he spoke another stone disappeared, and the hole was larger. Now in silence two pairs of hands worked at loosening the stones from the crumbling mortar.

'Ibc cobing through,' said Hugh suddenly; 'the hole's big edough.'

And he caught the little sword from the wall, and he set his knee on the bottom of the hole and through he went.

Through into a little room whose narrow window showed the blue daylit sky—a room with not much in it but a bed, a carved stool, and a boy of his own age, dressed in the kind of dress you see in the pictures of the little sons of Charles I.

'Why, you're me!' the strange boy said, and flung his arms round him. And Hugh felt that he spoke the truth. Then a sudden fear caught at him; he threw off the other boy, and turned to go back quickly into his own room, with the dancing firelight and the cough-mixture and the elder-flower tea.

And then a greater fear wiped out the first, as a great wave might wash out a tear-mark on the sea-sand. For the hole in the wall was no more there. All the wall was unbroken and straight and strongly stony. And the boy who had been so like him was there no longer. And he himself wore the laced breeches, the little handsome silk coat, the silk stockings and buckled shoes of that other boy. And at his side hung his own little left-handed sword.

'Oh, I'm dreaming,' said Hugh. 'That's all right. I wonder what I shall dream next!'

He waited. Nothing happened. Outside the sun shone, and a rainbow-throated pigeon perched in the window preened her bright feathers.

So presently he opened the heavy door and went down a winding stair. At its foot was a door opening on the arched gateway that he knew so well. A serving-man in brown came to him as he passed through the door.

'You lazy young lie-a-bed,' he said, 'my lady has asked for you three times already——'

'Where is my lady?' Hugh asked, without at all knowing that he was going to ask it.

'In her apartments, where any good son would have been with her,' said the serving-man.

'Show me where,' said Hugh.

The serving-man looked at him, and nodded to a group of men in armour who stood in the gatehouse.

''Mazed,' he said, touching his forehead, ''mazed with the cannons and the shoutings and the danger, and his father cold in the chapel, and . . . Come, lad,' he said, and took Hugh's hand in his.

Hugh found himself led into a long, low room, with a square wooden pattern on the ceiling, pictures along one side, and windows along the other. A lady, with long curls, a low-necked dress, and a lace collar, was stooping over an open chest from which came the gleam of gold and jewels. She rose as his shoes pattered on the floor.

'My son,' she said, and clasped him in her rich-clad arms, and her face, and her embrace, were the embrace and the face of his own mother, who wore blue cotton and washed the dishes in the little red-tiled castle house.

'All is lost,' said the lady, drawing back from the embrace. 'The wicked Roundheads have almost battered in the east wall. Two hours at least our men can keep them out. Your father's at peace, slain while you were asleep. All our wealth—I must hide it for you and for the upkeep of our ancient name. Ralph and Henry will see to it, while you and I read the morning prayers.'

Hugh is quite sure that in that long pleasant gallery, with the morning sun gay in the square garden outside, he and his mother read the prayers, while some serving-men staggered out with chest upon chest of treasure.

'Now,' his mother said, when the prayers were ended, 'all this is in the vault beneath your bed-chamber. We will go there, and I will lie down a little on your bed and rest, for, indeed, I am weary to death. Let no man enter.'

'No man shall enter. I will keep guard,' said Hugh, 'on the stairs without,' and felt proudly for his little sword at his side.

When they had come to that little room he kissed the silk-clad lady that was his mother, and then took up his station on the stairs outside.

And now he began to hear more and more loudly the thunder of artillery, the stamping and breathless shouting of fighting men. He sat there very still, and there was no sound from the chamber where his mother lay.

Long, very long, he waited there, and now there was no thought in him of its being a dream. He *was* Hugh de Drelincourt; the Roundheads were sacking his father's castle; his father lay in the chapel, dead, and his mother slept on the bed inside. He had promised that none should enter. Well, they should not.

And at long last came the clatter of mail on the stairs, and the heavy sound of great boots, and, one above another, heads in round steel caps, and shoulders in leather came round the newel of the little stair.

'A page-in-waiting,' cried the first man; 'where is your lady, my young imp?'

'My lady sleeps,' Hugh found himself saying.

'We have a word for your lady's ears,' said the round-capped man, trying to push past.

'Her ears are not to be soiled by your words,' Hugh was surprised to hear himself say.

'Don't thou crow so loud, my young cockerel,' the man said, 'and stand back, and make room for thy betters.'

The round caps and leather shoulders pushed upward, filling, crowding the staircase.

'Stand back!' they all cried, and the foremost drew a big sword, and pointed it, laughing, at the child.

''Tis thou shalt stand back!' Hugh cried, and drew his own little left-handed blade. A great shout of laughter echoed in the narrow staircase, and someone cried, 'Have a care, Jeremiah, lest he spit thee like a woodcock!'

Hugh looked at the coarse, laughing faces, and saw, without looking at it, the dear quiet face that lay in the room behind him.

'You shall *not* speak to her!' he cried, and thrust furiously with the little sword. The thrust was too fierce. It carried him forward on to the point of that big sword. There was a sharp pain in his side, a roaring in his ears: through it all he heard: 'This for our pains: a dead woman and a little child slain!' Then the roaring overpowered everything—the roaring and the pain, and to the sound of heavy feet that clattered down the stairs he went out of life, clutching to the last the little sword that had been drawn for her.

He was clutching the iron edge of his bed, his throat was parched and stiff, and the pain in his side was a burning pain, almost unbearable. 'Mother!' he called, 'Mother, I've had such a dreadful dream, and my side does hurt so!'

She was there even as he called—alive, living, tenderly caressing him. But not even in the comfort of her living presence, with the warmth of linseed poultices to the side that hurt, of warm lemon drink to the parched throat, could he tell a word of his dream. He has never told it to anyone but me.

'Now let this be a lesson to you, my darling,' his mother said; 'you must *not* climb about in those windy walls and arches, in this sort of weather. You're quite feverish. No wonder you've had bad dreams.'

But the odd thing is that nothing will persuade Hugh that this was only a dream. He says he knows it all happened—and indeed, the history books say so too. Of course, I should not believe that he had gone back into the past, as he says, and seen Drelincourt Castle taken by the Roundheads, but for one curious little fact.

When Hugh got well of his pleurisy, for that was the name the doctors gave to the pain that came from a dream sword-wound in his side, he let his mother have no peace till she sent for Mr Wraight, the builder at Dymchurch, and had all the stones taken out of that arch. And, sure enough, beyond it was a little room with a narrow window and no door. And the builder's men took up the stone floor, because nothing else would satisfy the boy, and sure enough again, there was a deep vault, and in it, piled on top of the other, chests upon chests of silver plate, and gold plate, and money, and jewels, so that now Lady Drelincourt can call herself by that gentle title, and Sir Hugh was able to go to Eton and to Oxford, where I met him, and where he told me this true tale.

And if you say that the mother of Hugh de Drelincourt, who died to defend his mother from the Roundheads, could not have been at all like the mother of little Hugh, who lived in the red-tiled castle house, and drank the elder-flower tea, and loved the left-handed sword that hung over his mantelpiece, I can only say, that mothers are very like mothers here, there, and everywhere else, all the world over, when all is said and done.

JOURNEY TO DRUID'S BOTTOM

Nina Bawden

At the beginning of the Second World War, Carrie, aged eleven, and Nick, her younger brother, are evacuated to Wales. There they have to stay with the bad-tempered shop-keeper, Mr Evans, and his kind, timid sister, Auntie Lou.

Nick had been born a week before Christmas. On his birthday Auntie Lou gave him a pair of leather gloves with fur linings and Mr Evans gave him a Holy Bible with a soft, red cover and pictures inside.

Nick said, 'Thank you, Mr Evans,' very politely, but without smiling. Then he put the Bible down and said, 'Auntie Lou, what *lovely* gloves, they're the best gloves I've ever had in my whole life. I'll keep them for ever and ever, even when I've grown too big for them. My tenth birthday gloves!'

Carrie felt sorry for Mr Evans. She said, 'The Bible's lovely too, you are lucky, Nick.' And later, when she and Nick were alone, 'It was kind of him, really. I expect when he was a little boy he'd rather have had a Bible for his birthday than anything else in the world, even a bicycle. So it was kind of him to think you might feel like that, too.'

'But I didn't want a Bible,' Nick said. 'I'd rather have had a knife. He's got some smashing knives in the shop on a card by the door. A Special Offer. I've been looking at them every day and hoping I'd get one and he knew that's what I was hoping. I looked at them and he saw me looking. It was just mean of him to give me a rotten old Bible instead.'

'You shall not speak to her!' he cried, and thrust furiously with the little sword. (p.14)

There was a box on the desk and inside it, resting on velvet, a small, ivory skull. (p.25)

'Perhaps he'll give you a knife for Christmas,' Carrie said, though she doubted it, in her heart. If Mr Evans really knew Nick wanted a knife, he was unlikely to give him one. He thought it was bad for people to get what they wanted. 'Want must be your master,' was what he always said.

Carrie sighed. She didn't like Mr Evans, no one could, but Nick hating him so much made her dislike him less. 'He's getting us a goose for Christmas,' she said, 'that'll be nice, won't it? I've never had a goose.'

'I'd rather have a turkey!' Nick said.

The goose was to come from Mr Evans's older sister who lived outside the town and kept poultry. Nick and Carrie had never heard of her until now. 'She's a bit of an invalid,' Auntie Lou said. 'Bed-fast much of the time now. Poor soul, I think of her but I daren't go to see her. Mr Evans won't have it. Dilys has made her bed and turned her back on her own people, is what he says, and that's that. She married Mr Gotobed, the mine-owner, you see.'

The children didn't see but didn't like to ask. It made Auntie Lou nervous to be asked direct questions. So they said, 'Gotobed's a funny name, isn't it?'

'English, of course,' Auntie Lou said. 'That upset Mr Evans to start with! An Englishman *and* a mine-owner, too! She married him just after our dad was killed down the pit—dancing on our father's grave, was what Mr Evans called it. The Gotobeds were bad owners, you see; our dad was killed by a rock fall that would never have happened, Mr Evans says, if they'd taken proper safety precautions. Not that it was young Mr Gotobed's fault, *his* father was alive then, and in charge of the mine, but Mr Evans says all that family was tarred with the same brush, only thinking of profits. So it made him hard against Dilys. Even now her husband's dead, he's not willing to let bygones be bygones.'

Though he was willing to accept a goose at Christmas, apparently. 'They're always fine birds,' Auntie Lou said—as if this was sufficient reason. 'Hepzibah Green rears them. She's good with poultry. Fine, light hand with pastry, too. You should taste her mince pies! Hepzibah looks after Dilys *and* the place best as she can. Druid's Bottom was a fine house once, though it's run down since Mr Gotobed passed on and Dilys took bad. Needs a man's eye, Mr Evans says, though he's not willing to give it, and Dilys won't ask, of course.' She sighed gently. 'They're both proud people, see?'

'Druid's *Bottom*,' Nick said, and giggled.

'Bottom of Druid's Grove,' Auntie Lou said. 'That's the cwm where the yew trees grow. Do you remember where we picked those blackberries up by the railway line? The deep cwm, just before the tunnel?'

Nick's eyes widened. He said, '*That dark place!*'

'It's the yews make it dark,' Auntie Lou said. 'Though it's a queer place, too. Full of the old religion still, people say—not a place to go after dark. Not alone, anyway. I know I'd not care to, though I wouldn't let Mr Evans hear me say it. Wicked foolishness, he calls that sort of talk. There's nothing to be afraid of on this earth he says, not for those who trust in the Lord.'

Carrie was excited; she loved old, spooky tales. 'I wouldn't be afraid of the Grove,' she boasted. 'Nick might be, he's a *baby*, but I'm not scared of anything. Can I come with you, Auntie Lou, when you go to fetch the goose?'

But as it turned out, she and Nick went alone. On what was, perhaps, the most important journey they ever made together.

They were due to go to Druid's Bottom two days before Christmas, but Auntie Lou was ill. She coughed all morning and her eyes were red-rimmed. After midday dinner, Mr Evans came into the kitchen and looked at her, coughing over the sink. 'You're not fit to go out,' he said. 'Send the children.'

Auntie Lou coughed and coughed. 'I thought I'd go tomorrow instead. Hepzibah will know I'm not coming now it's getting so late. I'll be better tomorrow.'

'I'll want you in the shop, Christmas Eve,' Mr Evans said. 'The children can go. Earn their keep for a change.'

'It'll be a heavy goose, Samuel.'

'They can manage between them.'

There was a short silence. Auntie Lou avoided the children's eyes. Then she said, uneasily, 'It'll be dark before they get back.'

'Full moon,' Mr Evans said. He looked at the children, at Nick's horrified face, and then at Auntie Lou. She began to blush painfully. He said in a quiet and ominous voice, 'You've not been putting ideas in their heads, I do hope!'

Auntie Lou looked at the children, too. Her expression begged them not to give her away. Carrie felt impatient with her—no grown-up should be so weak and so silly—but she was sorry as well. She said innocently, 'What ideas, Mr Evans? Of course we'd love to go, we don't mind the dark.'

'There's nothing *to* mind,' she said to Nick as they trudged along the railway line. 'What is there to be scared of? Just a few old trees.'

Nick said nothing; only sighed.

Carrie said, 'All that queer place stuff is just Auntie Lou being superstitious. You know how superstitious she is, touching wood and not walking under ladders and throwing salt over her shoulder when she's spilled some. I'm not surprised Mr Evans gets cross with her sometimes. She's so scared, she'd jump at her own shadow.'

But when they reached the Grove, Carrie felt a little less bold. It was growing dusk; stars were pricking out in the cold sky above them. And it was so quiet, suddenly, that their ears seemed to be singing.

Carrie whispered, 'There's the path down. By that stone.'

Nick's pale face glimmered as he looked up at her. He whispered back, 'You go. I'll wait here.'

'Don't be silly.' Carrie swallowed—then pleaded with him. 'Don't you want a nice mince pie? We might get a mince pie. And it's not far. Auntie Lou said it wasn't far down the hill. Not much more than five minutes.'

Nick shook his head. He screwed up his eyes and put his hands over his ears.

Carrie said coldly, 'All right, have it your own way. But it'll be dark soon and you'll be really scared then. Much more scared by yourself than you would be with me. Druids and ghosts coming to get you! Wild animals too—you don't *know*! I wouldn't be surprised if there were wolves in these mountains. But *I* don't care. Even if I hear them howling and snapping their jaws I shan't hurry!'

And she marched off without looking back. White stones marked the path through the yew trees and in the steep places there were steps cut in the earth and shored up with wood. She hadn't gone far when she heard

Nick wailing behind her. 'Carrie, wait for me, *wait* . . .' She stopped and he skidded into her back. 'Don't leave me, Carrie!'

'I thought it was you leaving *me*,' she said, making a joke of it, to comfort him, and he tried to laugh but it turned into a sob in his throat.

He hung on to the back of her coat, whimpering under his breath as she led the way down the path. The yew trees grew densely, some of them covered with ivy that rustled and rattled. Like scales, Carrie thought; the trees were like live creatures with scales. She told herself not to be stupid, but stopped to draw breath. She said, 'Do be quiet, Nick.'

'Why?'

'I don't know,' Carrie said. 'Something . . .'

She couldn't explain it. It was such a strange feeling. As if there was something here, something *waiting*. Deep in the trees or deep in the earth. Not a ghost—nothing so simple. Whatever it was had no name. Something old and huge and nameless, Carrie thought, and started to tremble.

Nick said, 'Carrie . . .'

'Listen.'

'What for?'

'*Sssh* . . .'

No sound at first. Then she heard it. A kind of slow, dry whisper, or sigh. As if the earth were turning in its sleep. Or the huge, nameless thing were breathing.

'Did you hear?' Carrie said. 'Did you *hear*?'

Nick began to cry piteously. Silence now, except for his weeping.

Carrie said, dry-mouthed, 'It's gone now. It wasn't anything. There's nothing there, really.'

Nick gulped, trying hard to stop crying. Then he clutched Carrie. 'Yes, there is! There is *now*!'

Carrie listened. It wasn't the sound she had heard before but something quite different. A queer, throaty, chuckling, gobbling sound that seemed to come from somewhere above them, higher up the path. They stood still as stone. The sound was coming closer.

'*Run*,' Carrie said. She began to run, stumbling. The big bag they had brought for the goose caught between her legs and almost threw her down but she recovered her balance, her feet slipping and sliding. She ran, and Nick ran behind her, and the creature, whatever it was, the gobbling *Thing*, followed them. It seemed to be calling to them and Carrie thought of fairy tales she had read—you looked back at something behind you and were caught in its spell! She gasped, 'Don't look back, Nick, whatever you do.'

The path widened and flattened as it came out of the Grove and she caught Nick's hand to make him run faster. Too fast for his shorter legs and he fell on his knees. He moaned, as she pulled him up, 'I can't, I *can't*, Carrie . . .'

She said, through chattering teeth, 'Yes you *can*. Not much farther.'

They saw the house then, its dark, tall-chimneyed bulk looming up, and lights in the windows. One light quite high up and one low down, at the side. They ran, on rubbery legs, through an open gate and across a dirt yard towards the lit window. There was a door but it was shut. They flung themselves against it.

Gobble-Gobble was coming behind them, was crossing the yard.

'Please,' Carrie croaked. 'Please.' Quite sure that it was too late, that the creature would get them.

But the door opened inward, like magic, and they fell through it to light, warmth, and safety.

★ ★ ★ ★

A warm, safe, lighted place.

Hepzibah's kitchen was always like that, and not only that evening. Coming into it was like coming home on a bitter cold day to a bright, leaping fire. It was like the smell of bacon when you were hungry; loving arms when you were lonely; safety when you were scared . . .

Not that they stopped being scared at once, that first, frightened time. They were indoors, it was true, but the door was still open. And the woman seemed in no hurry to close it and shut out the dangerous night; she simply stood, looking down at the children and smiling. She was tall with shining hair the colour of copper. She wore a white apron, the sleeves of her dress were rolled up, showing big, fair, freckled arms, and there was flour on her hands.

Carrie saw her, then the room. A big, stone-flagged kitchen, shadowy in the corners but bright near the fire. A dresser with blue and white plates; a scrubbed, wooden table; a hanging oil lamp. And Albert Sandwich, sitting at the table with an open book where the light fell upon it.

He opened his mouth to speak but Carrie had turned. She said, 'Shut the door!' The woman looked puzzled—people were always so *slow*, Carrie thought. She said desperately, 'Miss Evans sent us for the goose. But something chased us. We ran and ran but it chased us. Sort of *gobbling*.'

The woman peered where she pointed, out into the night.

'Oh, shut the *door*,' Carrie cried. 'It'll come *in*.'

The woman smiled broadly. She had lovely, white teeth with a gap in the middle. 'Bless you, love, it's only Mister Johnny. I didn't know he was out.'

'He went to shut up the chickens,' Albert Sandwich said. 'I expect he went for a walk after.'

'But it wasn't a *person*,' Carrie said, speaking slowly to make them understand. She wasn't so frightened now. Albert had spoken so calmly that it made her calm too. She said, 'It didn't talk, it went *gobble-gobble*.'

'That's Mister Johnny's way of talking,' Albert Sandwich said. 'You must admit, Hepzibah, it could frighten someone.' He looked at Carrie, quite sternly. 'Though I expect you frightened him just as much. How would you feel if people ran away from you when you didn't mean to hurt them?'

Hepzibah called softly into the darkness. 'It's all right, Mister Johnny, all right, come on in.' Her voice wasn't Welsh. A different, throatier, accent.

Someone appeared in the doorway and stood close to Hepzibah, as if for protection. A small person in a tweed suit and a spotted bow tie with a shy, scrumpled-up face. He tried to smile but he couldn't smile properly: one side of his mouth seemed dragged down.

Hepzibah said, 'This is Mister Johnny Gotobed, children. Mister Johnny, say how-do-you-do to our visitors, will you?'

He looked at her and made that queer sound in his throat. Chuckle-gobble—only now it did seem like talking. Some strange, unknown language. He rubbed his right hand on his trousers and looked at it. Then held it out, shakily.

Carrie couldn't move. Though he wasn't a ghost she was still too scared to touch that small, shaky hand. But Nick said, 'Hallo, Mister Johnny,' and went up to him as if it were the easiest and most natural thing in the world. I'm Nick,' he said. 'Nicholas Peter Willow and I'm just ten. It was my birthday last week. And Carrie, my sister, will be twelve next May.'

'Hch. Harch-a. Chala. Larschla,' Mister Johnny said. He spat a bit as he spoke and Carrie dreaded the moment when she would have to shake hands and be spat at.

But Hepzibah saved her. She said, 'The goose is ready for you. But you'll take a little something first, won't you? Albert, take Carrie to fetch the goose while I set the table.'

Albert took a candle from the dresser and lit it. Carrie followed him, through a door at the back of the kitchen, down a stone passage into a dairy. The goose lay, neatly trussed, on a cold, marble slab. There were speckly eggs in trays on the shelf, slabs of pale, oozy butter, and a big bowl of milk with a skin of cream on the top.

Carrie felt hollow with hunger. She said, 'I thought Mr Gotobed was dead. Mr Evans's sister's husband.'

'That's not him,' Albert said. 'Mister Johnny is a sort of distant cousin of *that* Mr Gotobed. He used to live in Norfolk but when his parents died he came here with Hepzibah. She's been his nurse since he was born.' He looked at Carrie as he set the candle down to give himself two free hands for the goose. 'Bit of a shock, I suppose, the first time.'

Holding the bag open so he could put the goose in, Carrie said, 'Is he mad?'

'No more than a lot of people. Just a bit simpler than some. Innocent, is what Hepzibah calls him.' Albert pushed the goose down and tied the string round the top of the bag. 'She's a witch,' he said calmly.

'A *witch*?'

He grinned at her. 'Oh, not what you're thinking of. Not black cats and broomsticks! Just what country people call a wise woman. When I was ill she gave me some herbs made into a medicine and I got better quite quickly. The doctor was amazed—he had thought I was going to die. I never thought that lad would see the spring, was what he told Hepzibah.'

'So that's where you've been. In bed, ill!' Carrie said, and then blushed. This might sound, to Albert, as if she'd been looking for him.

She said quickly, 'What's been wrong with you?'

'Pneumonia. Rheumatic fever,' Albert said. 'Just about every medical crime in the calendar. It's lucky I was sent here, to Hepzibah, or I'd be pushing up daisies. Though it wasn't luck, altogether. I told the billeting officer I liked books and he said there was a library here. And there is. A proper library, in a *house*!' He spoke as if this still amazed him. 'Shall I show you?'

They left the goose in the dairy and went back along the passage and through a swing door with baize on one side into a wide, dark hall where a grandfather clock ticked in one corner and a small oil lamp threw shadows. 'Here,' Albert said, opening another door and holding his candle high so that Carrie could see. Books—shelves and shelves of books, reaching up to the ceiling, most of them bound in pale calf with gold lettering on the spines. 'Marvellous, isn't it?' Albert said in a reverent voice as if he were speaking in church. 'And to think no one uses it! Only me!'

'Where's Mrs Gotobed?' Carrie asked.

'*Gone* to bed.' Albert laughed and his spectacles flashed. 'She's dying, I think.'

The idea of someone dying, here in this house, frightened Carrie. She looked up at the ceiling and shivered.

Albert said, 'She's been ill for ages. I read to her sometimes when she isn't too tired. Do you like reading?'

'Not much,' Carrie said. This wasn't quite true but all these books made her heart sink. So many words written; it would take a lifetime to read them.

'What do you do then?' Albert asked in a tone of surprise. 'When you're not at school, I mean.'

'I help in the shop sometimes. Mr Evans's shop. Nick's not allowed now, but I am. And I play on the mountains and I slide down the slag heap.'

Albert looked as if he thought these were rather childish occupations. But he said, politely and kindly, 'If you don't care for books much, perhaps you'd like to see the screaming skull. There's an interesting story about it. Untrue, I daresay, but interesting all the same.'

He advanced into the room and set the candle down on a desk. Carrie hung back. 'It sounds horrible.'

'Oh it's only a skull,' Albert said. 'Come and see.'

There was a box on the desk and inside it, resting on velvet, a small, ivory skull. Pearly-smooth and grinning.

'Touch it,' Albert said, and Carrie touched the top lightly. It was warmer than she'd expected. She said, 'What's the story?'

'Ask Hepzibah,' Albert said. 'She tells it better than I would. It's supposed to be the skull of an African boy who was brought here during the slave trade, but I don't believe it. It's not a boy's skull. You just look.'

He picked the skull out of its velvet bed and showed it to Carrie. The bottom jaw was missing and some of the teeth from the top, but the sockets were there. 'It had sixteen teeth in the top jaw,' Albert said, 'which means its wisdom teeth too. And you don't get your wisdom teeth until you're eighteen at least. I looked it up in *Gray's Anatomy* and that's what it says. And you see those wiggly lines on the top? That's the sutures, where the bones are starting to join up. So it must have been a grown person's skull but it's too small and light for an adult male, so it must have been a woman. What I think is, there's an Iron Age settlement at the top of the Grove, and I think someone found this woman's skull there, and made up a story about it, the way people do.'

He put the skull back and looked at Carrie. 'That's *me* making up a story, of course. I don't *know*. But you can test the age of the bones. I'd like to take this skull to the British Museum one day and get them to test it. The British Museum can find anything out, it's the most marvellous place in the world. Have you been there?'

'Once,' Carrie said. She remembered going with her father one day, and being dreadfully bored. All those old things in glass cases. 'It's very interesting,' she said, to please Albert.

His eyes danced as if he guessed what she really had thought. He put the skull back in its box and the lid on the top. He said, 'Would your brother like to see it?'

'No, he'd be scared,' Carrie said. 'That sort of thing scares him.'

Scared her a little too, though she wouldn't admit it to Albert. Not the skull, but the thought of the live person it had once been: a woman with eyes and hair who was dead now. Just pale, shiny bone in a box in a dark, musty library where the shelves of old books reached up into shadow. She said, 'Shouldn't we go back to the kitchen? I expect tea's ready by now.'

And it was. The cloth on the table was so stiffly starched that it stuck out at the corners. There was a huge plate of mince pies, golden brown and dusted with sugar, a tall jug of milk, a pink ham, and slices of bread thickly spread with the lovely, pale, sweaty butter Carrie had seen in the dairy. Nick was already at the table, tucking in, and Mister Johnny sat beside him, a white napkin round his neck. He chuckled excitedly as Carrie came in and she said, 'Hallo, Mister Johnny, can I sit next to you?'

Albert looked at her approvingly. He said, 'Hepzibah, I've been showing Carrie the skull. Tell her that old tale, will you? She'd like to hear it. Though it's a lot of old nonsense, of course!'

Hepzibah put a brown teapot down on the table and aimed a fake blow at his ear. 'I'll give you nonsense, my lad! Mister Albert Uppity-Know-All. You don't know so much yet, or you'd know that wise people don't mock what they don't understand!'

'Charsh, hcha,' Johnny Gotobed said.

'That's right, Mister Johnny.' Hepzibah bent over him, cutting up the ham on his plate. 'You've got more sense in your little finger than he's got in his clever young head.'

'I'm sorry, Hepzibah,' Albert said. 'Please tell Carrie.'

'Oh, it's a foolish tale, his young Lordship thinks.' Hepzibah sat down, smiling at Carrie and smoothing her copper hair back. She had a rather broad face, pale as cream, and dotted with freckles. Carrie thought she looked beautiful: so warm and friendly and kind.

She said, 'Please, Miss Green.'

'Hepzibah. That's my name.'

'Please, Hepzibah.'

'Well then. Perhaps I might, since you ask me so nicely. Fill up your plate now—go on, you can manage a bit more, growing girl like you. It's not home-cured ham, I'm sorry to say, though it would have been once. They had a good home farm, the Gotobeds. They made their money out of sugar and slaves and then moved here and made a fine place of the house. I heard about them long before I came to live here. When I was in service in Norfolk with Mister Johnny's parents, they used to tell me about their rich cousins in Wales and the screaming skull and the curse on the house. It's a queer old story, too . . .'

She sipped her tea thoughtfully, staring in front of her and frowning a little. Then she put her cup down and began to speak in a soft, sad, dreaming voice that seemed to weave a spell of silence in the room. 'He was brought here, the African boy, when he was ten or so. It was the fashion at that time for rich people to have a little black page, dressed up in silks and satins and riding on the step of their carriage. So they fetched this poor innocent away from his family, across the sea, to a strange land. And of course he cried, as any child might cry, taken from his mother. The Gotobeds weren't hard people, the young ladies gave him sweets and toys and made a real pet of him, but they couldn't comfort him, and in the end they said he could go back home one day. Perhaps they meant it, but he died of a fever his first winter here and it must have seemed to him that they'd broken a promise. So he put a curse on the house. He said, on his death-bed, that they could bury his body but when his flesh had rotted they must dig up his skull and keep it in the house or some dreadful disaster would come. The walls would crumble. And they believed him, people believed in curses then, and they did what he said. The skull has been kept in the library ever since—it only left the house once, when old Mr Gotobed's grandmother was a girl. She couldn't abide the thought of it, sitting there grinning, it gave her bad dreams she said, so she took it one morning and hid it in the stable loft. Nothing happened at all, she waited all day to see, and then went to bed, no doubt very pleased with herself. But in the middle of the night there was a great scream—like a screech owl—and a loud crashing sound. When the family came running down in their night-clothes, all the crockery was smashed in the kitchen, all the glass in the dining-room, every mirror in the house cracked to pieces! Then of course the girl said what she'd done and they fetched the skull back and had no trouble after . . .'

'With sixteen teeth in its upper jaw,' Albert said. 'Count your teeth, Nick. You're the same age as that boy would have been, see if *you've* got sixteen!'

Nick blinked at him.

Carrie said, 'It's a lovely story, Albert Clever Sandwich, don't you dare spoil it!' Though she thought, secretly, that it was a comfort to know it might not be true. She said in a sentimental voice, 'A lovely *sad* story. Poor little African boy, all that way from home!'

Nick sighed, very deeply. Then he got down from his chair and went to stand by Hepzibah. He put his head on her shoulder and she turned and picked him up and sat him on her broad lap, her arms tight about him. She rocked him gently and he nestled close and put his thumb in his mouth. The room was quiet except for the hiss of the fire. Even Mister Johnny sat still, as if the story had lulled him, though perhaps it was only the soft sound of Hepzibah's voice.

Carrie looked at Nick on Hepzibah's lap and felt jealous. Of Nick, because she would like to be sitting there, she wasn't too big. And of Hepzibah, because she was comforting Nick in a way she knew she could never do.

She said, 'We ought to go, really. Auntie Lou knew we might stay to tea but it's getting late now and she'll start to worry.'

Then she thought of going back, through the dark trees, and her stomach seemed to sink down inside her. That noise she had heard, that deep, sighing breath!

Perhaps what she was feeling showed in her face because Albert said, 'I'll come with you if you like. As far as the railway.'

'Not with your chest, you won't,' Hepzibah said.

Albert grinned. 'I could hardly go without it, could I? Go on, Hepzibah, I'm strong as a horse now and I could do with some air.'

'Not night air,' Hepzibah said. 'Besides, I want you to come and read to Mrs Gotobed while I settle her, it puts her mind at rest for the night. Mister Johnny will see them safe through the Grove.' She smiled at Carrie, her eyes so bright, suddenly, that Carrie felt they saw straight into her mind. Though this was an odd feeling, it wasn't frightening somehow. Hepzibah said, 'You'll be all right with him. No harm of the kind you're afraid of, ever comes near the innocent.'

Carrie said, 'Mr Evans says no harm can ever come to those who trust in the Lord.'

'Perhaps that's another way of saying the same thing,' Hepzibah said. She gave Nick a last hug and tipped him off her lap. 'Come again, love. Both of you, whenever you like. Are you ready, Mister Johnny?'

He seemed to understand her. He was on his feet, holding out his hand to Nick who went to him and took it trustingly.

DICING WITH DEATH

Rider Haggard

Deep in the rock beneath a gigantic mountain in eastern Africa lay two secret, connecting chambers—the Chamber of the Dead, housing the ancestors of the Kukuana tribe, and the Treasure House of King Solomon, where tons of gold, diamonds and ivory were stored. To this frightening but intriguing place three Britishers had come in search of a lost comrade: Allan Quatermain, the narrator of the following story, Sir Henry Curtis and Captain John Good, of the Royal Navy. Despite warnings from Infadoos, a friendly officer in the Kukuana Army, the three had allowed themselves to be led into the Treasure House by an aged sorceress. Now this treacherous crone had lowered a heavy stone slab, barring the entrance, and they were trapped.

I can give no adequate description of the horrors of the night which followed. Mercifully they were to some extent mitigated by sleep, for even in such a position as ours wearied nature will sometimes assert itself. But I, at any rate, found it impossible to sleep much. Putting aside the terrifying thought of our impending doom—for the bravest man on earth might well quail from such a fate as awaited us, and I never made any pretensions to be brave—the *silence* itself was too great to allow of it.

Reader, you may have lain awake at night and thought the quiet oppressive, but I say with confidence that you can have no idea what a vivid, tangible thing is perfect stillness. On the surface of the earth there is always some sound or motion, and though it may in itself be imperceptible, yet it deadens the sharp edge of absolute silence. But here there was none. We were buried in the bowels of a huge snow-clad peak. Thousands of feet above us the fresh air rushed over the white snow, but no sound of it reached us. We were separated by a long tunnel and five feet of rock even from the awful Chamber of the Dead; and the dead make no noise. The crashing of all the artillery of earth and heaven could not have come to our ears in our living tomb. We were cut off from every echo of the world—we were as men already in the grave.

Then the irony of the situation forced itself upon me. There around us lay treasures enough to pay off a moderate national debt, or to build a fleet of iron-clad ships, and yet we would have bartered them all gladly for the faintest chance of escape. Soon, doubtless, we should be rejoiced to exchange them for a bit of food or a cup of water, and, after that, even for the privilege of a speedy end to our sufferings. Truly wealth, which men spend their lives in acquiring, is a valueless thing at the last.

And so the night wore on.

'Good,' said Sir Henry's voice at last, to the captain, and it sounded awful in the intense stillness, 'how many matches have you in the box?'

'Eight, Curtis.'

'Strike one and let us see the time.'

He did so, and in contrast to the dense darkness the flame nearly blinded us. It was five o'clock by my watch. The beautiful dawn was now blushing on the snow-wreaths far over our heads, and the breeze would be stirring the night mists in the hollows.

'We had better eat something and keep up our strength,' I suggested.

'What is the good of eating?' answered Good; 'the sooner we die and get it over the better.'

'While there is life there is hope,' said Sir Henry.

Accordingly we ate and sipped some water, and another period of time passed. Then Sir Henry suggested that it might be well to get as near the door as possible and yell, on the faint chance of somebody catching a sound outside. Accordingly Good, who, from long practice at sea, has a fine piercing note, groped his way down the passage and set to work. I must say that he made a most diabolical noise. I never heard such yells; but it might have been a mosquito buzzing for all the effect they produced.

After a while he gave it up and came back very thirsty, and had to drink. Then we stopped yelling, as it encroached on the supply of water.

So we sat down once more against the chests of useless diamonds in that dreadful inaction which was one of the hardest circumstances of our fate; and I am bound to say that, for my part, I gave way in despair. Laying my head against Sir Henry's broad shoulder I burst into tears; and I think that I heard Good gulping away on the other side, and swearing hoarsely at himself for doing so.

Ah, how good and brave that great man was! Had we been two frightened children, and he our nurse, he could not have treated us more tenderly. Forgetting his own share of miseries, he did all he could to soothe our broken nerves, telling stories of men who had been in somewhat similar circumstances, and miraculously escaped; and when these failed to cheer us, pointing out how, after all, it was only anticipating an end which must come to us all, that it would soon be over, and that death from exhaustion was a merciful one (which is not true). Then, in a diffident sort of way, as once before I had heard him do, he suggested that we should throw ourselves on the mercy of a higher power, which for my part I did with great vigour.

His is a beautiful character, very quiet, but very strong.

And so somehow the day went as the night had gone, if, indeed, one can use these terms where all was densest night, and when I lit a match to see the time it was seven o'clock.

Once more we ate and drank, and as we did so an idea occurred to me.

'How is it,' said I, 'that the air in this place keeps fresh? It is thick and heavy, but it is perfectly fresh.'

'Great heavens!' said Good, starting up, 'I never thought of that. It can't come through the stone door, for it's air-tight, if ever a door was. It must come from somewhere. If there were no current of air in the place we should have been stifled or poisoned when we first came in. Let us have a look.'

It was wonderful what a change this mere spark of hope wrought in us. In a moment we were all three groping about on our hands and knees, feeling for the slightest indication of a draught.

For an hour or more we went on feeling about, till at last Sir Henry and I gave it up in despair, having been considerably hurt by constantly knocking our heads against tusks, chests, and the sides of the chamber. But Good still persevered, saying, with an approach to cheerfulness, that it was better than doing nothing.

'I say, you fellows,' he said presently, in a constrained sort of voice, 'come here.'

Needless to say we scrambled towards him quickly enough.

'Quatermain, put your hand here where mine is. Now, do you feel anything?'

'I *think* I feel air coming up.'

'Now listen.' He rose and stamped upon the place, and a flame of hope shot up in our hearts. *It rang hollow.*

With trembling hands I lit a match. I had only three left, and we saw that we were in the angle of the far corner of the chamber, a fact that accounted for our not having noticed the hollow sound of the place during our former exhaustive examination. As the match burnt we scrutinized the spot. There was a join in the solid rock floor, and, great heavens! There, let in level with the rock, was a stone ring. We said no word, we were too excited, and our hearts beat too wildly with hope to allow us to speak. Good had a knife, at the back of which was one of those hooks that are made to extract stones from horses' hoofs. He opened it, and scratched round the ring with it. Finally he worked it under, and levered away gently for fear of breaking the hook. The ring began to move. Being of stone it had not rusted fast in all the centuries it had lain there, as would have been the case had it been of iron. Presently it was upright. Then he thrust his hands into it and tugged with all his force, but nothing budged.

'Let me try,' I said impatiently, for the situation of the stone, right in the angle of the corner, was such that it was impossible for two to pull at once. I took hold and strained away, but no results.

Then Sir Henry tried and failed.

Taking the hook again, Good scratched all round the crack where we felt the air coming up.

'Now, Curtis,' he said, 'tackle on, and put your back into it; you are as strong as two. Stop,' and he took off a stout black silk handkerchief, which, true to his habits of neatness, he still wore, and ran it through the ring. 'Quatermain, get Curtis round the middle and pull for dear life when I give the word. *Now.*'

Sir Henry put out all his enormous strength, and Good and I did the same, with such power as nature had given us.

'Heave! heave! It's giving,' gasped Sir Henry; and I heard the muscles of his great back cracking. Suddenly there was a grating sound, then a rush of air, and we were all on our backs on the floor with a heavy flagstone upon the top of us. Sir Henry's strength had done it, and never did muscular power stand a man in better stead.

'Light a match, Quatermain,' he said, as soon as we had picked our-

'Here's the bottom,' he said. 'Thank goodness!' (p.35)

He spread out his hood more than ever and Rikki-tikki saw the spectacle-mark on the back of it. *(p.41)*

selves up and got our breath; 'carefully, now.'

I did so, and there before us, heaven be praised! was the *first step of a stone stair*.

'Now what is to be done?' asked Good.

'Follow the stair, of course, and trust to providence.'

'Stop!' said Sir Henry; 'Quatermain, get the bit of biltong [dried meat] and the water that is left; we may want them.'

I went, creeping back to our place by the chests for that purpose, and as I was coming away an idea struck me. We had not thought much of the diamonds for the last twenty-four hours or so; indeed, the very idea of diamonds was nauseous, seeing what they had entailed upon us; but, reflected I, I may as well pocket some in case we ever should get out of this ghastly hole. So I just put my fist into the first chest and filled all the available pockets of my old shooting-coat and trousers, topping up—this was a happy thought—with a few handful of big ones out of the third chest. Also, by an afterthought, I stuffed a basket, which, except for one water-gourd and a little biltong, was empty now, with great quantities of the stones.

'I say, you fellows,' I sang out, 'won't you take some diamonds with you? I've filled my pockets and the basket.'

'Oh, come on, Quatermain, and hang the diamonds!' said Sir Henry. 'I hope that I may never see another.'

As for Good, he made no answer. And curious as it may seem to you, my reader, sitting at home at ease and reflecting on the vast, indeed the immeasurable, wealth which we were thus abandoning, I can assure you that if you had passed some twenty-eight hours with next to nothing to eat and drink in that place, you would not have cared to cumber yourself with diamonds whilst plunging down into the unknown bowels of the earth, in the wild hope of escape from an agonizing death. If from the habits of a lifetime, it had not become a sort of second nature with me never to leave anything worth having behind if there was the slightest chance of my being able to carry it away, I am sure that I should not have bothered to fill my pockets and that basket.

'Come on, Quatermain,' repeated Sir Henry, who was already standing on the first step of the stone stair. 'Steady, I will go first.'

'Mind where you put your feet, there may be some awful hole underneath,' I answered.

'Much more likely to be another room,' said Sir Henry, while he descended slowly, counting the steps as he went.

When he got to 'fifteen' he stopped. 'Here's the bottom,' he said. 'Thank goodness! I think it's a passage. Follow me down.'

Good went next, and I came last, carrying the basket, and on reaching the bottom lit one of the two remaining matches. By its light we could just see that we were standing in a narrow tunnel, which ran right and left at right angles to the staircase we had descended. Before we could make out any more, the match burnt my fingers and went out. Then arose the delicate question of which way to go. Of course, it was impossible to know what the tunnel was, or where it led to, and yet to turn one way might lead us to safety, and the other to destruction. We were utterly perplexed, till suddenly it struck Good that when I had lit the match the draught of the passage blew the flame to the left.

'Let us go against the draught,' he said; 'air draws inwards, not outwards.'

We took this suggestion, and feeling along the wall with our hands, whilst trying the ground before us at every step, we departed from that accursed treasure chamber on our terrible quest for life. If ever it should be entered again by living man, which I do not think probable, he will find tokens of our visit in the open chests of jewels, the empty lamp, and the white bones of poor Foulata.

When we had groped our way for about a quarter of an hour along the passage, suddenly it took a sharp turn, or else was bisected by another which we followed only in course of time to be led into a third. And so it went on for some hours. We seemed to be in a stone labyrinth which led nowhere. What all these passages are, of course I cannot say, but we thought that they must be the ancient workings of a mine, of which the various shafts and adits travelled hither and thither as the ore led them. This is the only way in which we could account for such a multitude of galleries.

At length we halted, thoroughly worn out with fatigue and with that hope deferred which makes the heart sick, and ate up our poor remaining piece of biltong and drank our last sup of water, for our throats were like lime-kilns. It seemed to us that we had escaped death in the darkness of the treasure chamber only to meet him in the darkness of the tunnels.

As we stood, once more utterly depressed, I thought that I caught a sound, to which I called the attention of the others. It was very faint and very far off, but it *was* a sound, a faint, murmuring sound, for the others heard it too, and no words can describe the blessedness of it after all those house of utter, awful stillness.

'By heaven! It's running water,' said Good.. 'Come on.'

Off we started again in the direction from which the faint murmur seemed to come, groping our way as before along the rocky walls. I remember that I laid down the basket full of diamonds, wishing to be rid of its weight, but on second thoughts took it up again. One might as well die rich as poor, I reflected. As we went the sound became more and more audible, till at last it seemed quite loud in the quiet. On, yet on; now we could distinctly make out the unmistakable swirl of rushing water. And yet how could there be running water in the bowels of the earth? Now we were quite near it, and Good, who was leading, swore that he could smell it.

'Go gently, Good,' said Sir Henry, 'we must be close.' *Splash!* and a cry from Good.

He had fallen in.

'Good! Good! Where are you?' we shouted, in terrified distress. To our intense relief an answer came back in a choky voice.

'All right; I've got hold of a rock. Strike a light to show me where you are.'

Hastily I lit the last remaining match. Its faint gleam discovered to us a dark mass of water running at our feet. How wide it was we could not see, but there, some way out, was the dark form of our companion hanging on to a projecting rock.

'Stand clear to catch me,' sung out Good. 'I must swim for it.'

Then we heard a splash, and a great struggle. Another minute and he grabbed at and caught Sir Henry's outstretched hand, and we had pulled him up high and dry into the tunnel.

'My word!' he said, between his gasps, 'that was touch and go. If I hadn't managed to catch that rock, and known how to swim, I should have been done. It runs like a mill-race, and I could feel no bottom.'

We dared not follow the banks of the subterranean river lest we should fall into it again in the darkness. So after Good had rested a while, and we had drunk our fill of the water, which was sweet and fresh, and washed our faces, that needed it sadly, as well as we could, we started from the banks of this African Styx, and began to retrace our steps along the tunnel, Good dripping unpleasantly in front of us. At length we came to another gallery leading to our right.

'We may as well take it,' said Sir Henry wearily; 'all roads are alike here; we can only go on till we drop.'

Slowly, for a long, long while, we stumbled, utterly exhausted, along this new tunnel, Sir Henry now leading the way. Again I thought of abandoning that basket, but did not.

Suddenly he stopped, and we bumped up against him.

'Look!' he whispered, 'is my brain going, or is that light?'

We stared with all our eyes, and there, yes, there, far ahead of us, was a faint, glimmering spot, no larger than a cottage window pane. It was so faint that I doubt if any eyes, except those which, like ours, had for days seen nothing but blackness, could have perceived it at all.

With a gasp of hope we pushed on. In five minutes there was no longer any doubt; it *was* a patch of faint light. A minute more and a breath of real live air was fanning us. On we struggled. All at once the tunnel narrowed, Sir Henry went on his knees. Smaller yet it grew, till it was only the size of a large fox's earth—it was *earth* now, mind you: the rock had ceased.

A squeeze, a struggle, and Sir Henry was out, and so was Good, and so was I, dragging the basket after me; and there above us were the blessed stars, and in our nostrils was the sweet air. Then suddenly something gave, and we were all rolling over and over and over through grass and bushes and soft, wet soil.

The basket caught in something and I stopped. Sitting up I halloed lustily. An answering shout came from just below, where Sir Henry's wild career had been checked by some level ground. I scrambled to him, and found him unhurt, though breathless. Then we looked for Good. A little way off we discovered him also, jammed in a forked root. He was a good deal knocked about, but soon came to himself.

We sat down together, there on the grass, and the revulsion of feeling was so great that really I think we cried with joy. We had escaped from that awful dungeon, which was so near to becoming our grave. Surely some merciful power guided our footsteps to the jackal hole, for that is what it must have been, at the termination of the tunnel. And see, yonder on the mountains the dawn we had never thought to look upon again was blushing rosy red.

Presently the grey light stole down the slopes, and we saw that we were at the bottom, or rather, nearly at the bottom, of the vast pit in front of the entrance to the cave. Doubtless those awful passages, along which we had wandered the lifelong night, had been originally in some way connected with the great diamond mine. As for the subterranean river in the bowels of the mountain, heaven only knows what it is, or whence it flows, or whither it goes. I, for one, have no anxiety to trace its course.

Lighter it grew, and lighter yet. We would see each other now, and such a spectacle as we presented I have never set eyes on before or since. Gaunt-cheeked, hollow-eyed wretches, smeared all over with dust and mud, bruised, bleeding, the long fear of imminent death yet written on our countenances, we were, indeed, a sight to frighten the daylight. And yet it is a solemn fact that Good's eyeglass was still fixed in Good's eye. I doubt whether he had ever taken it out at all. Neither the darkness, nor the plunge in the subterranean river, nor the roll down the slope, had been able to separate Good and his eyeglass.

Presently we rose, fearing that our limbs would stiffen if we stopped there longer, and commenced with slow and painful steps to struggle up the sloping sides of the great pit. For an hour or more we toiled steadfastly up the blue clay, dragging ourselves on by the help of the roots and grasses with which it was clothed. But now I had no more thought of leaving the basket; indeed, nothing but death should have parted us.

At last it was done, and we stood by the great road.

At the side of the road, a hundred yards off, a fire was burning in front of some huts, and round the fire were figures. We staggered towards them, supporting one another, and halting every few paces. Presently one of the figures rose, saw us and fell on to the ground, crying out for fear.

'Infadoos, Infadoos! It is we, thy friends.'

He rose; he ran to us, staring wildly, and still shaking visibly with fear.

'Oh, my lords, my lords, it is indeed you come back from the dead! Come back from the dead!'

And the old warrior flung himself down before us, and clasping Sir Henry's knees, he wept aloud for joy.

RIKKI-TIKKI-TAVI

Rudyard Kipling

At the hole where he went in
Red-Eye called to Wrinkle-Skin.
Hear what little Red-Eye saith:
'Nag, come up and dance with death!'

Eye to eye and head to head,
    (*Keep the measure, Nag.*)
This shall end when one is dead;
    (*At thy pleasure, Nag.*)
Turn for turn and twist for twist—
    (*Run and hide thee, Nag.*)
Hah! The hooded Death has missed!
    (*Woe betide thee, Nag!*)

This is the story of the great war that Rikki-tikki-tavi fought single-handed, through the bathrooms of the big bungalow in Segowlee cantonment. Darzee, the tailor-bird, helped him, and Chuchundra, the musk-rat, who never comes out into the middle of the floor, but always creeps round by the wall, gave him advice; but Rikki-tikki did the real fighting.

He was a mongoose, rather like a little cat in his fur and his tail, but quite like a weasel in his head and his habits. His eyes and the end of his restless nose were pink; he could scratch himself anywhere he pleased, with any leg, front or back, that he chose to use; he could fluff up his tail till it looked like a bottle-brush, and his war-cry, as he scuttled through the long grass, was: '*Rikk-tikk-tikki-tikki-tchk!*'

One day, a high summer flood washed him out of the burrow where he lived with his father and mother, and carried him, kicking and clucking, down a roadside ditch. He found a little wisp of grass floating there, and clung to it till he lost his senses. When he revived, he was lying in the hot sun on the middle of a garden path, very draggled indeed, and a small boy was saying: 'Here's a dead mongoose. Let's have a funeral.'

'No,' said his mother; 'let's take him in and dry him. Perhaps he isn't really dead.'

They took him into the house, and a big man picked him up between his finger and thumb, and said he was not dead but half choked; so they wrapped him in cotton-wool, and warmed him, and he opened his eyes and sneezed.

'Now,' said the big man (he was an Englishman who had just moved into the bungalow); 'don't frighten him, and we'll see what he'll do.'

It is the hardest thing in the world to frighten a mongoose, because he is eaten up from nose to tail with curiosity. The motto of all the mongoose family is, 'Run and find out'; and Rikki-tikki was a true mongoose. He looked at the cotton-wool, decided that it was not good to eat, ran all round the table, sat up and put his fur in order, scratched himself, and jumped on the small boy's shoulder.

'Don't be frightened, Teddy,' said his father. 'That's his way of making friends.'

'Ouch! He's tickling under my chin,' said Teddy.

Rikki-tikki looked down between the boy's collar and neck, snuffed at his ear, and climbed down to the floor, where he sat rubbing his nose.

'Good gracious,' said Teddy's mother, 'and that's a wild creature! I suppose he's so tame because we've been kind to him.'

'All mongooses are like that,' said her husband. 'If Teddy doesn't pick him up by the tail, or try to put him in a cage, he'll run in and out of the house all day long. Let's give him something to eat.'

They gave him a little piece of raw meat. Rikki-tikki liked it immensely, and when it was finished he went out into the verandah and sat in the sunshine and fluffed up his fur to make it dry to the roots. Then he felt better.

'There are more things to find out about in this house,' he said to himself, 'than all my family could find out in all their lives. I shall certainly stay and find out.'

He spent all that day roaming over the house. He nearly drowned himself in the bath-tubs, put his nose into the ink on a writing-table, and burnt it on the end of the big man's cigar, for he climbed up in the big man's lap to see how writing was done. At nightfall he ran into Teddy's nursery to watch how kerosene-lamps were lit, and when Teddy went to bed Rikki-tikki climbed up too; but he was a restless companion, because he had to get up and attend to every noise all through the night, and find out what made it. Teddy's mother and father came in, the last thing, to look at their boy, and Rikki-tikki was awake on the pillow. 'I don't like that,' said Teddy's mother; 'he may bite the child.' 'He'll do no such thing,' said the father. 'Teddy's safer with that little beast than if he had a bloodhound to watch him. If a snake came into the nursery now——'

But Teddy's mother wouldn't think of anything so awful.

Early in the morning Rikki-tikki came to early breakfast in the verandah riding on Teddy's shoulder, and they gave him banana and some boiled egg; and he sat on all their laps one after the other, because every well-brought-up mongoose always hopes to be a house-mongoose some day and have rooms to run about in, and Rikki-tikki's mother (she used to live in the General's house at Segowlee) had carefully told Rikki what to do if ever he came across white men.

Then Rikki-tikki went out into the garden to see what was to be seen. It was a large garden, only half cultivated, with bushes as big as summer-houses of Marshal Niel roses, lime and orange trees, clumps of bamboos, and thickets of high grass. Rikki-tikki licked his lips. 'This is a splendid hunting-ground,' he said, and his tail grew bottle-brushy at the thought of it, and he scuttled up and down the garden, snuffing here and there till he heard very sorrowful voices in a thorn-bush.

It was Darzee, the tailor-bird, and his wife. They had made a beautiful nest by pulling two big leaves together and stitching them up the edges with fibres, and had filled the hollow with cotton and downy fluff. The nest swayed to and fro, as they sat on the rim and cried.

'What is the matter?' asked Rikki-tikki.

'We are very miserable,' said Darzee. 'One of our babies fell out of the nest yesterday, and Nag ate him.'

'H'm!' said Rikki-tikki, 'that is very sad—but I am a stranger here. Who is Nag?'

Darzee and his wife only cowered down in the nest without answering, for from the thick grass at the foot of the bush there came a low hiss—a horrid cold sound that made Rikki-tikki jump back two clear feet. Then inch by inch out of the grass rose up the head and spread hood of Nag, the big black cobra, and he was five feet long from tongue to tail. When he had lifted one-third of himself clear of the ground, he stayed balancing to and fro exactly as a dandelion-tuft balances in the wind, and he looked at Rikki-tikki with the wicked snake's eyes that never change their expression, whatever the snake may be thinking of.

'Who is Nag?' said he. '*I* am Nag. The great god Brahm put his mark upon all our people when the first cobra spread his hood to keep the sun off Brahm as he slept. Look, and be afraid!'

He spread out his hood more than ever, and Rikki-tikki saw the spectacle-mark on the back of it that looks exactly like the eye part of a hook-and-eye fastening. He was afraid for the minute; but it is impossible for a mongoose to stay frightened for any length of time, and though Rikki-tikki had never met a live cobra before, his mother had fed him on dead ones, and he knew that all a grown mongoose's business in life was to fight and eat snakes. Nag knew that too, and at the bottom of his cold heart he was afraid.

'Well,' said Rikki-tikki, and his tail began to fluff up again, 'marks or no marks, do you think it is right for you to eat fledglings out of a nest?'

Nag was thinking to himself, and watching the least little movement in the grass behind Rikki-tikki. He knew that mongooses in the garden meant death sooner or later for him and his family, but he wanted to get Rikki-tikki off his guard. So he dropped his head a little, and put it on one side.

'Let us talk,' he said. 'You eat eggs. Why should not I eat birds?'

'Behind you! Look behind you!' sang Darzee.

Rikki-tikki knew better than to waste time in staring. He jumped up in the air as high as he could go, and just under him whizzed by the head of Nagaina, Nag's wicked wife. She had crept up behind him as he was talking, to make an end of him; and he heard her savage hiss as the stroke missed. He came down almost across her back, and if he had been an old mongoose he would have known that then was the time to break her back with one bite; but he was afraid of the terrible lashing return-stroke of the cobra. He bit, indeed, but did not bite long enough, and he jumped clear of the whisking tail, leaving Nagaina torn and angry.

'Wicked, wicked Darzee!' said Nag, lashing up as high as he could reach toward the nest in the thorn-bush; but Darzee had built it out of reach of snakes, and it only swayed to and fro.

Rikki-tikki felt his eyes growing red and hot (when a mongoose's eyes grow red, he is angry), and he sat back on his tail and hind legs like a little kangaroo, and looked all round him, and chattered with rage. But Nag and Nagaina had disappeared into the grass. When a snake misses its stroke, it never says anything or gives any sign of what it means to do next. Rikki-tikki did not care to follow them, for he did not feel sure that he could manage two snakes at once. So he trotted off to the gravel path near the house, and sat down to think. It was a serious matter for him.

If you read the old books of natural history, you will find they say that when the mongoose fights the snake and happens to get bitten, he runs off and eats some herb that cures him. That is not true. The victory is only a matter of quickness of eye and quickness of foot—snake's blow against mongoose's jump—and as no eye can follow the motion of a snake's head when it strikes, that makes things much more wonderful than any magic herb. Rikki-tikki knew he was a young mongoose, and it made him all the more pleased to think that he had managed to escape a blow from behind. It gave him confidence in himself, and when Teddy came running down the path, Rikki-tikki was ready to be petted.

But just as Teddy was stooping, something flinched a little in the dust, and a tiny voice said: 'Be careful. I am death!' It was Karait, the dusty brown snakeling that lies for choice on the dusty earth; and his bite is as dangerous as the cobra's. But he is so small that nobody thinks of him, and so he does the more harm to people.

Rikki-tikki's eyes grew red again, and he danced up to Karait with the peculiar rocking, swaying motion that he had inherited from his family. It looks very funny, but it is so perfectly balanced a gait that you can fly off from it at any angle you please; and in dealing with snakes this is an advantage. If Rikki-tikki had only known, he was doing a much more dangerous thing than fighting Nag, for Karait is so small, and can turn so quickly, that unless Rikki bit him close to the back of the head, he would get the return-stroke in his eye or lip. But Rikki did not know: his eyes were all red, and he rocked back and forth, looking for a good place to hold. Karait struck out. Rikki jumped sideways and tried to run in, but the wicked little dusty grey head lashed within a fraction of his shoulder, and he had to jump over the body, and the head followed his heels close.

Teddy shouted to the house: 'Oh, look here! Our mongoose is killing a snake'; and Rikki-tikki heard a scream from Teddy's mother. His father ran out with a stick, but by the time he came up, Karait had lunged out once too far, and Rikki-tikki had sprung, jumped on the snake's back, dropped his head far between his forelegs, bitten as high up the back as he could get hold, and rolled away. That bite paralysed Karait, and Rikki-tikki was just going to eat him up from the tail, after the cutom of his family at dinner, when he remembered that a full meal makes a slow mongoose, and if he wanted all his strength and quickness ready, he must keep himself thin.

He went away for a dust-bath under the castor-oil bushes, while Teddy's father beat the dead Karait. 'What is the use of that?' thought Rikki-tikki. 'I have settled it all'; and then Teddy's mother picked him up from the dust and hugged him, crying that he had saved Teddy from death, and Teddy's father said that he was a providence, and Teddy looked on with big scared eyes. Rikki-tikki was rather amused at all the fuss, which, of course, he did not understand. Teddy's mother might just as well have petted Teddy for playing in the dust. Rikki was thoroughly enjoying himself.

That night, at dinner, walking to and fro among the wine-glasses on the table, he could have stuffed himself three times over with nice things; but he remembered Nag and Nagaina, and though it was very pleasant to be patted and petted by Teddy's mother, and to sit on Teddy's shoulder, his eyes would get red from time to time, and he would go off into his long war-cry of '*Rikk-tikk-tikki-tikki-tchkâ*'

Teddy carried him off to bed, and insisted on Rikki-tikki sleeping under his chin. Rikki-tikki was too well bred to bite or scratch, but as soon as Teddy was asleep he went off for his nightly walk round the house, and in the dark he ran up against Chuchundra, the musk-rat, creeping round by the wall. Chuchundra is a broken-hearted little beast. He whimpers and cheeps all the night, trying to make up his mind to run into the middle of the room, but he never gets there.

'Don't kill me,' said Chuchundra, almost weeping. 'Rikki-tikki, don't kill me.'

'Do you think a snake-killer kills musk-rats?' said Rikki-tikki.

'Those who kill snakes get killed by snakes,' said Chuchundra, more sorrowfully than ever. 'And how am I to be sure that Nag won't mistake me for you some dark night?'

'There's not the least danger,' said Rikki-tikki; 'but Nag is in the garden, and I know you don't go there.'

'My cousin Chua, the rat, told me——' said Chuchundra, and then he stopped.

'Told you what?'

'H'sh! Nag is everywhere, Rikki-tikki. You should have talked to Chua in the garden.'

'I didn't—so you must tell me. Quick, Chuchundra, or I'll bite you!'

Chuchundra sat down and cried till the tears rolled off his whiskers. 'I am a very poor man,' he sobbed. 'I never had spirit enough to run out into the middle of the room. H'sh! I mustn't tell you anything. Can't you *hear*, Rikki-tikki?'

Rikki-tikki listened. The house was as still as still, but he thought he could just catch the faintest *scratch-scratch* in the world—a noise as faint as that of a wasp walking on a window pane—the dry scratch of a snake's scales on brickwork.

'That's Nag or Nagaina,' he said to himself; 'and he is crawling into the bathroom sluice. You're right, Chuchundra; I should have talked to Chua.'

He stole off to Teddy's bathroom, but there was nothing there, and then to Tddy's mother's bathroom. At the bottom of the smooth plaster wall there was a brick pulled out to make a sluice for the bath-water, and as Rikki-tikki stole in by the masonry curb where the bath is put, he heard Nag and Nagaina whispering together outside in the moonlight.

'When the house is emptied of people,' said Nagaina to her husband, '*he* will have to go away, and then the garden will be our own again. Go in quietly, and remember that the big man who killed Karait is the first one to bite. Then come out and tell me, and we will hunt for Rikki-tikki together.'

'But are you sure that there is anything to be gained by killing the people?' said Nag.

'Everything. When there were no people in the bungalow, did we have any mongoose in the garden? So long as the bungalow is empty, we are king and queen of the garden; and remember that as soon as our eggs in the melon-bed hatch, as they may tomorrow, our children will will need room and quiet.'

'I had not thought of that,' said Nag. 'I will go, but there is no need that we should hunt for Rikki-tikki afterward. I will kill the big man and his wife, and the child if I can, and come away quietly. Then the bungalow will be empty, and Rikki-tikki will go.'

Rikki-tikki tingled all over with rage and hatred at this, and then Nag's head came through the sluice, and his five feet of cold body followed it. Angry as he was, Rikki-tikki was very frightened as he saw the size of the big cobra. Nag coiled himself up, raised his head, and looked into the bathroom in the dark, and Rikki could see his eyes glitter.

'Now, if I kill him here, Nagaina will know; and if I fight him on the open floor, the odds are in his favour. What am I to do?' said Rikki-tikki-tavi to himself.

Nag waved to and fro, and then Rikki-tikki heard him drinking from the biggest water-jar that was used to fill the bath. 'That is good,' said the snake. 'Now, when Karait was killed, the big man had a stick. He may have that stick still, but when he comes in to bathe in the morning he will not have a stick. I shall wait here till he comes. Nagaina—do you hear me?—I shall wait here in the cool till daytime.'

There was no answer from outside, so Rikki-tikki knew Nagaina had gone away. Nag coiled himself down, coil by coil, round the bulge at the bottom of the water-jar, and Rikki-tikki stayed still as death. After an hour he began to move, muscle by muscle, toward the jar. Nag was asleep, and Rikki-tikki looked at his big back, wondering which would be the best place for a good hold. 'If I don't break his back at the first jump,' said Rikki, 'he can still fight; and if he fights—O Rikki!' He looked at the thickness of the neck below the hood, but that was too much for him; and a bite near the tail would only make Nag savage.

'It must be the head,' he said at last; 'the head above the hood; and when I am once there, I must not let go.'

Then he jumped. The head was lying a little clear of the water-jar, under the curve of it; and, as his teeth met, Rikki braced his back against the bulge of the red earthenware to hold down the head. This gave him just one second's purchase, and he made the most of it. Then he was battered to and fro as a rat is shaken by a dog—to and fro on the floor, up and down, and round in great circles; but his eyes were red, and he held on as the body cart-whipped over the floor, upsetting the tin dipper and the soap-dish and the flesh-brush, and banged against the side of the tin bath. As he held he closed his jaws tighter and tighter, for he made sure he would be banged to death, and, for the honour of his family, he preferred to be found with his teeth locked. He was dizzy, aching, and felt shaken to pieces when something went off like a thunderclap just behind him; a hot wind knocked him senseless, and red fire singed his fur. The big man had been wakened by the noise, and had fired both barrels of a shotgun into Nag just behind the hood.

Rikki-tikki held on with his eyes shut, for now he was quite sure he was dead; but the head did not move, and the big man picked him up and said: 'It's the mongoose again, Alice; the little chap has saved *our* lives now.' Then Teddy's mother came in with a very white face, and saw what was left of Nag, and Rikki-tikki dragged himself to Teddy's bedroom and spent half the rest of the night shaking himself tenderly to find out whether he really was broken into forty pieces, as he fancied.

When morning came he was very stiff, but well pleased with his doings. 'Now I have Nagaina to settle with, and she will be worse than five Nags, and there's no knowing when the eggs she spoke of will hatch. Goodness! I must go and see Darzee,' he said.

Without waiting for breakfast, Rikki-tikki ran to the thorn-bush where Darzee was singing a song of triumph at the top of his voice. The news of Nag's death was all over the garden, for the sweeper had thrown the body on the rubbish-heap.

'Oh, you stupid tuft of feathers!' said Rikki-tikki angrily. 'Is this the time to sing?'

'Nag is dead—is dead—is dead!' sang Darzee. 'The valiant Rikki-tikki caught him by the head and held fast. The big man brought the bang-stick, and Nag fell in two pieces! He will never eat my babies again.'

'All that's true enough; but where's Nagaina?' said Rikki-tikki, looking carefully round him.

'Nagaina came to the bathroom sluice and called for Nag,' Darzee went on; 'and Nag came out on the end of a stick—the sweeper picked him up on the end of a stick and threw him upon the rubbish-heap. Let us sing about the great, the red-eyed Rikki-tikki!' and Darzee filled his throat and sang.

'If I could get up to your nest, I'd roll all your babies out!' said Rikki-tikki. 'You don't know when to do the right thing at the right time. You're safe enough in your nest there, but it's war for me down here. Stop singing a minute, Darzee.'

'For the great, the beautiful Rikki-tikki's sake I will stop,' said Darzee. 'What is it, O killer of the terrible Nag?'

'Where is Nagaina, for the third time?'

'On the rubbish-heap by the stables, mourning for Nag. Great is Rikki-tikki with the white teeth.'

'Bother my white teeth! Have you ever heard where she keeps her eggs?'

'In the melon-bed, on the end nearest the wall, where the sun strikes nearly all day. She hid them there weeks ago.'

'And you never thought it worth while to tell me? The end nearest the wall, you said?'

'Rikki-tikki, you are not going to eat her eggs?'

'Not eat exactly; no. Darzee, if you have a grain of sense you will fly off to the stables and pretend that your wing is broken, and let Nagaina chase you away to this bush. I must get to the melon-bed, and if I went there now she'd see me.'

Darzee was a feather-brained little fellow who could never hold more than one idea at a time in his head; and just because he knew that Nagaina's children were born in eggs like his own, he didn't think at first that it was fair to kill them. But his wife was a sensible bird, and she knew that cobra's eggs meant young cobras later on; so she flew off from the nest, and left Darzee to keep the babies warm, and continue his song about the death of Nag. Darzee was very like a man in some ways.

She fluttered in front of Nagaina by the rubbish-heap, and cried out, 'Oh, my wing is broken! The boy in the house threw a stone at me and broke it.' Then she fluttered more desperately than ever.

Nagaina lifted up her head and hissed, 'You warned Rikki-tikki when I would have killed him. Indeed and truly, you've chosen a bad place to be lame in.' And she moved toward Darzee's wife, slipping along over the dust.

'The boy broke it with a stone!' shrieked Darzee's wife.

'Well! It may be some consolation to you when you're dead to know that I shall settle accounts with the boy. My husband lies on the rubbish-heap this morning, but before night the boy in the house will lie very still. What is the use of running away? I am sure to catch you. Little fool, look at me!'

Darzee's wife knew better than to do *that*, for a bird who looks at a snake's eyes gets so frightened that she cannot move. Darzee's wife fluttered on, piping sorrowfully, and never leaving the ground, and Nagaina quickened her pace.

Rikki-tikki heard them going up the path from the stables, and he raced for the end of the melon-patch near the wall. There, in the warm litter about the melons, very cunningly hidden, he found twenty-five eggs, about the size of a bantam's eggs, but with whitish skin instead of shell.

'I was not a day too soon,' he said; for he could see the baby cobras curled up inside the skin, and he knew that the minute they were hatched they could each kill a man or a mongoose. He bit off the tops of the eggs as fast as he could, taking care to crush the young cobras, and turned over the litter from time to time to see whether he had missed any. At last there were only three eggs left, and Rikki-tikki began to chuckle to himself, when he heard Darzee's wife screaming:

'Rikki-tikki, I led Nagaina toward the house, and she has gone into the verandah, and—oh, come quickly—she means killing!'

Rikki-tikki smashed two eggs, and tumbled backward down the melon-bed with the third egg in his mouth, and scuttled to the verandah as hard as he could put foot to the ground. Teddy and his mother and father were there at early breakfast; but Rikki-tikki saw that they were not eating anything. They sat stone-still, and their faces were white. Nagaina was coiled up on the matting by Teddy's chair, within easy striking distance of Teddy's bare leg, and she was swaying to and fro singing a song of triumph.

'Son of the big man that killed Nag,' she hissed, 'stay still. I am not ready yet. Wait a little. Keep very still, all you three. If you move I strike, and if you do not move I strike. Oh, foolish people, who killed my Nag!'

Teddy's eyes were fixed on his father, and all his father could do was to whisper, 'Sit still, Teddy. You mustn't move. Teddy, keep still.'

Then Rikki-tikki came up and cried: 'Turn round, Nagaina; turn and fight!'

'All in good time,' said she, without moving her eyes. 'I will settle my account with *you* presently. Look at your friends, Rikki-tikki. They are still and white; they are afraid. They dare not move, and if you come a step nearer I strike.'

'Look at your eggs,' said Rikki-tikki, 'in the melon-bed near the wall. Go and look, Nagaina.'

The big snake turned half round, and saw the egg on the verandah. 'Ah-h! Give it to me,' she said.

Rikki-tikki put his paws one on each side of the egg, and his eyes were blood-red. 'What price for a snake's egg? For a young cobra? For a young king-cobra? For the last—the very last of the brood? The ants are eating all the others down by the melon-bed.'

Nagaina spun clear round, forgetting everything for the sake of the one egg; and Rikki-tikki saw Teddy's father shoot out a big hand, catch Teddy by the shoulder, and drag him across the little table with the tea-cups, safe and out of reach of Nagaina.

'Tricked! Tricked! Tricked! *Rikk-tck-tck!*' chuckled Rikki-tikki. 'The boy is safe, and it was I—I—I that caught Nag by the hood last night in the bathroom.' Then he began to jump up and down, all four feet together, his head close to the floor. 'He threw me to and fro, but he could not shake me off. He was dead before the big man blew him in two. I did it. *Rikki-tikki-tck-tck!* Come then, Nagaina. Come and fight with me. You shall not be a widow long.'

Nagaina saw that she had lost her chance of killing Teddy, and the egg lay between Rikki-tikki's paws. 'Give me the egg, Rikki-tikki. Give me the last of my eggs, and I will go away and never come back,' she said, lowering her hood.

'Yes, you will go away, and you will never come back; for you will go to the rubbish-heap with Nag. Fight, widow! The big man has gone for his gun! Fight!'

Rikki-tikki was bounding all round Nagaina, keeping just out of reach of her stroke, his little eyes like hot coals. Nagaina gathered herself together, and flung out at him. Rikki-tikki jumped up and backward. Again and again and again she struck, and each time her head came with a whack on the matting of the verandah, and she gathered herself together like a watch-spring. Then Rikki-tikki danced in a circle to get behind her, and Nagaina spun round to keep her head to his head, so that the rustle of her tail on the matting sounded like dry leaves blown along by the wind.

He had forgotten the egg. It still lay on the verandah, and Nagaina came nearer and nearer to it, till at last, while Rikki-tikki was drawing breath, she caught it in her mouth, turned to the verandah steps, and flew like an arrow down the path, with Rikki-tikki behind her. When the cobra runs for her life, she goes like a whiplash flicked across a horse's neck.

Rikki-tikki knew that he must catch her, or all the trouble would begin again. She headed straight for the long grass by the thorn-bush, and as he was running Rikki-tikki heard Darzee still singing his foolish little song of triumph. But Darzee's wife was wiser. She flew off her nest as Nagaina came along, and flapped her wings about Nagaina's head. If Darzee had helped they might have turned her; but Nagaina only lowered her hood and went on. Still, the instant's delay brought Rikki-tikki up to her, and as she plunged into the rat-hole where she and Nag used to live, his little white teeth were clenched on her tail, and he went down with her—and very few mongooses, however wise and old they may be, care to follow a cobra into its hole. It was dark in the hole; and Rikki-tikki never knew when it might open out and give Nagaina room to turn and strike at him. He held on savagely, and struck out his feet to act as brakes on the dark slope of the hot, moist earth.

Then the grass by the mouth of the hole stopped waving, and Darzee said: 'It is all over with Rikki-tikki! We must sing his death-song. Valiant Rikki-tikki is dead! For Nagaina will surely kill him underground.'

So he sang a very mournful song that he made up on the spur of the minute, and just as he got to the most touching part the grass quivered again, and Rikki-tikki, covered with dirt, dragged himself out of the hole leg by leg, licking his whiskers. Darzee stopped with a little shout. Rikki-tikki shook some of the dust out of his fur and sneezed. 'It is all over,' he said. 'The widow will never come out again.' And the red ants that live between the grass stems heard him, and began to troop down one after another to see if he had spoken the truth.

Rikki-tikki curled himself up in the grass and slept where he was—slept and slept till it was late in the afternoon, for he had done a hard day's work.

'Now,' he said, when he awoke, 'I will go back to the house. Tell the coppersmith, Darzee, and he will tell the garden that Nagaina is dead.'

The coppersmith is a bird who makes a noise exactly like the beating of a little hammer on a copper pot; and the reason he is always making it is because he is the town-crier to every Indian garden, and tells all the news to everybody who cares to listen. As Rikki-tikki went up the path, he heard his 'attention' notes like a tiny dinner-gong; and then the steady '*Ding-dong-tock!* Nag is dead—*dong!* Nagaina is dead! *Ding-dong-tock!*' That set all the birds in the garden singing, and the frogs croaking; for Nag and Nagaina used to eat frogs as well as little birds.

When Rikki got to the house, Teddy and Teddy's mother (she looked very white still, for she had been fainting) and Teddy's father came out and almost cried over him; and that night he ate all that was given him till he could eat no more, and went to bed on Teddy's shoulder, where Teddy's mother saw him when she came to look late at night.

'He saved our lives and Teddy's life,' she said to her husband. 'Just think, he saved all our lives.'

Rikki-tikki woke up with a jump, for all the mongooses are light sleepers.

'Oh, it's you,' said he. 'What are you bothering for? All the cobras are dead; and if they weren't, I'm here.'

Rikki-tikki had a right to be proud of himself; but he did not grow too proud, and he kept that garden as a mongoose should keep it, with tooth and jump and spring and bite, till never a cobra dared show its head inside the walls.

TEMPEST

Charles Dickens

Of all Dickens's books David Copperfield *was the author's own favourite. As a child David had become friendly with the family of his faithful nurse Peggotty, and one of his happiest recollections was of the time he had spent with them in the upturned boat at Yarmouth that was their home. Mr Peggotty, Peggotty's brother, was an honest and good fisherman who had brought up his niece Emily and nephew Ham. Emily and Ham were engaged to be married when David introduced Steerforth, a dashing friend whom he had known at school.*

The result is disaster: Emily abandons the unfortunate Ham and goes abroad with Steerforth, only to be deserted by him in due course; and Mr Peggotty devotes his life to finding his niece. Emily eventually returns, and Mr Peggotty decides that they should both emigrate. Ham has meantime given a message to David for Emily, and this is on David's mind as this chapter, which is the book's climax, opens. It describes the deaths of both Ham and Steerforth.

I now approach an event in my life so indelible, so awful, so bound by an infinite variety of ties to all that has preceded it, in these pages, that, from the beginning of my narrative, I have seen it growing larger and larger as I advanced, like a great tower in a plain, and throwing its fore-cast shadow even on the incidents of my childish days.

For years after it occurred, I dreamed of it often. I have started up so vividly impressed by it, that its fury has yet seemed raging in my quiet room, in the still night. I dream of it sometimes, though at lengthened and uncertain intervals, to this hour. I have an association between it and a stormy wind, or the lightest mention of a sea-shore, as strong as any of which my mind is conscious. As plainly as I behold what happened, I will try to write it down. I do not recall it, but see it done; for it happens again before me.

The time drawing on rapidly for the sailing of the emigrant ship, my good old nurse (almost broken-hearted for me, when we first met) came up to London. I was constantly with her, and her brother, and the Micawbers (they being very much together); but Emily I never saw.

One evening, when the time was close at hand, I was alone with Peggotty and her brother. Our conversation turned on Ham. She described to us how tenderly he had taken leave of her and how manfully and quietly he had borne himself. Most of all, of late, when she believed he was most tried. It was a subject of which the affectionate creature never tired; and our interest in hearing the many examples which she, who was so much with him, had to relate, was equal to hers in relating them.

My aunt and I were at that time vacating the two cottages at Highgate; I intending to go abroad, and she to return to her house at Dover. We had a temporary lodging in Covent Garden. As I walked home to it, after this evening's conversation, reflecting on what had passed between Ham and myself when I was last at Yarmouth, I wavered in the original purpose I had formed, of leaving a letter for Emily when I should take leave of her uncle on board the ship, and thought it would be better to write to her now. She might desire, I thought, after receiving my communication, to send some parting word by me to her unhappy lover. I ought to give her the opportunity.

I therefore sat down in my room, before going to bed, and wrote to her. I told her that I had seen him, and that he had requested me to tell her what I have already written in its place in these sheets. I faithfully repeated it. I had no need to enlarge upon it, if I had had the right. Its deep fidelity and goodness were not to be adorned by me or any man. I left it out, to be sent round in the morning; with a line to Mr Peggotty, requesting him to give it to her; and went to bed at daybreak.

I was weaker than I knew then; and, not falling asleep until the sun was up, lay late, and unrefreshed, next day. I was roused by the silent presence of my aunt at my bedside. I felt it in my sleep, as I suppose we all do feel such things.

'Trot, my dear,' she said, when I opened my eyes, 'I couldn't make up my mind to disturb you. Mr Peggotty is here; shall he come up?'

I replied yes, and he soon appeared.

'Mas'r Davy,' he said, when we had shaken hands, 'I giv Em'ly your letter, sir, and she writ this heer; and begged of me fur to ask you to read it, and if you see no hurt in't, to be so kind as take charge on't.'

'Have you read it?' said I.

He nodded sorrowfully. I opened it, and read as follows:

> 'I have got your message. Oh, what can I write, to thank you for your good and blessed kindness to me!
>
> I have put the words close to my heart. I shall keep them till I die. They are sharp thorns, but they are such comfort. I have prayed over them, oh, I have prayed so much. When I find what you are, and what uncle is, I think what God must be, and can cry to Him.
>
> Good-bye for ever. Now, my dear friend, good-bye for ever in this world. In another world, if I am forgiven, I may wake a child and come to you. All thanks and blessings. Farewell, evermore!'

This, blotted with tears, was the letter.

'May I tell her as you doen't see no hurt in't, and as you'll be so kind as take charge on't, Mas'r Davy?' said Mr Peggotty when I had read it.

'Unquestionably,' said I—'but I am thinking——'

'Yes, Mas'r Davy?'

'I am thinking,' said I, 'that I'll go down again to Yarmouth. There's time, and to spare, for me to go and come back before the ship sails. My mind is constantly running on him, in his solitude; to put this letter of her writing in his hand at this time, and to enable you to tell her, in the moment of parting, that he has got it, will be a kindness to both of them. I solemnly accepted his commission, dear good fellow, and cannot discharge it too completely. The journey is nothing to me. I am restless, and shall be better in motion. I'll go down tonight.'

Though he anxiously endeavoured to dissuade me, I saw that he was of my mind; and this, if I had required to be confirmed in my intention, would have had the effect. He went round to the coach-office at my request, and took the box-seat for me on the mail. In the evening I started, by that conveyance, down the road I had travelled under so many changes of fortune.

'Don't you think that,' I asked the coachman, in the first stage out of London, 'a very remarkable sky? I don't remember to have seen one like it.'

'Nor I—not equal to it,' he replied. 'That's wind, sir. There'll be mischief done at sea, I expect, before long.'

It was a murky confusion—here and there blotted with a colour like the colour of the smoke from damp fuel—of flying clouds tossed up into most remarkable heaps, suggesting greater heights in the clouds than there were depths below them to the bottom of the deepest hollows in the earth, through which the wild moon seemed to plunge headlong, as if, in a dread disturbance of the laws of nature, she had lost her way and were frightened. There had been a wind all day; and it was rising then, with an extraordinary great sound. In another hour it had much increased, and the sky was more overcast, and it blew hard.

But as the night advanced, the clouds closing in and densely overspreading the whole sky, then very dark, it came on to blow, harder and harder. It still increased, until our horses could scarcely face the wind. Many times, in the dark part of the night (it was then late in September, when the nights were not short), the leaders turned about, or came to a dead stop; and we were often in serious apprehension that the coach would be blown over. Sweeping gusts of rain came up before this storm, like showers of steel; and, at those times, when there was any shelter of trees or lee walls to be got, we were fain to stop, in a sheer impossibility of continuing the struggle.

When the day broke, it blew harder and harder. I had been in Yarmouth when the seamen said it blew great guns, but I have never known the like of this, or anything approaching it. We came to Ipswich—very late, having had to fight every inch of ground since we were ten miles out of London—and found a cluster of people in the market-place, who had risen from their beds in the night, fearful of falling chimneys. Some of these, congregating about the inn-yard while we changed horses, told us of great sheets of lead having been ripped off a high church-tower, and flung into a by-street, which they then blocked up. Others had to tell of country people, coming in from neighbouring villages, who had seen great trees lying torn out of the earth, and whole ricks scattered about the roads and fields. Still, there was no abatement in the storm, but it blew harder.

As we struggled on, nearer and nearer to the sea, from which this mighty wind was blowing dead on shore, its force became more and more terrific. Long before we saw the sea, its spray was on our lips, and showered salt rain upon us. The water was out, over miles and miles of the flat country adjacent to Yarmouth; and every sheet and puddle lashed its banks, and had its stress of little breakers setting heavily towards us. When we came within sight of the sea, the waves on the horizon, caught at intervals above the rolling abyss, were like glimpses of another shore with towers and buildings. When at last we got into the town, the people came out to their doors, all aslant, and with streaming hair, making a wonder of the mail that had come through such a night.

I put up at the old inn, and went down to look at the sea; staggering along the street, which was strewn with sand and seaweed, and with flying blotches of foam; afraid of falling slates and tiles; and holding by people I met, at angry corners. Coming near the beach, I saw not only the boatmen but half the people of the town, lurking behind buildings; some, now and then braving the fury of the storm to look away to sea, and blown sheer out of their course in trying to get zigzag back.

Joining these groups, I found bewailing women whose husbands were away in herring or oyster boats, which there was too much reason to think might have foundered before they could run in anywhere for safety. Grizzled old sailors were among the people, shaking their heads as they looked from water to sky, and muttering to one another; shipowners, excited and uneasy; children, huddling together, and peering into old faces; even stout mariners, disturbed and anxious, levelling their glasses at the sea from behind places of shelter, as if they were surveying an enemy.

The tremendous sea itself, when I could find sufficient pause to look at it, in the agitation of the blinding wind, the flying stones and sand, and the awful noise, confounded me. As the high watery walls came rolling in, and, at their highest, tumbled into surf, they looked as if the least would engulf the town. As the receding wave swept back with a hoarse roar, it seemed to scoop out deep caves in the beach, as if its purpose was to undermine the earth. When some white-headed billows thundered on, and dashed themselves to pieces before they reached the land, every fragment of the late whole seemed possessed by the full might of its wrath, rushing to be gathered to the composition of another monster. Undulating hills were changed to valleys, undulating valleys (with a solitary storm-bird sometimes skimming through them) were lifted up to hills; masses of water shivered and shook the beach with a booming sound; every shape tumultuously rolled on, as soon as made, to change its shape and place, and beat another shape and place away; the ideal shore on the horizon, with its towers and buildings, rose and fell; the clouds flew fast and thick; I seemed to see a rending and up-heaving of all nature.

Not finding Ham among the people whom this memorable wind—for it is still remembered down there as the greatest ever known to blow upon that coast—had brought together, I made my way to his house. It was shut; and as no one answered to my knocking, I went, by back ways and by-lanes, to the yard where he worked. I learned, there, that he had gone to Lowestoft, to meet some sudden exigency of ship-repairing in which his skill was required; but that he would be back tomorrow morning, in good time.

I went back to the inn; and when I had washed and dressed, and tried to sleep, but in vain, it was five o'clock in the afternoon. I had not sat five minutes by the coffee-room fire, when the waiter coming to stir it, as an excuse for talking, told me that two colliers had gone down, with all hands, a few miles away; and that some other ships had been seen labouring hard in The Roads, and trying, in great distress, to keep off shore. Mercy on them, and on all poor sailors, said he, if we had another night like the last!

I was very much depressed in spirits; very solitary; and felt an uneasiness in Ham's not being there, disproportionate to the occasion. I was seriously affected, without knowing how much, by late events; and my long exposure to the fierce wind had confused me. There was that jumble in my thoughts and recollections, that I had lost the clear arrangement of time and distance. Thus, if I had gone out into the town, I should not have been surprised, I think, to encounter someone who I knew must be then in London. So to speak, there was in these respects a curious inattention in my mind. Yet it was busy, too, with all the remembrances the place naturally awakened; and they were particularly distinct and vivid.

In this state, the waiter's dismal intelligence about the ships immediately connected itself, without any effort of my volition, with my uneasiness about Ham. I was persuaded that I had an apprehension of his returning from Lowestoft by sea, and being lost. This grew so strong with me that I resolved to go back to the yard before I took my dinner, and ask the boat-builder if he thought his attempting to return by sea at all likely? If he gave me the least reason to think so, I would go over to Lowestoft and prevent it by bringing him with me.

I hastily ordered my dinner, and went back to the yard. I was none too soon; for the boat-builder, with a lantern in his hand, was locking the yard-gate. He quite laughed when I asked him the question, and said there was no fear; no man in his senses, or out of them, would put off in such a gale of wind, least of all Ham Peggotty, who had been born to sea-faring.

So sensible of this, beforehand, that I had really felt ashamed of doing what I was nevertheless impelled to do, I went back to the inn. If such a wind could rise, I think it was rising. The howl and roar, the rattling of the doors and windows, the rumbling in the chimneys, the apparent rocking of the very house that sheltered me, and the prodigious tumult of the sea, were more fearful than in the morning. But there was now a great darkness besides; and that invested the storm with new terrors, real and fanciful.

I could not eat, I could not sit still, I could not continue steadfast to anything. Something within me, faintly answering to the storm without, tossed up the depth of my memory, and made a tumult in them. Yet, in all the hurry of my thoughts, wild running with the thundering sea—the storm, and my uneasiness regarding Ham, were always in the foreground.

My dinner went away almost untasted, and I tried to refresh myself with a glass or two of wine. In vain. I fell into a dull slumber before the fire, without losing my consciousness, either of the uproar out of doors, or of the place in which I was. Both became overshadowed by a new and indefinable horror; and when I awoke—or rather when I shook off the lethargy that bound me in my chair—my whole frame thrilled with objectless and unintelligible fear.

I walked to and fro, tried to read an old gazetteer, listened to the awful noises: looked at faces, scenes, and figures in the fire. At length, the steady ticking of the undisturbed clock on the wall tormented me to that degree that I resolved to go to bed.

It was reassuring, on such a night, to be told that some of the inn-servants had agreed together to sit up until morning. I went to bed, exceedingly weary and heavy; but, on my lying down, all such sensations vanished, as if by magic, and I was broad awake.

For hours I lay there, listening to the wind and water: imagining, now, that I heard shrieks out at sea; now, that I distinctly heard the firing of signal guns; and now, the fall of houses in the town. I got up, several times, and looked out; but could see nothing, except the reflection in the window-panes of the faint candle I had left burning, and of my own haggard face looking in at me from the black void.

At length, my restlessness attained to such a pitch that I hurried on my clothes, and went downstairs. In the large kitchen, where I dimly saw bacon and ropes of onions hanging from the beams, the watchers were clustered together, in various attitudes, about a table, purposely moved away from the great chimney, and brought near the door. A pretty girl, who had her ears stopped with her apron, and her eyes upon the door, screamed when I appeared, supposing me to be a spirit; but the others had more presence of mind, and were glad of an addition to their company. One man, referring to the topic they had been discussing, asked me whether I thought the souls of the collier-crews who had gone down, were out in the storm?

I remained there, I dare say, two hours. Once, I opened the yard-gate, and looked into the empty street. The sand, the seaweed, and the flakes of foam were driving by; and I was obliged to call for assistance before I could shut the gate again, and make it fast against the wind.

There was a dark gloom in my solitary chamber, when I at length returned to it; but I was tired now, and, getting into bed again, fell—off a tower and down a precipice—into the depths of sleep. I have an impression that for a long time, though I dreamed of being elsewhere and in a variety of scenes, it was always blowing in my dream. At length, I lost that feeble hold upon reality, and was engaged with two dear friends, but who they were I don't know, at the siege of some town in a roar of cannonading.

The thunder of the cannon was so loud and incessant, that I could not hear something I much desired to hear, until I made a great exertion and awoke. It was broad day—eight or nine o'clock; the storm raging, in lieu of the batteries; and someone knocking and calling at my door.

'What is the matter?' I cried.

'A wreck! Close by!'

I sprang out of bed, and asked, 'What wreck?'

'A schooner, from Spain or Portugal, laden with fruit and wine.

Make haste, sir, if you want to see her! It's thought, down on the beach, she'll go to pieces every moment.'

The excited voice went clamouring along the staircase; and I wrapped myself in my clothes as quickly as I could, and ran into the street.

Numbers of people were there before me, all running in one direction, to the beach. I ran the same way, outstripping a good many, and soon came facing the wild sea.

The wind might by this time have lulled a little, though not more sensibly than if the cannonading I had dreamed of, had been diminished by the silencing of half-a-dozen guns out of hundreds. But the sea, having upon it the additional agitation of the whole night, was infinitely more terrific than when I had seen it last. Every appearance it had then presented, bore the expression of being *swelled*; and the height to which the breakers rose, and, looking over one another, bore one another down, and rolled in, in interminable hosts, was most appalling.

In the difficulty of hearing anything but wind and waves, and in the crowd, and the unspeakable confusion, and my first breathless efforts to stand against the weather, I was so confused that I looked out to sea for the wreck, and saw nothing but the foaming heads of the great waves. A half-dressed boatman, standing next to me, pointed with his bare arm (a tattooed arrow on it, pointing in the same direction) to the left. Then, O great heaven, I saw it, close in upon us!

One mast was broken short off, six or eight feet from the deck, and lay over the side, entangled in a maze of sail and rigging; and all that ruin, as the ship rolled and beat—which she did without a moment's pause, and with a violence quite inconceivable—beat the side as if it would stave it in. Some efforts were even then being made to cut this portion of the wreck away; for, as the ship, which was broadside on, turned towards us in her rolling, I plainly descried her people at work with axes, especially one active figure with long curling hair, conspicuous among the rest. But, a great cry, which was audible even above the wind and water, rose from the shore at this moment; the sea, sweeping over the rolling wreck, made a clean breach, and carried men, spars, casks, planks, bulwarks, heaps of such toys, into the boiling surge.

The second mast was yet standing, with the rags of a rent sail, and a wild confusion of broken cordage flapping to and fro. The ship had struck once, the same boatman hoarsely said in my ear, and then lifted in and struck again. I understood him to add that she was parting amidships, and I could readily suppose so, for the rolling and beating were too tremendous for any human work to suffer long. As he spoke, there was another great cry of pity from the beach; four men arose with the wreck out of the deep, clinging to the rigging of the remaining mast; uppermost the active figure with the curling hair.

There was a bell on board; and as the ship rolled and dashed, like a desperate creature driven mad, now showing us the whole sweep of her deck, as she turned on her beam-ends towards the shore, now nothing but her keel, as she sprang wildly over and turned towards the sea, the bell rang; and its sound, the knell of those unhappy men, was borne towards us on the wind. Again we lost her, and again she rose. Two men were gone. The agony on shore increased. Men groaned, and clasped their hands; women shrieked, and turned away their faces. Some ran wildly up and down along the beach, crying for help where no help could be. I found myself one of these, frantically imploring a knot of sailors whom I knew, not to let those two lost creatures perish before our eyes.

They were making out to me, in an agitated way—I don't know how, for the little I could hear I was scarcely composed enough to understand—that the lifeboat had been bravely manned an hour ago, and could do nothing; and that as no man would be so desperate as to attempt to wade off with a rope, and establish a communication with the shore, there was nothing left to try; when I noticed that some new sensation moved the people on the beach, and saw them part, and Ham come breaking through them to the front.

I ran to him—as well as I know, to repeat my appeal for help. But, distracted though I was, by a sight so new to me and terrible, the determination in his face, and his look, out to sea—exactly the same look as I remembered in connection with the morning after Emily's flight—awoke me to a knowledge of his danger. I held him back with both arms; and implored the men with whom I had been speaking, not to listen to him, not to do murder, not to let him stir from off that sand!

Another cry arose on shore; and looking to the wreck, we saw the cruel sail, with blow on blow, beat off the lower of the two men, and fly up in triumph round the active figure left alone upon the mast.

Against such a sight, and against such determination as that of the calmly desperate man who was already accustomed to lead half the people present, I might as hopefully have entreated the wind. 'Mas'r Davy,' he said, cheerily grasping me by both hands, 'if my time is come, 'tis come. If 'tan't I'll bide it. Lord above bless you, and bless all! Mates, make me ready! I'm a-going off!'

I was swept away, but not unkindly, to some distance, where the people around me made me stay; urging, as I confusedly perceived, that he was bent on going, with help or without, and that I should endanger the precautions for his safety by troubling those with whom they rested. I don't know what I answered, or what they rejoined; but, I saw hurry on the beach, and men running with ropes from a capstan that was there, and penetrating into a circle of figures that hid him from me. Then, I saw him standing alone, in a seaman's frock and trousers: a rope in his hand, or slung to his wrist: another round his body: and several of the best men holding, at a little distance, to the latter, which he laid out himself, slack upon the shore, at his feet.

The wreck, even to my unpractised eye, was breaking up. I saw that

'Mates, make me ready!' said Ham. 'I'm a-going off!'

she was parting in the middle, and that the life of the solitary man upon the mast hung by a thread. Still, he clung to it. He had a singular red cap on—not like a sailor's cap, but of a finer colour; and as the few yielding planks between him and destruction rolled and bulged, and his anticipative death-knell rang, he was seen by all of us to wave it. I saw him do it now, and thought I was going distracted, when his action brought an old remembrance to my mind of a once dear friend.

Ham watched the sea, standing alone, with the silence of suspended breath behind him, and the storm before, until there was a great retiring wave, when, with a backward glance at those who held the rope which was made fast round his body, he dashed in after it, and in a moment was buffeting with the water; rising with the hills, falling with the valleys, lost beneath the foam; then drawn again to land. They hauled in hastily.

He was hurt. I saw blood on his face, from where I stood; but he took no thought of that. He seemed hurriedly to give them some directions for leaving him more free—or so I judged from the motion of his arm—and was gone as before.

And now he made for the wreck, rising with the hills, falling with the valleys, lost beneath the rugged foam, borne in towards the shore, borne on towards the ship, striving hard and valiantly. The distance was nothing, but the power of the sea and wind made the strife deadly. At length he neared the wreck. He was so near, that with one more of his vigorous strokes he would be clinging to it—when a high, green, vast hillside of water, moving on shoreward, from beyond the ship, he seemed to leap up into it with a mighty bound, and the ship was gone!

Some eddying fragments I saw in the sea, as if a mere cask had been broken, in running to the spot where they were hauling in. Consternation was in every face. They drew him to my very feet—insensible—dead. He was carried to the nearest house; and, no one preventing me now, I remained near him, busy, while every means of restoration were tried; but he had been beaten to death by the great wave, and his generous heart was stilled for ever.

As I sat beside the bed, when hope was abandoned and all was done, a fisherman, who had known me when Emily and I were children, and ever since, whispered my name at the door.

'Sir,' said he, with tears starting to his weather-beaten face, which, with his trembling lips, was ashy pale, 'will you come over yonder?'

The old remembrance that had been recalled to me, was in his look. I asked him, terror-stricken, leaning on the arm he held out to support me:

'Has a body come ashore?'

He said, 'Yes.'

'Do I know it?' I asked then.

He answered nothing.

But, he led me to the shore. And on that part of it where she and I had looked for shells, two children—on that part of it where some lighter fragments of the old boat, blown down last night, had been scattered by the wind—among the ruins of the home he had wronged—I saw him lying with his head upon his arm, as I had often seen him lie at school.

THE FIRST LADY OF FLYING

Graeme Cook

By 1928 the Atlantic Ocean had been crossed by air no fewer than ten times, but even so it was still a dangerous undertaking. There were, however, men prepared to take the risk to list their names amongst the pioneers headed by Alcock and Brown. Two such men were Americans Lou Gordon and Wilmer Stultz, who planned to make the crossing in that year.

It occurred to the two men and their friend and aviation enthusiast George Putnam Palmer, a New York publisher, that only *men* had so far flown the Atlantic. What a gimmick and boost for the prestige of American womanhood if they could take a woman along with them. The more they thought about it, the more enthusiastic they became. But there was a problem. Where would they get a young woman willing to risk possible death amid the Atlantic waves?

At once a nationwide search began, led by Palmer, who interviewed a host of willing candidates. Alas, none of them was really suitable. Above all they needed a stable, 'down-to-earth' woman with just the right degree of self-confidence and one who would not panic in an emergency. So far none of the girls Palmer had interviewed had all the necessary qualities. When he had almost exhausted his supply of candidates, he searched his mind for others, running through the list of lady friends he had. It was then that he remembered a young girl teacher and social worker he had known for some time. He decided to get in touch with her and see if she was interested.

Palmer's friend had, he remembered, flown with Frank Hawkes, one of America's famous barn-stormers who performed feats of daring in the air to excited crowds across America. Then, he recalled, she had herself become a pilot but lack of money had forced her to give it up. This girl, he thought, might just be the one he was looking for. Little did he know then that she was to become one of the most famous pilots ever to take to the air. Her name was Amelia Earhart.

So it was that the tall, thirty-year-old girl with the short, unkempt tawny hair walked eagerly into his office, trying desperately not to show too much enthusiasm and excitement. Amelia was attractive in a boyish way with her short hair, her freckled face and open grey eyes. She certainly didn't look her thirty years.

Palmer and Amelia talked at some length about her experience of flying; what she had done, whom she had flown with and the most important question of all—whether or not she would like to fly the Atlantic with Gordon and Stultz. For Amelia the question need never have been asked. It was obvious to Palmer, a particularly good judge of character, that he had found his girl. She was just what he had been looking for. The answer was an emphatic 'yes'. Palmer pointed out the many hazards she was likely to face on such a trip but Amelia merely replied that she would not consider going on the trip if there was not an element of danger. She loved a challenge and regarded life as not worth living without one.

Soon everything was arranged and the long, tiring flight with all its dangers took place. Throughout the flight, the inexhaustible Amelia spent most of her time helping the pilots and bombarding them with hosts of questions about this and that instrument or navigational problem and even about the aircraft's engines.

Although she took no real part in the flying of the aircraft, the very fact that she had actually flown the Atlantic made Amelia world-famous almost overnight. She was asked to go on lecture tours of America, telling of her experiences, and to write articles for newspapers and magazines, all of which brought her in the money she needed to continue her flying.

But there was more to Amelia's wish to become a better pilot than hopes of short-haul trips in America. Spurred on by her Atlantic flight, she determined that one day she would fly the Atlantic again, but this time she would do it alone. At the very suggestion of this, Palmer was staggered. By then his relationship with Amelia had grown into something more than just friendship and he did all in his power to persuade her to forget this foolish venture. But Amelia was made of strong and stubborn stuff. She continued flying until she became a first-class pilot and certainly the match for any man.

As time went by and Amelia gained more and more distinctions by completing long cross-country flights in America, the desire to fulfil her ambition grew. Palmer did all in his power to dissuade her from undertaking the trip, but her resolution won the day and in 1931 she declared that she was ready for the flight. Realizing that he could never stop her, Palmer at last gave her his blessing, doing everything he could to help her. But before committing himself too far, he asked her to marry him. After due consideration, Amelia accepted his proposal of marriage, but not without certain conditions, which she even went to the extent of putting down in writing! He was in no way to interfere with her flying. A 'beaten man', Palmer agreed to her conditions and they were duly married.

The truth of the matter was that Palmer fully understood Amelia's desire for freedom and need for an ever-present challenge. Palmer had won fame for his courage during two Arctic expeditions which he had undertaken, so the lust for adventure was in him, too.

The following year, 1932, Amelia achieved her dream. She flew solo across the Atlantic in only thirteen and a half hours, shattering a world record and becoming the world's first lady of aviation. The trip was not without its difficulties. Like many others before her she had faced abominable weather, howling gales, fierce rain-storms and dense cloud. To make matters worse, her altimeter and petrol gauge had failed, then an exhaust pipe on her Lockheed Monoplane split open and choking fumes and flames crept into the cockpit. Only her superb skill as a pilot and her dogged tenacity brought her through the ordeal.

After her epic flight, the name of Amelia Earhart became a household word. But she determined not to stop there. There were other challenges to overcome, other oceans to cross. She made many more dramatic flights and became an expert on aircraft engines, showing a particular interest in the autogyro, the forerunner of the modern-day helicopter. She actually flew the autogyro on several occasions and gave many technical lectures throughout the country.

Amelia Earhart was, above all, determined to show that aviation was not a world exclusively set aside for men. She did all in her power to encourage other women to take up flying . . . not because she was an ardent advocate of 'women's liberation', but because she wanted other women to experience the thrill of flight as she had done.

In 1935, Amelia once more staggered the world when she flew solo across the Pacific Ocean from Hawaii to California, the first person ever to do so. World records fell to her as the years went by and Amelia kept on with the same resolve she had shown in earlier years. She was aiming for the one achievement which, until then, had eluded her. She wanted to fly right around the world.

This, she promised her husband, would be the last long-distance trip she would make. Amelia could not have foreseen then that what she said would come literally true—but in a tragic way.

The route she was to fly from Oakland, California was to take her across the American continent, down to Brazil, over the South Atlantic to Africa then east across the world, culminating in a flight across the Pacific Ocean. She was to take with her as navigator one of the most skilled in the business, Fred Noonan.

In 1937, Amelia was presented with a brand new twin-engined Lockheed aircraft for her services to aviation. She christened it *Electra*. It was in this aircraft that she planned to make her round-the-world trip. On 1 June 1937, she and Fred Noonan took off from Oakland and the epic adventure began . . .

In spite of adverse conditions much of the way, the trip round the world to the Pacific Ocean went according to plan. It was this vast expanse of ocean that was to prove the final challenge to Amelia Earhart. The weather alone, as they waited to take off from Lae, in New Guinea, seemed to herald disaster. Their next stop in the hops across the Pacific was to be Howland, a tiny coral island over 2,500 miles from Lae. The weather was appalling. From the airstrip which had been hastily cut out

All her skill was required to get the fuel-laden aircraft over the trees.

of the jungle, they experienced the full force of a Pacific storm. It rained incessantly while thunder boomed and lightning streaked the storm-blackened sky.

While she and Fred waited for the storm to abate, Amelia set about checking their flight plan, provisions and safety equipment for the journey. This was to be the longest single lap of the journey and she was taking every precaution. The vital radio was checked along with the rubber dinghy, Very pistol, signalling lamps, iron rations and the many other things that went to make for a safer trip. Nothing had been left to chance. If they were forced down into the sea, they would have all the equipment necessary for survival.

She wrote to her husband: 'The whole width of the world has passed beneath us, except this broad ocean. I shall be glad when we have the hazard of its navigation behind us.'

It was not until the morning of 2 July that the weather brightened and Amelia and Fred could contemplate taking off. The take-off alone presented considerable difficulties for the intrepid flier. The space which had been cleared for a runway was small and further complicated by the towering trees which surrounded it. All Amelia's skill was going to be required to get the fuel-laden aircraft up and over the trees.

The lumbering aircraft trundled along the runway and lifted into the air, barely skimming the tops of the trees then made off into the blue sky dotted with puffy white clouds. The weather for the hop to Howland was reasonable and there seemed to be no problems ahead of them, save for the gargantuan task Fred Noonan had to face in navigating across the vast waste of rolling waves.

The difficulty of navigation was an enormous one but Noonan was equal to the task. He had pioneered the San Francisco–Manila run for Pan-American Airways. If it were humanly possible to navigate across the trackless wastes of ocean, Noonan was the man to do it, and he had planned his route for the last leg of the journey with meticulous care.

A coastguard cutter, the *Itasca*, was riding at anchor off Howland with orders to help guide Amelia's aircraft in to the airstrip. The boat was equipped with high-powered radio equipment and capable of transmitting weather information to the *Electra*. The whole schedule of the operation had been worked out in detail. Commander Thompson, the captain of the cutter, was given explicit instructions which were to be followed to the letter. They read:

'Earhart's call letters are K.H.A.Q.Q. Earhart to broadcast her position on 3105 kilocycles at every 15 and 45 minutes past the hour. *Itasca* to broadcast weather and homing signal on 3105 and 7500 kilocycles on the hour and half-hour.'

The system seemed without fault and incapable of misinterpretation —but problems were to arise. Something happened to the *Electra* with disastrous consequences . . .

In the radio cabin of the *Itasca*, the operator tried in vain to contact *Electra* for seven hours after she had left Lae. No reply came. In desperation, Thompson contacted a radio direction finder unit at Howland to see if they had any more promising news, but he drew a blank. They had not heard a thing.

At one o'clock in the morning of 4 July, Thompson put out a call to the coastguard on the Californian coast indicating that he had heard nothing from Amelia but that he was not unduly concerned because, according to the schedule, they were at that time still 1,000 miles away.

Following the message to the coastguard he broadcast to *Electra* the weather conditions which were 'excellent'. Then he waited . . . and waited . . . but nothing was heard from Amelia until just before three o'clock in the morning, when a faint voice was heard through heavy static on the radio. It was Amelia.

'Encountering headwinds . . . cloudy and overcast.' Then the voice died out. More messages were transmitted from *Electra* but they were so distorted by static that they were almost unintelligible. Then at 6.15 a.m. Howland time came the most coherent message of the night.

'We are about 100 miles out. Please take a bearing on us and report in half an hour. I will transmit in the microphone.' The message was short and clipped . . . too short for the Howland operators to get a proper radio 'fix' on the aircraft.

From then on there was complete silence. In a bid to find the tiny aircraft, the radio direction finder unit swept the sky with its beams, only to encounter utter silence. As far as they were concerned, the *Electra* was lost but they were determined not to give up trying and continued the search. Then came a stroke of luck; Amelia's voice came through with startling clarity at 7.42 . . .

'We must be right on top of you but we can't see you. Our gas is running low and we've only about thirty minutes left. Have been unable to reach you by radio. We are flying at an altitude of 1,000 feet. Please take a bearing.' Then the din of static started up again and Amelia's voice was lost. Shortly afterwards came yet another message . . .

'We are circling but still cannot see you! Go ahead on 7500 kilocycles either now or on the scheduled half-hourly time!'

The *Itasca*, at the duly appointed time, transmitted Amelia's call sign in Morse code in the hope that it would not be affected by static, but it was still impossible to get a bearing. Then Amelia made a transmission . . .

'We are receiving your signals but we are unable to get a minimum. Please take a bearing and answer with voice on 3105.'

Not long after, at 8.45, Amelia was heard for the last time. She said in a weak voice . . .

'We are in a line of position 157-337, repeat 157-337. Will repeat this message now on 6210 kilocycles. We are running north and south. We have only half an hour's fuel left and we cannot see land.'

Amelia Earhart and Fred Noonan were never heard or seen again.

As the minutes ticked by into hours it was obvious to all that they had ditched into the sea. But that did not necessarily mean they were doomed. Everyone hoped that they had survived the crash and were waiting to be picked up in their life-raft. There was still a chance that they were alive.

It must be remembered that the search procedures in the 1930s were not the elaborate ones they are today. There was, however, one ray of hope. The fuel tanks of the *Electra* would be empty and therefore provide considerable buoyancy for the aircraft. If only the crash-landing was successful then there was a fair chance that they might still be alive, if not in the life-raft then waiting on the buoyant wings of the aircraft for rescue. However, a full-scale search by ships and aircraft revealed nothing. In spite of attempts by radio 'hams' all around the Pacific coastline, there was no sign of life from Amelia's radio.

A whole string of suspected calls from K.H.A.Q.Q. were heard or reported as having been heard. The most promising of these was . . .

'We are on a coral reef just below the equator . . . we are okay but a little weak.'

However, none of the reported messages led to anything. Wild rumours about their fate were rife throughout the world but one particularly sinister one came from the island of Saipan, which lies north of Howland Island. Years later someone on the island, while discussing the mysterious disappearance of Amelia Earhart, remembered an incident which occurred in 1937 when a light aircraft carrying a man and a woman crash-landed in the sea just off the island coast. Then another person recalled seeing an aircraft crash-land in the sea and a man and woman emerge from it to be arrested by armed Japanese, who were at that time building an airstrip on the island. This witness saw the couple taken into the woods by the Japanese and there followed two shots. Nothing more was heard of them. Putting two and two together they surmised that the couple were none other than Amelia and Fred Noonan. But this posed a question. Why should the Japanese murder them out of hand? Was it to hide the fact that they were illegally building an airstrip on the island? If word of that got out there would surely be an international incident. It was a horrific possibility.

The rumours grew to alarmist proportions and there were suggestions that both Amelia and Fred Noonan were in fact American spies who had been using the round-the-world trip to cover up their true mission . . . to seek out the islands on which the Japanese were carrying out their unlawful work. There are those who, even now, believe that this was the case. It is said that the Japanese military authorities held a complete dossier on Amelia Earhart. Why would they have such a thing on a female whose sole interest in life was flying? Could it have been that she was a Japanese spy? There are those who believe this version to be true and also believe that the aircraft she was flying did not crash-land but was shot down by American fighters to cover up her duplicity!

Knowing of Amelia's love for adventure and the thrill of a challenge, it is not too difficult to believe that she may have been implicated or engaged in spying on behalf of the Americans, but the very suggestion that she was in any way connected with the Japanese is too ridiculous to be considered. Amelia Earhart was an American in every sense of the word, loyal and abundantly proud of her country.

Was Amelia Earhart spying or was she, as many hold to be true, killed with Fred Noonan when their aircraft crashed into the sea? Perhaps somewhere there is hidden the truth—but it seems unlikely that the mysterious disappearance of the world's greatest woman pilot will ever be solved.

THE COMPUTER SUSPECTS

Betsy Byars

When Kate, a doctor's daughter, plays with a computer in her father's surgery she begins to receive messages from BB-9. Who can be contacting her? Kate and her friend, Linda, have their suspects.

'Wait a minute! This is exactly like something I saw on television.'

It was noon, and Kate and her friend Linda were walking into the school cafeteria. 'See,' Linda went on, pausing to get a tray, 'this boy and girl started communicating by computer, and they met in McDonald's and fell in love. That's about all I got to see. My sister claimed she had to watch *General Hospital* for extra credit in Science, and my mom believed her. My mom believes everything my sister says. My sister goes, "My geography teacher wants us to watch *Dallas*," and my mom'll go, "Linda, turn off *Nova* this minute. Your sister's got to watch *Dallas*."'

'Linda, this is nothing like that programme. I don't know who sent this message. It could have been a girl or a boy or a ninety-year-old man. You don't understand—'

'Of course I don't understand. How could I? I have never in my life touched a computer that it didn't go, "Illegal Command." Even games. "Bad input." I finally agreed—this was over at Roz Hammond's—to play Yatze on her Apple because I used to like it when we had the little pads of paper and the dice and—'

'Linda, will you hush for a minute and listen?'

'Listening is not what I do best.'

'Well try. This was *not* a game. This was somebody trying to contact me, somebody I don't even know, and all my mom could say was, "Don't give out your name. It's some weirdo."'

'What did your dad say?'

'My dad did not say anything. My dad was depressed because he looked fat on television.'

'Your dad looks fat off television too. Don't tell him I said that.'

'I won't.'

'You know what my dad's depressed about?'

'Your grades?'

'No, that's what he ought to be depressed about. He's depressed because he thinks his chin is disappearing.' She laughed.

'There's nothing wrong with your dad's chin.'

'He thinks there is. So, listen, this was so funny. His picture was in the newspaper last week, and me and my sisters saw it first, and we took an eraser and gently erased his chin—you couldn't tell we'd touched it—and then we folded the newspaper back up and put it in the driveway, and when my dad opened it and saw himself without a chin—well, we had to go in the kitchen, we laughed so hard.'

Kate said, 'I'll have pizza,' to the cafeteria worker and turned back to Linda. 'Come with me to my dad's office this afternoon and we'll see if the message comes through again.'

'I can't.'

'Please, Linda.'

'I *can't*. My mom's got me a tutor. My mom managed to find the ugliest maths tutor in the entire university. He looks like—who is that man in M★A★S★H who dresses in women's clothes?'

'Klinger.'

'He looks like Klinger. He—' Suddenly Linda stopped. The plate containing her hamburger rattled on her tray. She said, 'I know who contacted you.'

'What?'

'On the computer yesterday. I know who it was.'

'Who?'

'Are you ready for this? Frank Wilkins.'

'Oh, Linda.'

'It has to be. He's always fooling around with computers. All he talks about is his software and floppy disks. He's as bad a nut as you are. And don't forget that time he sat by you on the bus and told you he loved you.'

'Linda, he was being initiated into a club and he had to sit by the first girl he came to, and I just happened to be—'

'I know it's him. I have an instinct about these things. I tell you what we'll do. Let's walk out of the cafeteria the same time as he does—see, he's sitting right over there with Bubba Joe Riley. Bubba Joe is so disgusting. He's licking pizza sauce off his wrist. Anyway, we will just very casually, very naturally bump into him, and when he looks at you and you look at him we'll know. Come on. Eat fast.'

'Linda,' Kate said. She pulled out her chair and sat. 'You don't understand computers. You can't communicate with just anybody. There are lines connecting computers. You—'

'Listen, if people can rob banks by computer and steal atomic secrets by computer—which I learned on *In the News* Saturday morning during the Bugs Bunny show—well, then Frank Wilkins can send you a message.'

Kate looked down at her pizza. 'Linda, this is stupid. I would be the last person Frank Wilkins would contact. Ever since he had to tell me he loved me, he's hated me.'

'Oh, he's getting up. They're through. Come on. We can eat outside. Hurry or we'll miss our chance.'

'Linda, this is stupid.'

'Come on. I'll make it look natural. Leave everything to me.'

'Linda tore across the cafeteria, pulling Kate behind her like a toy. They dodged people, chairs, tables until they were directly behind Frank Wilkins and Bubba Joe Riley. Then they slowed to a walk.

'Just act natural,' Linda said.

'Bubba Joe was licking pizza sauce off his shirt cuff now. Frank was saying, 'Moss claims I was in on it, but I went straight home after school. I worked on my program. My mom will swear I—'

Linda took Kate by the arm. Kate felt as helpless as if she were in a game of Crack the Whip.

With her eyes on Frank's back, Linda closed the remaining distance, waiting for the right moment. 'Get ready,' she said. Frank lifted his milk carton to drink. 'Go!'

Linda pushed Kate forward at the exact moment when Frank stopped by the trash can to finish his chocolate milk.

She hit Frank Wilkins full force. He swirled around, and she stumbled backwards. He was scowling. He had chocolate milk dripping down his blue sweater. He wiped his chin. He said, 'What's wrong with you?'

Kate kept backing into the cafeteria. She flicked her hair behind her ears. Her face burned.

'Why don't you look where you're going?' He glared from Kate to his sweater, then in distaste at his wet hand.

'She stumbled,' Linda said. 'She just, you know, stumbled. She's sorry.'

'Yeah, she's sorry all right.'

Frank slam-dunked his milk carton into the trash can and walked into the hall. Still wiping his sweater, he said, 'I sat by that stupid girl one time on the school bus, and she's been after me ever since.'

Kate and Linda watched in silence as the boys disappeared down the hall.

'Oh, Linda, that was horrible!' Kate said.

'Well, how did I know he was going to stop so suddenly?'

'Did you hear what he said? He thinks I'm after him!'

'He thinks everybody's after him. Anyway, we have narrowed the possibilities. I think we can safely say it is not Frank Wilkins who is contacting you.' Linda leaned against the doorway. She began to laugh. 'Did you see the expression on his face? It was so funny!'

'He was furious!'

'Frank Wilkins cannot stand to have a hair out of place. He thinks he's Mr Perfect. Did you see your pizza stuck on his back?

Kate looked down in horror at the paper napkin in her hand. Her slice of pizza was gone.

'I wish I could be there when he finds out he has been walking around school with a piece of pizza on his back. He has *noooo* sense of humour. In English we will be sitting there laughing at something, and he'll be going, "What's everybody laughing at? What's so funny?" And Ervin Bubeck will tell him, and he'll go, "Oh", and start combing his hair.'

'I just feel terrible, Linda.'

'I don't. It made my day. Anyway, do not worry. We will find the answer to who is contacting you on the computer. I promise you that. I am making it my own personal project.'

To Kate, it sounded somehow like a threat. She threw her napkin in the trash can and, head lowered, followed Linda down the hall.

* * * *

It was Saturday morning, and rain had been coming down for three hours, a cold, solid October rain that brought winter closer.

Kate came into her father's office, shaking rain from her slicker. She threw back her hood and crossed to the door to the computer room. 'It is pouring,' she said to Miss Markham.

'I'm surprised your mother let you out on a day like this.'

'She almost didn't. She said, "Just because your father is a doctor is no reason to take chances with your health . . . blah . . . blah . . . blah." And I said, "I never take chances with my health because when I get sick I have to take free samples."'

'Kate!'

'That's what my mother said. "Kate!" Anyway, it's true I have never had drugstore medicine in my life. How much longer are you going to be?'

'Until I finish the bills.'

'But that'll be hours!'

'Well, I'm going to take a break in five minutes. How about that?'

'That's better.'

Kate walked over to the window. She looked out at the rain-swept street. She closed the blinds, opened them to the same scene, closed them.

'What is wrong with you?' Miss Markham asked without looking around. 'Why are you so restless?'

'I'm not restless. I just want to know who sent me that message. And I would like to find out before Linda completely ruins me. Yesterday she—' Kate broke off.

'She what?'

'Nothing.'

Kate opened the blinds again. The memory of being pushed into

Frank Wilkins, of leaving a slice of pizza on his back, had been returning like an echo to embarrass her again and again. Even now her cheeks reddened. She turned from the window with a sigh.

'Okay, okay, the computer is yours. I need to make some phone calls anyway. Mrs Brown thinks Arthur swallowed some of the dog's worm pills.' She slipped out the accounting program. 'I'll be back in twenty minutes, Kate.'

Kate slid into the chair as Miss Markham got up. She took a deep breath and exhaled. Before Miss Markham was out of the room, she had begun to type.

THIS IS THE COMPUTER NUT. DOES
SOMEBODY OUT THERE HAVE A MESSAGE
FOR ME?

She waited, watching the screen. She moistened her dry lips. She typed again.

REPEAT. THIS IS THE COMPUTER NUT. IS
THERE A MESSAGE FOR ME?

She waited. When nothing happened, she gave a mock scream of impatience.

'Give it a chance,' Miss Markham called from her desk.

'I *hate* to wait for anything. You know that.' Kate turned back to the screen. She drummed her fingers on the desk. 'I just *hate* to—'

Suddenly Kate straightened. Words were appearing on the screen.

COMPUTER NUT, THAT IS AFFIRMATIVE. THIS
IS BB-9 AND I WAS TRYING TO CONTACT YOU.

'BB-9?' Kate asked herself. 'I wonder what that stands for—some sort of program?'

She typed:

I AM UNFAMILIAR WITH BB-9. WHAT DOES
THAT STAND FOR?

The answer came at once:

BB-9 IS A SHORTENED VERSION OF MY
DESIGNATION. MY FULL DESIGNATION IS

BB-947-82-A-1070-BLX-09. THAT IS A CODE THAT
WOULD HAVE NO MEANING TO YOU AT THIS
TIME. LET ME SAY THAT YOU ARE IN
CONTACT WITH A PEACEABLE BEING
WITHOUT MALICE OF INTENT WHOSE
INTEREST IS IN MUTUAL EXCHANGE OF
INFORMATION.

Kate paused. Suddenly she wished Linda were there with her to laugh, to wonder at the real identity of BB-9, to yell, 'I know who it is, Kate!' She swallowed and typed:

HOW DID YOU HAPPEN TO SEE MY
SELF-PORTRAIT?

She waited.

I SAW IT ON MY MASTER CONSOLE WHICH
MONITORS ALL TERRESTRIAL TERMINALS.
YOUR SELF-PORTRAIT WAS THE ONLY
INTERESTING THING ON THE MASTER
CONSOLE AT 16:39 THURSDAY. ALSO YOU
LOOKED AS IF YOU HAD A SENSE OF HUMOUR,
AS IF YOU WOULD ENJOY A GOOD LAUGH.
THAT IS WHY I DECIDED TO CONTACT YOU.

Kate stared at the words. 'Somebody is putting me on.'

'Oh, is your message coming?' Miss Markham called from the outer office.

'*Something's* coming.'

'Well, tell me about it when you get through.'

Kate let out her breath between her teeth, then typed:

WHERE, EXACTLY, IS THIS MASTER CONSOLE?
HOW FAR AWAY?

She put one hand under her chin and watched the screen. 'Well?'

THE MASTER CONSOLE IS 2591.82 MILES
DIRECTLY ABOVE YOU AT THIS MOMENT,
MOVING IN A GEOSYNCHRONOUS ORBIT.

'Oh, come on. You expect me to believe that?' Kate put her hands on the keyboard.

WHAT ARE YOU? A SATELLITE? A—

'I'm ready to use the computer now, Kate,' Miss Markham called. 'I'm almost through.'

The answer was coming. Kate leaned forward.

NO SATELLITE, COMPUTER NUT. I AM IN A SELF-CONTAINED UNIT, A STAR SHIP, AS YOU EARTHLINGS WOULD SAY, AND I HAVE BEEN MONITORING EARTH'S COMPUTERS IN PREPARATION FOR AN OCTOBER LANDING.

Kate snorted with disgust. 'An October landing. Who does he think he is? E.T.?'

AND JUST HOW, WHEN, AND WHERE ARE YOU GOING TO MAKE THIS LANDING?

She waited, leaning forward on her elbows.

THE ACTUAL DETAILS OF MY LANDING CANNOT BE REVEALED AT THIS TIME. HOWEVER, I WOULD BE GLAD TO DEPICT MY SPACE TRANSPORT. IT IS NOT AN UNUSUAL VEHICLE—MUCH LIKE OTHERS THAT HAVE COME TO YOUR PLANET—BUT IF IT WOULD BE OF INTEREST TO YOU. . .

Kate typed:

IT WOULD DEFINITELY BE OF INTEREST.

'Kate, are you finished?' Miss Markham called.

'Just let me see this spaceship,' Kate called back.

'Spaceship?'

'Yes, some nut is pretending to be from outer space, and he is going to draw his spaceship. It's nothing out of the ordinary, just some little vehicle he's been tooling around the galaxy in.'

'This I must see.'

Miss Markham came into the room and stood behind Kate. They watched the screen as lines began to appear. For a moment there was not a sound in the office.

Then, when the picture was finished, Miss Markham let out her breath in a low whistle. 'Well,' she said, 'as space vehicles go, that is not bad.'

Kate slapped her hands down on the desk. 'I hate it when people try to put me on. I *hate* it.'

'Don't be so intense, hon. You take life too seriously. It's just somebody playing a joke on you. Go along with it. Ask him to send a picture of himself, of his planet.'

Kate kept staring at the spaceship until the picture disappeared and words replaced it on the screen.

WHAT DID YOU THINK OF MY SPACESHIP,
COMPUTER NUT? WAS IT A DISAPPOINTMENT?
WAS IT AS YOU EXPECTED?

'Tell him, "Yes." Tell him you'd like to go for a ride. Tell him you'll meet him out in front of the office. Ask him if he's got an alien friend for me.' Miss Markham broke off and let her hands drop on to Kate's shoulders. 'I am getting carried away. Whatever you tell him will have to be some other time. I need the computer now.'

Kate typed:

COMPUTER NUT LOGGING.

'There.' Kate got up and walked over to the window. She stared out at the wet street.

'You'll find out who it is,' Miss Markham said.

Kate flicked her hair behind her ears. 'I'm beginning to wonder,' she said.

★ ★ ★ ★

'I have had the most humongously horrible morning of my life,' Linda said.

'Me too,' Kate answered. 'I just got back from my dad's office, and remember that person who—'

'Wait. Let me tell mine first,' Linda said. 'Mine's the worst.'

'Oh, all right.'

Kate settled herself on the sofa and stretched out her legs. In her years of friendship with Linda, Kate had gotten used to going second. She propped the phone against a pillow and prepared for a long story.

'Well, this was the day for my maths tutor. Remember I told you about him? So he comes and we sit at the kitchen table, which is the absolute centre of the universe! Everybody comes through and makes fun of me—my sisters, their friends. My mom is pretending to cook. My dad is pretending to fix the disposal. And in the middle of all this, I am supposed to be learning long division. Big numbers—14,988 divided by 4,521! Which is ridiculous. When am I ever going to have that many of anything?'

Linda drew in a deep breath. 'Anyway, I could not get one right—some of them didn't even come out even. And my mom started yelling, "You're not trying . . . blah . . . blah . . . blah." She's like *Mommie Dearest* when she gets mad, and Dad started yelling, "What do you expect? She's *your* daughter." And the tutor yelled, "She got one! She got one!" And while I was sitting there wondering which one I got, he gave me twenty-five problems as homework and left. I am really depressed.'

'You ought to get a computer.'

'Can your dad's computer do long division?'

'Linda, I have a Mickey Mouse computer from first grade that can do long division.'

'Can I borrow it?'

'Sure.'

'That makes me feel better. If it were cute—the tutor—I wouldn't mind so much. I learn better when I have a cute teacher. Well, it's your turn. What terrible thing happened to you?'

'Oh.' Kate sat up. 'Remember I told you about the computer message?'

'Vaguely.'

'Well, this morning I walked through the pouring rain, seven blocks, and it turned out to be some kook pretending to be from outer space. He drew a picture of his spaceship and talked about his orbit and—'

Linda took a deep breath. 'Kate, I know who it is!'

'Linda, don't start that again.'

'The minute you said "kook", it came to me.'

'Linda—'

'You are going to hate this, Kate, because it is somebody we both scorn, but the minute you said "kook", you know who I thought of?'

'Who?'

'Willie Lomax!'

'Willie Lomax! Don't be ridiculous.'

'It *has* to be him. He loves practical jokes—remember that time in home room with the fish bowl and the toilet paper? Remember that anonymous call to the principal about the stink bomb? And he's great with computers. He was at computer camp with you—you told me so. It is definitely Willie.'

Kate dangled her legs off the sofa. She dropped her shoes to the floor and eyed her feet critically. Her socks had got wet during the walk to her dad's office, and her shoes had dyed them brown.

'Mmmmmm,' she said, pretending not to be interested. She did not want Linda to suspect that she liked Willie Lomax a lot. After computer camp she had told Linda that Willie was funny, and Linda had said, 'Don't tell me you *like* Willie Lomax!' 'No, I just think he's funny,' Kate had said quickly, and Linda had answered, 'I was afraid you had lost your smarts.'

'It *is* him,' Linda went on enthusiastically. 'And I know how we can prove it.'

'No!' Kate got to her feet. 'Absolutely no!'

The thought of Willie Lomax saying something like, 'That stupid girl's been after me ever since computer camp,' made her face burn.

'You are not pushing me into Willie Lomax! I mean it, Linda. Yesterday Frank Wilkins came up to me and told me that if the pizza sauce didn't come out of his sweater, I was going to have to pay for it.'

'He told me the same thing. I think I dislike him intensely. Anyway, here's what I have in mind.'

'I don't want to hear it.'

'Yes, you do. It's perfect. Willie Lomax is in Honour Society, and tomorrow afternoon they are having a dog wash to make money. So we take our dogs over to be washed. What could be more natural than that?'

'It would be a lot more natural, Linda, if you had a dog.'

'So we take your dog. Three dollars a dog—you have to admit that's a bargain. All we have to do is make sure that Willie is the one who washes Harvey. Then, while the washing is in progress, you casually make some comment about computers and watch his reaction. The plan is foolproof. You find out if it's Willie and get a clean dog at the same time. If you want him dipped in flea dip, it's a dollar more.'

'I don't know, Linda,' Kate said slowly. She sat back down.

'Don't you want to find out who it is?'

'Yes.'

She admitted to herself that she also wanted to see Willie Lomax washing dogs. Still she hesitated. With Linda along, the possibility of something going wrong was great.

'Don't you want to eliminate Willie Lomax as a possibility?'

'Yes, of course.'

'Then let's go to the dog wash. It'll be something to do. Sunday afternoons are so boring anyway.'

'I just don't think it's Willie, Linda. He's got an Apple computer, and there is no way he could connect it to my dad's.'

'You just don't want to think it's Willie. You want to think it's somebody new and good-looking.'

'Not really.'

'Come on. Let's go.'

Kate smiled at the thought of Willie Lomax washing a dog. She said, 'Oh, all right.'

'Great! I'll be over tomorrow afternoon. Look at it this way—what can go wrong?'

* * * *

Linda and Kate were making their way towards the parking-lot of the school. It was Sunday afternoon, three o'clock, and the dog wash had been in progress for an hour.

'Not so fast,' Linda said. 'I don't want to get there until we spot Willie Lomax.'

Kate had already spotted him in the last line with his sleeves rolled up, his hair falling over his forehead. 'I don't want to get there at all,' she said. She tugged Harvey's leash. 'Calm down, Harvey.'

Harvey had been straining his leash ever since they had rounded the corner and he had caught sight of the group in the school parking-lot—dogs, dozens of them. He pulled forwards, choked on his collar and, unconcerned, pulled forwards again. He thought he saw and smelled several old enemies in the ragged lines.

'Sit, Harvey,' Kate said.

Harvey was beyond obeying. Behind his fringe, his black eyes were bright, beady, intent. He threw himself forward.

'Hold him back,' Linda said. 'Honestly, I'm sorry we brought him.'

'We could hardly come to a dog wash without him.'

'Did you tell me he graduated from obedience school or dropped out? Oh, look, there's Willie.'

'Where?'

'In the last line, and he's only got two dogs waiting—a Boston terrier and a poodle. They ought to go fast.'

Linda and Kate crossed the street with Harvey, leash stretched tight, in the lead. They made their way across the school yard and got in the last line behind the poodle. The woman glanced at Harvey and quickly picked up her poodle.

'Muffin's allergic to other dogs,' the woman explained. Harvey lifted his leg in the direction of her shoe.

'Harvey!' Kate pulled him back against her leg and shortened his leash. She could feel his eager breath hot against her ankle.

'Willie is not much of a dog washer,' Linda commented behind her hand. 'Look at him. He looks like he's kneading dough.' She laughed.

Kate let herself look at Willie for the first time. He was washing a schnauzer. His rolled-up sleeves were damp with water. 'Almost through, Nicky,' he told the struggling dog. The dog's tongue was hanging out the side of his mouth; his eyes rolled towards his master.

'You want the flea dip?' Willie asked. He wiped soap suds off his cheek with the back of one hand. 'It's a dollar more.'

'Yes.'

'Sorry, pal,' Willie told the schnauzer.

Kate glanced down at Harvey. He was sniffing the spot where the poodle had been sitting. Smelling was one of his primary pleasures. Suddenly he caught a different scent. He looked up.

His tail stopped wagging. His beady eyes sharpened. His ears pointed forward. Boomer, his worst enemy in the world, was at the front of the next line, pressed against his owner, his tail curled between his legs.

Harvey twitched with excitement. He barked once. Boomer was too upset to notice. The smell of dog shampoo and flea dip had reduced him to a blob of dread. His long legs trembled like twigs.

Willie Lomax lowered the schnauzer into the garbage can of flea dip, then dried him. He glanced up. 'Who's next?'

'Inger's next,' the lady with the Boston terrier said.

As Willie reached up to take Inger, he caught sight of Linda and Kate at the back of his line. Quickly he ducked his head.

'Now did you see that?' Linda asked. 'As soon as he saw you, he looked down. He could not meet your eyes. That is a sure sign of guilt. Ask any psychologist.'

'Maybe,' Kate said. She herself had looked away at the same moment.

'It's him, all right.'

Willie took the Boston terrier. The boy beside Willie was washing a sheepdog and said, 'Hey, Willie, how come you get all the little dogs?'

'This is the express lane, man, nothing over five kilos.' Willie turned the hose on the terrier. Inger's eyes bulged in panic.

'See,' Linda said, 'he is so flustered that he sprayed that little dog right in the face.'

Harvey's eyes had not left Boomer. Boomer was now under the hose himself. He had begun to whimper with fear. Harvey had never heard his enemy make such a sound. He tried to take a few steps forward but could not move on his shortened leash.

Kate said absently, 'Sit, Harvey.' She had begun to feel it had been a mistake to come. If Willie *was* sending the messages, then she would probably scare him off by . . .

'Now, when we get up there,' Linda said, 'you make some comment about computers that will let him know you're on to him.'

'If I can think of anything.'

'*If* you can! I thought you already had!'

The boy next to Willie said, 'Come on, Lomax, help me get this dog in the garbage can. You've been goofing off all afternoon.'

'Wait till I finish Inger. You want the flea dip, ma'am?'

'Inger doesn't have fleas.'

'Well, there you are then.'

Willie walked over to where his friend was struggling to get Boomer into the garbage can. He hiked up his wet sleeves.

'Grab his legs, Willie.'

'Right.' Willie took Boomer by the hind legs. 'This dog does not want to be dipped. He's holding on with his toes. Did you ever see that Road Runner cartoon where Coyote was . . .'

Harvey twitched with excitement. He had never seen his enemy in such peril. Boomer's ears were flattened against his head. His eyes, wide with fear, rolled from side to side. A steady moan came from his throat. It was obviously the moment to attack.

Harvey lunged forwards. He was held tight by the leash, but he twisted suddenly in a move that had brought him success in the past. His head slipped out of his collar, and he dashed towards Boomer and the garbage can.

In three strides he was there. A powerful leap lifted his short legs off the ground, and he aimed straight for the white of Boomer's trembling throat.

'Harvey!' Kate started after him.

Willie and his friend were lowering Boomer into the flea dip. 'This is like dipping an octopus.' Willie said. 'He's got more legs than any dog I ever—'

'*Harvey!*'

Then Willie looked up. He was just in time to see Harvey fling himself into the air, to hear the thud against the garbage can, and to feel the warm wave of flea dip slap into his chest. He fell backwards with the garbage can and Boomer in his lap. He struggled to get up while Boomer and Harvey waged an awkward dog fight in his lap.

'Harvey! Come!' Kate caught him by the back legs and pulled him, struggling, out of the way. Then she looked down at Willie.

'Oh, I'm so sorry. My dog slipped out of his collar. Let me get this garbage can. Let me—'

'No, you've done enough already.' Willie did not glance up. The wave of laughter from the other dog washers hurt more than the jolt of his fall. Trying not to show pain, he got to his feet.

Kate darted forwards. 'Let me—'

'*No!*'

The force of the word caused Kate to step back as if she had been slapped. She watched helplessly as Willie shook water from his arms, wrung out his shirttail. Someone took Boomer. 'Thank you,' he managed to say. Then he looked at Kate.

'If you want to do something, you can take your dog to somebody else's line.'

'Look, she said she was sorry,' Linda said. 'You don't have to be so irritable.'

'Yeah, Lomax, at least you got rid of your fleas,' a dog washer called.

Linda laughed and then trailed off as Willie turned his cold glance on her.

Kate looked away. Her eyes stung with tears. Spots of colour flushed her cheeks. She bent and worked Harvey's collar over his head. 'Let's go,' she said without looking up.

'We don't have to leave just because Willie Lomax got a little flea dip on—'

'Come!'

Kate spoke so sharply that Harvey thought it was a command. Dutifully he began to trot forwards. The event had not turned out exactly as he had hoped. He had got his teeth into Boomer, but Boomer had tasted like flea dip. Well, a partial success . . .

With one final glance at the dog wash, Harvey took the lead for home.

SPECTRE LOVERS

Joseph Sheridan le Fanu

There lived some fifteen years since, in a small and ruinous house little better than a hovel, an old woman who was reported to have considerably exceeded her eightieth year, and who rejoiced in the name of Alice, or popularly, Ally Moran. Her society was not much courted, for she was neither rich, nor, as the reader may suppose, beautiful. In addition to a lean cur and a cat she had one human companion, her grandson, Peter Brien, whom, with laudable good nature, she had supported from the period of his orphanage down to that of my story which finds him in his twentieth year.

Peter was a good-natured slob of a fellow, much more addicted to wrestling, dancing, and love-making than to hard work, and fonder of whisky punch than good advice. His grandmother had a high opinion of his accomplishments, which indeed was but natural, and also of his genius, for Peter had of late years begun to apply his mind to politics; and as it was plain that he had a mortal hatred of honest labour, his grandmother predicted, like a true fortune-teller, that he was born to marry an heiress, and Peter himself (who had no mind to forego his freedom even on such terms) that he was destined to find a pot of gold.

Upon one point both agreed, that being unfitted by the peculiar bias of his genius for work, he was to acquire the immense fortune to which his merits entitled him by means of a pure run of good luck. This solution of Peter's future had the double effect of reconciling both himself and his grandmother to his idle courses, and also of maintaining that even flow of hilarious spirits which made him everywhere welcome, and which was in truth the natural result of his consciousness of approaching affluence.

It happened one night that Peter had enjoyed himself to a very late hour with two or three choice spirits near Palmerstown. They had talked politics and love, sung songs, and told stories, and, above all, had swallowed, in the chastened disguise of punch, at least a pint of good whisky, every man.

It was considerably past one o'clock when Peter bid his companions good-bye, with a sigh and a hiccough, and lighting his pipe set forth on his solitary homeward way.

The bridge of Chapelizod was pretty nearly the midway point of his night march, and from one cause or another his progress was rather slow, and it was past two o'clock by the time he found himself leaning over its old battlements, and looking up the river, over whose winding current and wooded banks the soft moonlight was falling.

The cold breeze that blew lightly down the stream was grateful to him. It cooled his throbbing head, and he drank it in at his hot lips. The scene, too, had, without his being well sensible of it, a secret fascination. The village was sunk in the profoundest slumber, not a mortal stirring, not a sound afloat, a soft haze covered it all, and the fairy moonlight hovered over the entire landscape.

In a state between rumination and rapture, Peter continued to lean over the battlements of the old bridge, and as he did so he saw, or fancied he saw, emerging one after another along the river-bank in the little gardens and enclosures in the rear of the street of Chapelizod, the queerest little white-washed huts and cabins he had ever seen there before. They had not been there that evening when he passed the bridge on the way to his merry tryst. But the most remarkable thing about it was the odd way in which these quaint little cabins showed themselves.

First he saw one or two of them just with the corner of his eye, and when he looked full at them, strange to say, they faded away and disappeared. Then another and another came in view, but all in the same coy way, just appearing and gone again before he could well fix his gaze upon them; in a little while, however, they began to bear a fuller gaze, and he found, as it seemed to himself, that he was able to by an effort of attention to fix the vision for a longer and a longer time, and when they waxed faint and nearly vanished he had the power of recalling them into light and substance, until at last their vacillating indistinctness became less and less, and they assumed a permanent place in the moonlit landscape.

'Be the hokey,' said Peter, lost in amazement, and dropping his pipe into the river unconsciously, 'them is the quarist bits iv mud cabins I ever seen, growing up like musharoons in the dew of an evening, and poppin' up here and down again there, and up again in another place, like so many white rabbits in a warren; and there they stand at last as firm and fast as if they were there from the deluge; bedad it's enough to make a man a'most believe in the fairies.'

This latter was a large concession from Peter, who was a bit of a freethinker, and spoke contemptuously in his ordinary conversation of that class of agencies.

Having treated himself to a long last stare at these mysterious fabrics, Peter prepared to pursue his homeward way; having crossed the bridge and passed the mill, he arrived at the corner of the main street of the little town, and casting a careless look up the Dublin road, his eye was arrested by a most unexpected spectacle.

There was no other than a column of foot-soldiers, marching with perfect regularity towards the village, and headed by an officer on horseback. They were at the far side of the turnpike, which was closed; but much to his perplexity he perceived that they marched on through it without appearing to sustain the least check from that barrier.

On they came at a slow march; and what was most singular in the matter was, that they were drawing several cannons along with them; some held ropes, others spoked the wheels, and others again marched in front of the guns and behind them, with muskets shouldered, giving a stately character of parade and regularity to this, as it seemed to Peter, most unmilitary procedure.

It was owing either to some temporary defect in Peter's vision, or to some illusion attendant upon mist and moonlight, or perhaps to some other cause, that the whole procession had a certain waving and vapoury character which perplexed and tasked his eyes not a little. It was like the pictured pageant of a phantasmagoria reflected upon smoke. It was as if every breath disturbed it; sometimes it was blurred, sometimes obliterated; now here, now there. Sometimes, while the upper part was quite distinct, the legs of the column would nearly fade away or vanish outright, and then again they would come out into clear relief, marching on with measured tread, while the cocked hats and shoulders grew, as it were, transparent, and all but disappeared.

Notwithstanding these strange optical fluctuations, however, the column continued steadily to advance. Peter crossed the street from the corner near the old bridge, running on tip-toe, and with his body stopped to avoid observation, and took up a position upon the raised footpath in the shadow of the houses, where, as the soldiers kept the middle of the road, he calculated that he might, himself undetected, see them distinctly enough as they passed.

'What the div——, what on airth,' he muttered, checking the irreligious ejaculation with which he was about to start, for certain queer misgivings were hovering about his heart, notwithstanding the artificial courage of the whisky bottle. 'What on airth is the manin' of all this? Is it the French that's landed at last to give us a hand and help us in airnest to this blessed repale? If it is not them, I simply ask who the div——, I mane who on airth are they, for such sogers as them I never seen before in my born days?'

By this time the foremost of them were quite near, and truth to say they were the queerest soldiers he had ever seen in the course of his life. They wore long gaiters and leather breeches, three-cornered hats bound with silver lace, long blue coats with scarlet facings and linings, which latter were sewn by a fastening which held together the two opposite corners of the skirt behind; and in front the breasts were in like manner connected at a single point, where and below which they sloped back, disclosing a long-flapped waistcoat of snowy whiteness; they had very large, long cross-belts, and wore enormous pouches of white leather hung extraordinarily low, and on each of which a little silver star was glittering.

But what struck him as most grotesque and outlandish in their costume was their extraordinary display of shirt-frill in front, and of ruffle about their wrists, and the stranger manner in which their hair was frizzled out and powdered under their hats, and clubbed up into great rolls behind. But one of the party was mounted. He rode a tall white horse, with high action and arching neck; he had a snow-white feather in this three-cornered hat, and his coat was shimmering all over with a profusion of silver lace. From these circumstances Peter concluded that he must be the commander of the detachment, and examined him attentively as he passed. He was a slight, tall man, whose legs did not half fill his leather breeches, and he appeared to be at the wrong side of sixty. He had a shrunken, weather-beaten, mulberry-coloured face, carried a large black patch over one eye, and turned neither to the right nor to the left, but rode on at the head of his men, with a grim, military inflexibility.

The countenances of these soldiers, officers as well as men, seemed all full of trouble, and, so to speak, scared and wild. He watched in vain for a single contented or comely face. They had, one and all, a melancholy and hang-dog look; and as they passed by, Peter fancied that the air grew cold.

He had seated himself upon a stone bench, from which, staring with all his might, he gazed upon the grotesque and noiseless procession as it filed by him. Noiseless it was; he could neither hear the jingle of accoutrements, the tread of feet, nor the rumble of the wheels; and when the old colonel turned his horse a little, and made as though he were giving the word of command, and a trumpeter, with a swollen blue nose and white feather fringe round his hat, who was walking beside him, turned about and put his bugle to his lips, still Peter heard nothing, although it was plain the sound had reached the soldiers, for they instantly changed their front to three abreast.

'Botheration!' muttered Peter, 'is it deaf I'm growing?'

But that could not be, for he heard the sighing of the breeze and the rush of the neighbouring Liffey plain enough.

'Well,' said he, in the same cautious key, 'by the piper, this bangs Banagher fairly! It's either the French Army that's in it, come to take the town iv Chapelizod by surprise, an' makin' no noise for feard iv wakenin' the inhabitants; or else it's—it's—what it's—somethin' else. But, tundher-an-ouns, what's gone wrong wid Fitzpatrick's shop across the way?'

The brown dingy stone building at the opposite side of the street looked newer and cleaner than he had been used to see it; the front door of it stood open, and a sentry in the same grotesque uniform, with shouldered musket, was pacing noiselessly to and fro before it. At the angle of this building, in like manner, a wide gate (of which Peter had no recollection whatever) stood open, before which, also, a similar sentry was gliding and into this gateway the whole column gradually passed, and Peter finally lost sight of it.

'I'm not asleep; I'm not dhramin',' said he, rubbing his eyes, and stamping slightly on the pavement, to assure himself that he was wide awake. 'It is a quare business, whatever it is; an' it's not alone that, but everything about the town looks strange to me. There's Tresham's house new painted, bedad, an' them flowers in the windies! An' Delaney's house, too, that had not a whole pane of glass in it this morning, and scarce a slate on the roof of it! It is not possible it's that it's dhrunk I am. Sure there's the big tree, and not a leaf of it changed since I passed, and the stars overhead, all right. I don't think it is in my eyes it is.'

And so looking about him, and every moment finding or fancying new food for wonder, he walked along the pavement, intending, without further delay, to make his way home.

But his adventures for the night were not concluded. He had nearly reached the angle of the short lane that leads up to the church, when for the first time he perceived that an officer, in the uniform he had just seen, was walking before, only a few yards in advance of him.

The officer was walking along at an easy, swinging gait, and carried his sword under his arm, and was looking down on the pavement with an air of reverie.

In the very fact that he seemed unconscious of Peter's presence, and disposed to keep his reflection to himself, there was something reassuring. Besides, the reader must please to remember that our hero had a sufficient quantity of good punch before his adventure commenced, and was thus fortified against those qualms and terrors under which, in a more reasonable state of mind, he might not impossibly have sunk.

The idea of the French invasion revived in full power in Peter's fuddled imagination, as he pursued the nonchalant swagger of the officer.

'Be the powers iv Molly Kelly, I'll ax him what it is,' said Peter, with a sudden accession of rashness. 'He may tell me or not, as he plases, but he can't be offinded, anyhow.'

With this reflection having inspired himself, Peter cleared his voice and begun:

'Captain!' said he, 'I ax your pardon, an' maybe you'd be so condescindin' to my ignorance as to tell me, if it's plasin' to yer honour, whether your honour is not a Frenchman, if it's plasin' to you.'

This he asked, not thinking that, had it been as he suspected, not one word of his question in all probability would have been intelligible to the person he addressed. He was, however, understood, for the officer answered him in English, at the same time slackening his pace and moving a little to the side of the pathway, as if to invite his interrogator to take his place beside him.

'No; I am an Irishman,' he answered.

'I humbly thank your honour,' said Peter, drawing nearer—for the affability and the nativity of the officer encouraged him—'but maybe your honour is in the sarvice of the King of France?'

'I serve the same king as you do,' he answered, with a sorrowful significance which Peter did not comprehend at the time; and, interrogating in turn, he asked, 'But what calls you forth at this hour of the day?'

'The day, your honour!—the night, you mane.'

'It was always our way to turn night into day, and we keep to it still,' remarked the soldier. 'But no matter, come up here to my house; I have a job for you, if you wish to earn some money easily. I live here.'

As he said this, he beckoned authoritatively to Peter, who followed almost mechanically at his heels, and they turned up a little lane near the old Roman Catholic chapel, at the end of which stood, in Peter's time, the ruins of a tall, stone-built house.

Like everything else in the town, it had suffered a metamorphosis. The stained and ragged walls were now erect, perfect, and covered with pebble-dash; window-panes glittered coldly in every window; the green hall-door had a bright knocker on it. Peter did not know whether to believe his previous or his present impressions: seeing is believing, and Peter could not dispute the reality of the scene. All the records of his memory seemed but the images of a tipsy dream. In a trance of astonishment and perplexity, therefore, he submitted himself to the chances of his adventure.

The door opened, the officer beckoned with a melancholy air of authority to Peter, and entered. Our hero followed him into a sort of hall, which was very dark, but he was guided by the steps of the soldier, and, in silence, they ascended the stairs. The moonlight, which shone in at the lobbies, showed an old, dark wainscoting, and a heavy, oak banister. They passed by closed doors at different landing-places, but all was dark and silent as, indeed, became that late hour of the night.

Now they ascended to the topmost floor. The captain paused for a minute at the nearest door, and, with a heavy groan, pushing it open, entered the room. Peter remained at the threshold. A slight female form in a sort of loose, white robe, and with a great deal of dark hair hanging loosely about her, was standing in the middle of the floor with her back towards them.

The soldier stopped short before he reached her, and said, in a voice of great anguish, 'Still the same, sweet bird—sweet bird! Still the same.' Whereupon, she turned suddenly, and threw her arms about the neck of the officer, with a gesture of fondness and despair, and her frame was agitated as if by a burst of sobs. He held her close to his breast in silence; and honest Peter felt a strange terror creep over him, as he witnessed these mysterious sorrows and endearments.

'Tonight, tonight—and then ten years more—ten long years—another ten years.'

The officer and the lady seemed to speak these words together; her voice mingled with his in a musical and fearful wail, like a distant summer wind, in the dead hour of night wandering through ruins. Then he heard the officer say, alone in a voice of anguish:

'Upon me be it all, for ever, sweet birdie, upon me.'

And again they seemed to mourn together in the same soft and desolate wail, like sounds of grief heard from a great distance.

Peter was thrilled with horror, but he was also under a strange fascination, and an intense and dreadful curiosity held him fast.

The moon was shining obliquely into the room, and through the window Peter saw the familiar slopes of the Park, sleeping mistily under its shimmer. He could also see the furniture of the room with tolerable distinctness—the old balloon-backed chairs, a four-post bed in a sort of recess, and a rack against the wall, from which hung some military clothes and accoutrements; and the sight of all these homely objects reassured him somewhat and he could not help feeling unspeakably curious to see the face of the girl whose long hair was streaming over the officer's epaulet.

Peter, accordingly, coughed, at first slightly, and afterward more loudly, to recall her from her reverie of grief, and, apparently, he succeeded; for she turned round, as did her companion, and both, standing hand in hand, gazed upon him fixedly. He thought he had never seen such large, strange eyes in all his life; and their gaze seemed to chill the very air around him, and arrest the pulses of his heart. An eternity of misery and remorse was in the shadowy faces that looked upon him.

If Peter had taken less whisky by a single thimbleful, it is probable that he would have lost heart altogether before these figures, which seemed every moment to assume a more marked and fearful, though hardly definable, contrast to ordinary human shapes.

'What is it you want with me?' he stammered.

'To bring my lost treasure to the churchyard,' replied the lady, in a silvery voice of more than mortal desolation.

The word 'treasure' revived the resolution of Peter, although a cold sweat was covering him, and his hair was bristling with horror; he believed, however, that he was on the brink of fortune, if he could but command nerve to brave the interview to its close.

'And where,' he gasped, 'is it hid—where will I find it?'

They both pointed to the sill of the window, through which the moon was shining at the far end of the room, and the soldier said:

'Under that stone.'

Peter drew a long breath, and wiped the cold dew from his face, preparatory to passing to the window, where he expected to secure the reward of his protracted errors. But looking steadfastly at the window, he saw the faint image of a new-born child sitting upon the sill in the moonlight, with its little arms stretched toward him, and a smile so heavenly as he never beheld before.

At sight of this, strange to say, his heart entirely failed him, he looked on the figures that stood near, and beheld them gazing on the infantine form with a smile so guilty and distorted, that he felt as if he were entering alive among the scenery of hell, and, shuddering, he cried in an irrepressible agony of horror:

'I'll have nothing to say with you, and nothing to do with you; I

He saw the faint image of a new-born child.

don't know what yez are or what yez want iv me, but let me go this minute, every one of yez, in the name of God.'

With these words there came a strange rumbling and sighing about Peter's ears; he lost sight of everything, and felt that peculiar and not unpleasant sensation of falling softly, that sometimes supervenes in sleep, ending in a dull shock. After that he had neither dream nor consciousness till he wakened, chill and stiff, stretched between two piles of old rubbish, among the black and roofless walls of the ruined house. We need hardly mention that the village had put on its wonted air of neglect and decay, or that Peter looked around him in vain for traces of those novelties which had so puzzled and distracted him upon the previous night.

'Ay, ay,' said his grandmother, removing her pipe, as he ended his description of the view from the bridge, 'sure enough I remember myself, when I was a slip of a girl, these little white cabins among the gardens by the river-side. The artillery sogers that was married, or had not room in the barracks, used to be in them, but they're all gone long ago.'

'The Lord be merciful to us!' she resumed, when he had described the military procession, 'it's often I seen the regiment marchin' into the town, just as you saw it last night, acushla. Oh, voch, but it makes my heart sore to think iv them days; they were pleasant times, sure enough; but is not it terrible, avick, to think it's what it was the ghost of the rigiment you seen? The Lord betune us an' harm, for it was nothing else, as sure as I'm sittin' here.'

When he mentioned the peculiar figure of the old officer who rode at the head of the regiment:

'That,' said the old crone, dogmatically, 'was ould Colonel Grimshaw, the Lord preserve us! He's buried in the churchard iv Chapelizod, and well I remember him, when I was a young thing, an' a cross ould floggin' fellow he was wid the men, an' a devil's boy among the girls—rest his soul!'

'Amen!' said Peter; 'it's often I read his tombstone myself; but he's a long time dead.'

'Sure, I tell you he died when I was no more nor a slip iv a girl—the Lord betune us and harm!'

'I'm afeard it is what I'm not long for this world myself, afther seeing such a sight as that,' said Peter fearfully.

'Nonsense, avourneen,' retorted his grandmother, indignantly, though she had herself misgivings on the subject; 'sure there was Phil Doolan, the ferryman, that seen black Ann Scanlan in his own boat, and what harm ever kem of it?'

Peter proceeded with his narrative, but when he came to the description of the house, in which his adventure had had so sinister a conclusion, the old woman was at fault.

'I know the house and the ould walls well, an' I can remember the time there was a roof on it, and the doors an' windows in it, but it had a bad name about being haunted, but by who, or for what, I forget intirely.'

'Did you ever hear was there gold or silver there?' he inquired.

'No, no, avick, don't be thinking about the likes; take a fool's advice, and never go next or near them ugly black walls again the longest day you have to live; an' I'd take my davy, it's what it's the same word the priest himself I'd be afther sayin' to you if you wor to ax his raverence consarnin' it, for it's plain to be seen it was nothing good you seen there, and there's neither luck nor grace about it.'

Peter's adventure made no little noise in the neighbourhood, as the reader may well suppose; and a few evenings after it, being on an errand to old Major Vandeleur, who lived in a snug old-fashioned house, close by the river, under a perfect bower of ancient trees, he was called on to relate the story in the parlour.

The Major was, as I have said, an old man; he was small, lean, and upright, with a mahogany complexion, and a wooden inflexibility of face; he was a man, besides, of few words, and if he was old, it follows plainly that his mother was older still. Nobody could guess or tell how old, but it was admitted that her own generation had long passed away, and that she had not a competitor left. She had French blood in her veins, and although she did not retain her charms quite so well as Ninon de l'Enclos, she was in full possession of all her mental activity, and talked quite enough for herself and the Major.

'So, Peter,' she said, 'you have seen the dear old Royal Irish again in the streets of Chapelizod. Make him a tumbler of punch, Frank; and Peter, sit down, and while you take it let us have the story.'

Peter accordingly, seated near the door, with a tumbler of the nectarian stimulant steaming beside him, proceeded with marvellous courage, considering they had no light but the uncertain glare of the fire, to relate with minute particularity his awful adventure. The old lady listened at first with a smile of good-natured incredulity; her cross-examination touching the drinking-bout at Palmerstown had been teasing, but as the narrative proceeded she became attentive, and at length absorbed, and once or twice she uttered ejaculations of pity or awe. When it was over, the old lady looked with a somewhat sad and stern abstraction on the table, patting her cat assiduously meanwhile, and then suddenly looking upon her son, the Major, she said:

'Frank, as sure as I live, he has seen the wicked Captain Devereux.'

The major uttered an inarticulate expression of wonder.

'The house was precisely that he had described. I have told you the story often, as I heard it from your dear grandmother, about the poor young lady he ruined, and the dreadful suspicion about the little baby. She, poor thing, died in that house heartbroken, and you know he was shot shortly after in a duel.'

This was the only light that Peter ever received respecting his adventure. It was supposed, however, that he still clung to the hope that treasure of some sort was hidden about the old house, for he was often seen lurking about its walls, and at last his fate overtook him, poor fellow, in the pursuit; for climbing near the summit one day, his holding gave way, and he fell upon the hard uneven ground, fracturing a leg and a rib, and after a short interval died; he, like the other heroes of these true tales, lies buried in the little churchyard of Chapelizod.

WHAT A NIGHT!

Pat Smythe

The three Jays—Jimmy, his sister Jane, Jacqueline plus their friend Billy Noakes—had come up with me from Miserden in the Cotswolds and were at the Horse of the Year Show in the Haringey arena to compete for the Prince Philip Cup for riders under seventeen.

As non-riding captain of the team I knew they were up against tough opposition—all the more reason to avoid snags. But having had my permission to watch Jacky's cousin Darcy test-fly a new jet plane at Northolt during the afternoon, Jimmy, after some hair-raising adventures, had got back only just in time for the start of the competition at five past ten, while earlier in the day the hoof of a pony from another team had landed smack on Jane's right foot. What with Jimmy missing and Jane's badly swollen foot, it had seemed for a time that the Miserden team would have to scratch. But Jane was determined to go on. 'I'm going to get on my pony', she had said, 'and ride into the ring. And I'm not coming out till the competition's over!'

What a night it had been! And there was still the last exciting event to go—the climax to weeks of effort and hopes. I sank into my seat, feeling quite exhausted by the strain of it all and by Jimmy's sudden appearance just when I was sure he would never turn up in time. As the teams paraded, I glanced at the figures I had scribbled down in the margin of my programme. Of the four teams with this one round to go, the leaders had thirty-four points to date, Miserden had thirty-two, the third team had thirty and the other team had only twenty-three. That meant that Miserden, if they maintained the same average—and so did the other teams—would finish second overall. If somehow they could get back three points from the present leaders, they would win the Prince Philip Cup!

There were two enormous 'ifs' and they both pointed at Jane. Jimmy, I knew, was tough, and although he looked as though he had been through some harrowing experiences in the last few hours—judging by his torn and dirty clothes and the scratches on his hands—as long as he was physically sound he had a natural buoyancy that would lift him up in a crisis.

But Jane was the problem. She rode past with head erect, but her face was chalk-white and her lips were compressed. I suspected that she was still in great pain and I wondered whether she would be able to keep going.

The first event was the Grooms' Stakes. The number one in each team had to mount his own pony and then lead the number two's pony round four bending posts to the other end of the arena and hand over to the number two, who would lead the number three's pony back and hand over in turn—and so on until the number four completed the event by riding his own pony and leading the number one's past the finishing post.

This was not too bad for Jane and the others almost made up the yard or two lost by not being able to vault on. In a very tight finish Miserden came second, beating the team that was two points ahead of them by a length or so. Miserden had pulled back a valuable point.

Next came the Sharpshooters' Race. Two riders from each team would be mounted bareback on one pony. One rider from each pair would have to dismount and fling wooden balls at the Aunt Sallies until they were knocked flat. Then the riders had to remount and both pairs would gallop back to the start-line.

The Miserden team had worked it out in practice that the pairings should be Jane and Jimmy on one pony and Jacky and Billy on the other, with the two boys being the sharpshooters because of their superior throwing power. The choosing of this event was a lucky break for our team, for it meant that Jane would stay aboard her pony all the time and conserve her strength. And the luck held. The other teams had one boy apiece but otherwise had to rely on girls to knock down the Aunt Sallies. Whatever one's feelings about the ability of girls to ride better than boys, when it comes to throwing even the most ardent feminist has to admit that boys are usually superior.

So it was this time. Jimmy and Billy slid off the backs of the ponies, ran to the heaps of wooden balls on the arena floor and, with that side-arm flick that girls never seem to be able to manage, they began to fling the balls at the flat wooden targets. The crowd was roaring encouragement to the throwers and chuckling whenever a particularly wide throw sent a ball sailing into the stop-net at the back, thoughtfully provided by the arena party. It took Jimmy and Billy only three or four throws each to send their targets tilting backwards; then they turned, ran back, leap-frogged over their respective pony's quarters and grabbed Jane and Jacky round the waist as the ponies bounded towards the start-line.

Miserden finished a length ahead of the next team and the luckless pair who came last just couldn't hit their Aunt Sallies. The other teams had all finished and still they threw ever more wildly while the audience rocked with laughter. The two girls were brave enough to persevere, for they knew that every point was valuable and minutes later they managed to get the targets down.

The four valuable points they had gained put the Miserden team in the lead with thirty-nine points. One behind came the previous leaders, who had come third in the Sharpshooters' Race, and the next team had thirty-four points. Two more events to go and a one-point lead—a shudder of excitement ran through my limbs. Could they do it? Would Jane's bad foot stand up to the strain? Their present rivals were breathing down their necks, one point away. The crisis was on.

The arena party were marking out a circle with small bushes in wooden boxes and were planting one straight row of posts in the centre. I guessed that the next event was to be Musical Hats. Wide-brimmed straw hats were to be placed on top of the poles and there would be one hat fewer than the number of riders taking part. The riders had to circle round the ring and when the music stopped make a dash to the centre and grab a hat off a pole. The rider left hatless would be eliminated, one hat would then be removed and so on until two riders vied for the last hat. The team points were calculated on a cumulative basis, so that it did not follow that the team supplying the individual winner automatically won the whole event.

Jane was eliminated in the first round, although she usually excelled at this event, being able to keep her head and judge the right distance to the nearest hat when her rivals got flurried with excitement. However, on this occasion her injured foot must have been hurting her just when the music stopped, as she was not concentrating at that moment and was caught at the end of the arena farthest from the hats. Jacky went out before long after tearing half the brim off a hat in her mad rush past. Unluckily for her, another competitor had already gripped it firmly, so Jacky was left waving the brim while her grinning rival donned the rest of the hat.

Jimmy, too, had misfortune and was knocked out soon after. The music seemed to stop and he bolted for the centre, only to find that the band was just breaking into a waltz. While he was still turning back outside the circle, the music really did stop and poor Jimmy was left facing the wrong way in the rush.

By cantering slowly whenever he was facing the band and speeding up whenever he had to turn a corner away from them, Billy was cunning enough to survive to the last two but, when the points were added up, it turned out that Miserden came third over all. Their chief rivals came second and that brought them up to level pegging—with one event to go. The other two teams were no longer in the hunt, the nearer one being four points behind the joint leaders at this stage. And so, in the next three or four minutes, one of them was going to win the Prince Philip Cup.

My throat was dry and my heart seemed to be knocking against my ribs. And then my erratically beating heart sank. I saw the arena party laying out four sacks on the centre line. The final event was to be the Sack Race—and none of the twelve events listed could have been worse from Jane's point of view. Each rider in turn had to dash for the centre line, dismount, climb into a sack and then hobble or hop to the far end, leading his pony. On crossing the far line, he would hand the sack over to the next rider who in turn rode for the centre line, dismounted and hopped the rest of the course; and so on until number four crossed the last line, leading his pony.

Jimmy must have spotted that something was wrong with Jane's foot, for I saw him go into a whispered huddle with Billy and then talk urgently to the other two. Jane shook her head but the others seemed to persuade her. Were they going to withdraw? I wondered. It would be an anti-climax to all their efforts but it might save Jane from further pain. But then I realized that Jimmy and Billy had changed the order. Instead of going second Jane was to go to last. Perhaps they hoped to have built up such a lead when her turn came that she could take things easy. I licked my dry lips and waited.

The starter dropped the handkerchief and the leading riders in the four teams were away. Jimmy had practised a flying getaway on his pony, training it to spring from a standing start like a polo pony. He picked up a yard on their rivals. slid off and, leading his pony at arm's length so that it would not tread on the sack, he hopped up to the far end, gaining another yard in the process. A quick handover and Jacky was away next. She pulled Pickles into a 'four-wheel skid' at the centre line, dismounted, climbed into the sack and went like a dangeroo for the far end. As Jimmy had done, she gained another two yards for the Miserden team and slowly I began to breathe again.

Billy was his usual dependable self—neat, precise and determined not to risk all by losing his head. He reached the centre line, was off in a flash but very deliberately climbed into the sack. I wanted to yell at him to hurry, to get on with it—but I knew in my heart that he was right not to be rushed. He took small, controlled hops but he covered the ground and his pony trotted quietly alongside. The number three of their chief rivals may have picked up a couple of feet, even a yard, but Miserden held the lead.

And now it all hung on Jane. The packed arena was roaring encouragement at the teams and my shout of 'Come on, Jane!' was lost in the din. She grabbed the sack from Billy and shot away from the line. She sprang off her pony at the centre point and I could see her wince as her bad foot hit the ground. She climbed into the sack, a shade clumsily, and now her rival was only two yards behind.

Twenty yards to go to win the Prince Philip Cup—and perhaps twenty hops to do it in. Twenty times her injured foot would come crashing down on the hard ground and a searing pain would shoot up her leg. Just twenty yards and twenty hops—but each one a concentration of agony. Jane started off with one hand holding her pony's mane, so as to take some of the weight off her foot. I had to blink the misty tears from my eyes and concentrate on watching her face. She landed and her mouth screwed up with shock. On she went, gathering her strength and her nerve for each jump, landing awkwardly as she tried to take her weight on her sound left leg, tottering, then capturing her balance and repeating the effort. The pony sensed the excitement and Jane had to leave the support of the mane in order to control its head with the reins.

Twelve yards to go and now her rival was only a foot behind. Three more agonizing hops—and they were dead level. Jane made a supreme effort and for the next five yards she kept abreast. But her face had gone milk-white, her eyes were almost closed and she was swaying like a tired top at the end of its run. Three yards to go and the other number four went ahead. And then, as Jane made her last despairing effort, she pitched headlong. I thought she had fainted and I half-rose in my seat. But somehow she staggered to her feet, took two last hops, then fell across the line. She had come a gallant second, beaten by just a yard.

There was pandemonium in the arena—cheers for the winner and a roar of sympathy for Jane. She quickly recovered and was able to take part in the prize-giving ceremony and the tour of honour that followed.

It was nearly half an hour before I could commiserate with the Jays for the arena went dark, there was a roll on the drums and twin spotlights picked out the four state trumpeters and the drummer from the Royal Horse Guards who heralded the cavalcade which wound up the show. Into the ring came the great horses and riders of this and past years. They assembled in their pride and a strange hush settled over the audience as the well-known voice of Dorian Williams read out that splendid tribute to the horse, written by Ronald Duncan:

'Where in this wide world can man find nobility without pride, friendship without envy or beauty without vanity? Here, where grace is laced with muscle, and strength by gentleness confined.

'He serves without servility, he has fought without enmity. There is nothing so powerful, nothing less violent; there is nothing so quick, nothing more patient.

'England's past has been borne on his back. All our history is his industry. We are his heirs, he our inheritance. Ladies and Gentlemen—the Horse!'

So ended the Horse of the Year Show. On the following morning we started back for the Cotswolds, not at all down-hearted. Though we had not won the Cup the team had proved its worth against the toughest competition in Britain. And next time . . . 'Next time,' said Jane cheerily, 'nobody's pony is going to stamp on *me*, don't you worry!'

A NUN'S STORY

Lawrence Wilson

One fascinating thing about human life is the way in which genius crops up in the most unexpected places. It is not confined to the families of the rich or famous. Far from it. Admittedly Sir Winston Churchill was descended from the Dukes of Marlborough and St Francis of Assisi was the son of a wealthy cloth merchant; but the father of the poet John Keats had been a stable-boy, the artist William Turner was the son of a barber, Charles Dickens son of a clerk in the navy pay office, the composer Tchaikovsky son of an inspector of mines—and Mother Teresa of Calcutta was the daughter of an Albanian peasant.

The family, surnamed Bejaxhiu, consisted of one son and two daughters and lived in Skopje, Yugoslavia. Teresa's real name was Agnes, and she was born in 1910. At the age of twelve she became convinced that God was calling her to become a nun and that this vocation would in some way involve serving the poor. To start with, the idea did not appeal to her because her life in the family was so happy, but while at school in the following years she heard a great deal about the work of Christians helping the poor in India and became eager to follow their example. At eighteen she went to Ireland to prepare for her work and joined a religious order there called the Loreto nuns. A few months later she was sent to India.

As a nun, though, she had to do what she was told, and for some years there was no question of her working with the poor. In fact the opposite occurred. She was sent to a beautiful place called Darjeeling in the foothills of the Himalayas to teach geography and mathematics to the children of rich Indian parents. She found she enjoyed teaching very much and so, some years later, was glad to be sent to another convent school at Entally, a suburb of Calcutta. The place was clean, well organized, and set in a beautiful garden. But just beyond the convent wall was one of the worst slums in the city where people were literally dying in the streets of leprosy, malaria, tuberculosis, cholera—and starvation. 'Teresa' saw them and knew at once that here were the poorest of the poor that God had sent her to tend. What she did not know at that time was that in a city of seven million inhabitants (including the suburbs) there were nearly half a million of them.

At one time Calcutta was the capital of British-ruled India, and it is still a busy port and industrial centre. There have always been strong contrasts of wealth and poverty there, rich merchants' houses jostling slums where ragged poverty-striken people live and die in the streets or huddle together in makeshift shelters, their only possessions the odd cup and a few rusty cooking pots to be used when—and if—they have anything to cook. Only half the city has proper sanitation, otherwise sewage runs in open drains beside the streets. In the last four decades the squalor and poverty have been made much worse by an influx of refugees, including Hindus fleeing from the newly created state of Bangladesh (East Pakistan) and the victims of flood and famine in Calcutta's swampy hinterland. Already in 1946, when Teresa looked beyond her convent wall, the situation was bad enough—too bad for international or government aid to make much impression.

Yet here was a small, rather frail cloistered nun deciding that she alone had to do something for those desperate people. Men priding themselves on their sanity might well have called her crazy, and she would have agreed with them had she intended to compete with international airlines flying in sacks of wheat or those organizing large-scale relief. But she wasn't. There was a difference, and in this difference lies the crux of her story.

Right from the start Mother Teresa was determined to give the poor not only material help—food, shelter, clothing, medicines—but also love from person to person, believing that without it they would always feel rejected as outcasts. Let her speak as she did in 1970, after long experience:

'I have come more and more to realize that it is being unwanted that is the worst disease that any human being can ever suffer. Nowadays we have found medicines for leprosy and lepers can be cured. There's medicine for TB and consumptives can be cured. For all kinds of diseases there are medicines and cures. But for being unwanted, except there are willing hands to serve and there's a loving heart to love, I don't think this terrible disease can ever be cured.'

So, back in 1946, after the day's teaching was over, Mother Teresa would slip out into the streets to bring food and her loving concern to the starving people personally. Some weeks passed, and then, on a train journey to Darjeeling, she felt that God was calling her to give up teaching and devote her whole life to the poor. Two years later the Pope gave his blessing on her enterprise and she left the convent for ever. She had exactly five rupees (25p) in her pocket.

First, friends helped to send her to another town where she took a crash course in medical training. Then, back in Calcutta, she was given shelter by another order of nuns, the Little Sisters of the Poor, and started work immediately in the slums. Sister Agnes, now her principal assistant, remembers: 'She didn't know where she was going or what she was going to do in the future. Nothing. But she was not frightened. She knew God was calling her and would lead her where he wanted. She used to go out every day carrying something: a little bread, some medicine, things like that. And she used to walk from slum to slum to slum. Always working. Then always she would go to pray and eat the little food she had left, if any; she probably gave it all away.'

The work was hard and Mother Teresa made it even harder because, as she says, 'to be able to love the poor and to know the poor we must be poor ourselves.' This means that, to this day, she and her helpers exist on the barest necessities of life: the simplest food, hardly any personal possessions, no money of their own and, for clothes, a length of cheap white cotton wrapped round the body, like the sari which Hindu women wear. But in those early years, before her name became known throughout the world, many of her former pupils came to join her, promising to devote their whole lives to her work, some even while still studying for their exams. Surprisingly, a few were high-caste Indian girls who normally would have refused to go anywhere near the 'untouchables', as they were called by the Hindus.

Soon Mother Theresa set up a slum school for young children in an open space among dilapidated huts, teaching them at first only how to keep clean and some signs from the Bengali alphabet. These had to be written in the mud with a stick because there were no blackboards, and there were no chairs or benches either. But on the second day someone donated a table, then a chair, later a cupboard.

From the start she refused to accept payment from anyone, assuming anyone was able to pay, nor would she accept government money. As it was God's work she believed God would provide. and money certainly came, from friends, from people touched by the obvious value of her work, always enough, just enough to help her do what she wanted —and she wanted to do a great deal more. For the growing number of her dedicated helpers, the Missionaries of Charity as they were now called, she needed a place where they could live, a Mother House, and this was provided by a well-wisher at a nominal rent.

Above all, she needed a home for the dying. She knew that from personal experience. Once, when still teaching at Entally, she had picked up a sick woman in the streets, taken her back to the convent and given her her own bed. Then she found another woman with her feet half eaten away by rats and ants. Teresa had somehow got her to hospital and simply refused to leave till the doctors had taken her in. They were not callous or indifferent, but Calcutta's hospitals are always overcrowded, bursting at the seams. There is never room for everyone.

Now Teresa was determined to have a place where at least some of Calcutta's half-million derelicts could die in dignity, tended with loving care. They had to know they were wanted and loved, at least for the few hours left to them in this world. She had no desire to set up a big rescue operation, even if she had had the resources, because she knew that persons would be lost in sheer numbers and become simply mouths to feed. 'I do not agree,' she has said, 'with the big way of doing things. To us what matters is the individual.' And in the individual, however disgusting his or her sores and sickness, however repellent the personality, she sees nothing less than the spirit of Jesus Christ.

In 1952 the city corporation offered her a place for the dying. It had been a rest-house for pilgrims visiting the temple of a Hindu goddess and was at that time a doss-house for thugs, thieves and drug-addicts. They did not like having to move out and they made a lot of trouble, even threatening to kill her. 'All right,' she said, 'then kill me, but let us have an end to this nonsense.' Incredibly then they gave way and the home was set up and called Nirmal Hriday, 'The Place of the Pure Heart'.

When journalists visit the home today they are scared to start with, but after they have seen the long rows of mattresses, on each a dark figure quietly awaiting his time to leave this world, the Sisters flitting to and fro giving a drink here, a word of comfort there, and have felt the atmosphere of love, all agree that in Nirmal Hriday there is an indescribable sense of peace. In nearly twenty years 23,000 people have been taken there from the streets, most of them in the last stages of illness and disease, so that inevitably nearly half have died. But that is what the place is for: to give final comfort to the dying.

But to Mother Teresa this was by no means enough. She had only to go into a Calcutta street or one of the big railway stations to see there were thousands still uncared for. In the main hallways, instead of the bustling passengers seen in London, there were pathetic groups squatting everywhere, whole families living, dying and being born—among them many lepers.

Leprosy is a terrible infectious disease which attacks the central nervous system until bit by bit the whole body becomes involved. Deep ulcers form on the skin, fingers and toes lose their feeling and drop off, even the lungs and vocal cords are affected, so that the sufferer can barely speak. At one time, and still today in many places, when an Indian family saw the tell-tale patch on a member's skin they were so scared of infection that they simply pushed him out to wander the streets or the countryside. Whole colonies of these poor people would then cling together in utter hopelessness because there was nowhere among the fit and active for them to go. So Mother Teresa started to help, first with a humble shed in one of the slums for leper children, then with proper settlements in other areas where the lepers could be treated and given light work. Mobile dispensaries were set up, later still a hospital and rehabilitation centre entirely for lepers.

It would seem horrible as well as dangerous work being with such people, but Teresa's flock of nuns, ever growing in numbers, coming now from all over the world, strictly trained and dedicated, go about it with positive joy. Like her, they say quite simply that Jesus guides them and it is Jesus they serve in the lepers. Even in the most disreputable characters they can see something good. Recently a journalist was shown round a leper settlement. A patient was introduced. 'He's a murderer,' said the Sister cheerily. 'He has been in prison. He's deformed, but he has a heart of gold. Only yesterday he told me, "You Sisters have defeated me. You love even the wicked".'

The poor, the starving, the sick and small children—all come within the net of Mother Teresa's loving concern. She has set up homes for children abandoned in the streets, left with her by their parents, sent from hospitals, even rescued from dustbins. Many of the babies are born prematurely and when brought in are too feeble even to suck, so they have to be fed through the nose or by injection. Though the homes are crowded so far no child has ever been refused.

Slowly the work of the Missionaries of Charity became better known and began to spread throughout India and the rest of the world. Men as well as girls began to volunteer and went through the same strict training, took the same vows of poverty, chastity and obedience, with the same object: to give love and succour to the poor. By 1975 sixty-one centres were operating in India and more in other countries, in the slums of London and Belfast, in the USA, Australia, Italy, Israel, Bangladesh, Jordan, Venezuela, Peru, the Yemen, Mauritius, New Guinea, Tanzania and Ethiopia. Now, too, there are the Co-Workers of Mother Teresa, people everywhere, even in small English villages, who collect clothing, blankets, cigarette coupons, trading stamps and money for the great cause. School-children in England give money to buy bread for the starving; in West Germany they give the equivalent of a glass of milk per day or per week.

Mother Teresa has been nominated for the Nobel Peace Prize. Many other awards have been showered on her. But she shrugs it all off. All this recognition, she says, is not for her but for the poor whom she serves. And here once more we have to recognize the difference between international relief organized impersonally and what she and her helpers are doing throughout the world. They do not try to convert anyone to Christianity, but they themselves are committed Christians, believing that God gives them his own love to pass on to suffering individuals and that beneath their sores and the often hideous diseases the spirit of God is in them too, waiting to be served.

So from the conviction of one twelve-year-old girl, first felt over fifty years ago, that her destiny was to serve the poor, has grown a mighty world-wide band of helpers, joyous and powerful in their faith and self-sacrifice.

THE RESCUE OF LORNA DOONE

R. D. Blackmore

John Ridd had first seen Lorna Doone when as a boy he was returning home from Blundell's School; one of the Doones was carrying the little girl flung across his saddlebow. The Doones were a band of fierce and hated outlaws living in Glen Doone, and it was they who had murdered John's father. John, bent on revenge, finds his way into the Doone valley, and there meets Lorna. They continue to see each other secretly as they grow up and fall in love. When Lorna tells John one day that she is to be starved until she consents to marry Carver Doone, he decides the time has come to take her away from her captors.

To my great delight, I found the weather, not often friendly to lovers, and lately seeming so hostile, had in the most important matter done me a signal service. For when I had promised to take my love from the power of those wretches, the only way of escape apparent lay through the main Doone-gate. For though I might climb the cliffs myself, especially with the snow to aid me, I durst not try to fetch Lorna up them, even if she were not half-starved, as well as partly frozen; and as for Gwenny's door, as we called it (that is to say, the little entrance from the wooded hollow), it was snowed up long ago to the level of the hills around. Therefore I was at my wit's end, how to get them out; the passage by the Doone-gate being long, and dark, and difficult, and leading to such a weary circuit among the snowy moors and hills.

But now, being homeward-bound by the shortest possible track, I slipped along between the bonfire and the boundary cliffs, where I found a caved way of snow behind a sort of avalanche: so that if the Doones had been keeping watch (which they were not doing, but revelling) they could scarcely have discovered me. And when I came to my old ascent, where I had often scaled the cliff and made across the mountains, it struck me that I would just have a look at my first and painful entrance, to wit, the water-slide. I never for a moment imagined that this could help me now; for I never had dared to descend it, even in the finest weather; still I had a curiosity to know what my old friend was like, with so much snow upon him. But, to my very great surprise, there was scarcely any snow there at all, though plenty curling high over head from the cliff, like bolsters over it. Probably the sweeping of the north-east wind up the narrow chasm had kept the showers from blocking it, although the water had no power under the bitter grip of frost. All my water-slide was now less a slide than a path of ice; furrowed where the waters ran over fluted ridges; seamed where wind had tossed and combed them, even while congealing; and crossed with little steps wherever the freezing torrent lingered. And here and there the ice was fibred with the trail of sludge-weed, slanting from the side, and matted, so as to make resting-place.

Lo, it was easy track and channel, as if for the very purpose made, down which I could guide my sledge, with Lorna sitting in it. There were only two things to be feared; one, lest the rolls of snow above should fall in and bury us; the other lest we should rush too fast, and so be carried headlong into the black whirlpool at the bottom, the middle of which was still unfrozen, and looking more horrible by the contrast. Against this danger I made provision by fixing a stout bar across; but of the other we must take our chance, and trust ourselves to providence.

I hastened home at my utmost speed, and told my mother for God's sake to keep the house up till my return, and to have plenty of fire blazing, and plenty of water boiling, and food enough hot for a dozen people, and the best bed aired with the warming-pan. Dear mother smiled softly at my excitement, though her own was not much less, I am sure, and enhanced by sore anxiety. Then I gave very strict directions to Annie, and praised her a little, and kissed her; and I even endeavoured to flatter Eliza, lest she should be disagreeable.

After this I took some brandy, both within and about me; the former because I had sharp work to do; and the latter in fear of whatever might happen, in such great cold, to my comrades. Also I carried some other provisions, grieving much at their coldness; and then I went to the upper linhay, and took our new light pony-sled, which had been made almost as much for pleasure as for business; though God only knows how our girls could have found any pleasure in bumping along so. On the snow, however, it ran as sweetly as if it had been made for it; yet I durst not take the pony with it; in the first place, because his hoofs would break through the ever-shifting surface of the light and piling snow; and secondly, because those ponies, coming from the forest, have a dreadful trick of neighing, and most of all in frosty weather.

Therefore I girded my own body with a dozen turns of hay-rope, twisting both the ends in under at the bottom of my breast, and winding the hay on the skew a little, that the hemp thong might not slip between, and so cut me in the drawing. I put a good piece of spare rope in the sled, and the cross-seat with the back to it, which was stuffed with our own wool, as well as two or three fur coats: and then just as I was starting, out came Annie, in spite of the cold, panting for fear of missing me, and with nothing on her head, but a lanthorn in one hand.

'Oh, John, here is the most wonderful thing! Mother has never shown it before; and I can't think how she could make up her mind. She had gotten it in a great well of a cupboard, with camphor, and spirits, and lavender. Lizzie says it is a most magnificent sealskin cloak, worth fifty pounds, or a farthing.'

'At any rate it is soft and warm,' said I, very calmly flinging it into the bottom of the sled. 'Tell mother I will put it over Lorna's feet.'

'Lorna's feet! Oh, you great fool,' cried Annie, for the first time reviling me; 'over her shoulders; and be proud, you very stupid John.'

'It is not good enough for her feet,' I answered, with strong emphasis; 'but don't tell mother I said so, Annie. Only thank her very kindly.'

With that I drew my traces hard, and set my ashen staff into the snow, and struck out with my best foot foremost (the best one at snow-shoes, I mean), and the sled came after me as lightly as a dog might follow; and Annie with the lanthorn seemed to be left behind and waiting, like a pretty lamp-post.

The full moon rose as bright behind me as a patin of pure silver, casting on the snow long shadows of the few things left above, burned rock, and shaggy foreland, and the labouring trees. In the great white desolation, distance was a mocking vision: hills looked nigh, and valleys far; when hills were far and valleys nigh. And the misty breath of frost, piercing through the ribs of rock, striking to the pith of trees, creeping to the heart of man, lay along the hollow places, like a serpent sloughing.

Even as my own gaunt shadow (travestied as if I were the moonlight's daddy-long-legs) went before me down the slope; even I, the shadow's master, who had tried in vain to cough, when coughing brought good liquorice, felt a pressure on my bosom, and a husking in my throat.

However, I went on quietly, and at a very tidy speed; being only too thankful that the snow had ceased, and no wind as yet arisen. And from the ring of low white vapour girding all the verge of sky, and from the rosy blue above, and the shafts of starlight set upon a quivering bow, as well as from the moon itself and the light behind it, having learned the signs of frost from its bitter twinges, I knew that we should have a night as keen as ever England felt. Nevertheless, I had work enough to keep me warm if I managed it. The question was, could I contrive to save my darling from it?

Daring not to risk my sled by any fall from the valley-cliffs, I dragged it very carefully up the steep incline of ice, through the narrow chasm, and so to the very brink and verge where first I had seen my Lorna, in the fishing days of boyhood. As then I had a trident fork, for sticking of the loaches, so now I had a strong ash stake, to lay across from rock to rock, and break the speed of descending. With this I moored the sled quite safe, at the very lip of the chasm, where all was now substantial ice, green and black in the moonlight; and then I set off up the valley, skirting along one side of it.

The stack-fire still was burning strongly, but with more of heat than blaze; and many of the younger Doones were playing on the verge of it, the children making rings of fire, and their mothers watching them. All the grave and reverend warriors, having heard of rheumatism, were inside of log and stone, in the two lowest houses, with enough of candles burning to make our list of sheep come short.

All these I passed, without the smallest risk of difficulty, walking up the channel of drift which I spoke of once before. And then I crossed, with more care, and to the door of Lorna's house, and made the sign, and listened, after taking my snow-shoes off.

But no one came, as I expected, neither could I espy a light. And I seemed to hear a faint low sound, like the moaning of the snow-wind. Then I knocked again more loudly, with a knocking at my heart; and receiving no answer, set all my power at once against the door. In a moment it flew inwards, and I glided along the passage with my feet still slippery. There in Lorna's room I saw, by the moonlight flowing in, a sight which drove me beyond sense.

Lorna was behind a chair, crouching in the corner, with her hands up, and a crucifix, or something that looked like it. In the middle of the room lay Gwenny Carfax, stupid, yet with one hand clutching the ankle of a struggling man. Another man stood above my Lorna, trying to draw the chair away. In a moment I had him round the waist, and he went out of the window with a mighty crash of glass; luckily for him that window had no bars like some of them. Then I took the other man by the neck; and he could not plead for mercy. I bore him out of the house as lightly as I would bear a baby, yet squeezing his throat a little more than I fain would do to an infant. By the bright moonlight I saw that I carried Marwood de Whichehalse. For his father's sake I spared him, and because he had been my schoolfellow: but with every muscle of my body strung with indignation, I cast him, like a skittle, from me into a snowdrift, which closed over him. Then I looked for the other fellow, tossed through Lorna's window; and found him lying stunned and bleeding, neither able to groan yet. Charleworth Doone, if his gushing blood did not much mislead me.

It was no time to linger now: I fastened my shoes in a moment, and caught up my own darling with her head upon my shoulder, where she whispered faintly; and telling Gwenny to follow me, or else I would come back for her, if she could not walk the snow, I ran the whole distance to my sled, caring not who might follow me. Then by the time I had set up Lorna, beautiful and smiling, with the sealskin cloak all over her, sturdy Gwenny came along, having trudged in the track of my snow-shoes, although with two bags on her back. I set her in beside her mistress, to support her, and keep warm; and then with one look back at the glen, which had been so long my home of heart, I hung behind the sled, and launched it down the steep and dangerous way.

Though the cliffs were black above us, and the road unseen in front, and a great white grave of snow might at a single word come down, Lorna was as calm and happy as an infant in its bed. She knew that I was with her; and when I told her not to speak, she touched my hand in silence. Gwenny was in a much greater fright, having never seen such a thing before, neither knowing what it is to yield to pure love's confidence. I could hardly keep her quiet, without making a noise myself.

With my staff from rock to rock, and my weight thrown backward, I broke the sled's too rapid way, and brought my grown love safely out, by the self-same road which first had led me to her girlish fancy, and my boyish slavery.

Unpursued, yet looking back as if some one must be after us, we skirted round the black whirling pool, and gained the meadows beyond it. Here there was hard collar work, the track being all uphill and rough; and Gwenny wanted to jump out, to lighten the sled and to push behind. But I would not hear of it; because it was now so deadly cold, and I feared that Lorna might get frozen, without having Gwenny to keep her warm. And after all, it was the sweetest labour I had ever known in all my life, to be sure that I was pulling Lorna, and pulling her to our own farmhouse.

Gwenny's nose was touched with frost, before we had gone much further, because she would not keep it quiet and snug beneath the seal-skin. And here I had to stop in the moonlight (which was very dangerous) and rub it with a clove of snow, as Eliza had taught me; and Gwenny scolding all the time, as if myself had frozen it. Lorna was now so far oppressed with all the troubles of the evening, and the joy that followed them, as well as by the piercing cold and difficulty of breathing, that she lay quite motionless, like fairest wax in the moonlight—when we stole a glance at her, beneath the dark folds of the cloak; and I thought that she was falling into the heavy snow-sleep, whence there is no awaking.

Therefore I drew my traces tight, and set my whole strength to the business; and we slipped along at a merry pace, although with many joltings, which must have sent my darling out into the cold snow-drifts, but for the short strong arm of Gwenny. And so in about an hour's time, in spite of many hindrances, we came home to the old courtyard, and all the dogs saluted us. My heart was quivering, and my cheeks as hot as the Doones' bonfire, with wondering both what Lorna would think of our farmyard, and what my mother would think of her. Upon the former subject my anxiety was wasted, for Lorna neither saw a thing, nor even opened her heavy eyes. And as to what mother would think of her, she was certain not to think at all, until she had cried over her.

And so indeed it came to pass. Even at this length of time, I can hardly tell it, although so bright before my mind, because it moves my heart so. The sled was at the open door, with only Lorna in it: for Gwenny Carfax had jumped out, and hung back in the clearing, giving any reason rather than the only true one—that she would not be intruding. At the door were all our people; first of course Betty Muxworthy, teaching me how to draw the sled, as if she had been born in it, and flourishing with a great broom, wherever a speck of snow lay. Then dear Annie, and old Molly (who was very quiet, and counted almost for nobody), and behind them mother, looking as if she wanted to come first, but doubted how the manners lay. In the distance Lizzie stood, fearful of encouraging, but unable to keep out of it.

Betty was going to poke her broom right in under the sealskin cloak, where Lorna lay unconscious, and where her precious breath hung frozen, like a silver cobweb; but I caught up Betty's broom, and flung it clean away over the corn chamber; and then I put the others by, and fetched my mother forward.

'You shall see her first,' I said; 'is she not your daughter? Hold the light there, Annie.'

Dear mother's hands were quick and trembling, as she opened the shining folds; and there she saw my Lorna sleeping, with her black hair all dishevelled, and she bent and kissed her forehead, and only said, 'God bless her, John!' And then she was taken with violent weeping, and I was forced to hold her.

'Us may tich of her now, I rackon,' said Betty in her most jealous way: 'Annie, tak her by the head, and I'll tak her by the toesen. No taime to stand here like girt gawks. Don'ee tak on zo, missus. Ther be vainer vish in the zea—Lor, but her be a booty!'

With this, they carried her into the house, Betty chattering all the while, and going on now about Lorna's hands, and the others crowding round her, so that I thought I was not wanted among so many women, and should only get the worst of it, and perhaps do harm to my darling. Therefore I went and brought Gwenny in, and gave her a potful of bacon and peas, and an iron spoon to eat it with, which she did right heartily.

Then I asked her how she could have been such a fool as to let those two vile fellows enter the house where Lorna was; and she accounted for it so naturally, that I could only blame myself. For my agreement had been to give one loud knock (if you happen to remember) and after that two little knocks. Well, these two drunken rogues had come; and one, being very drunk indeed, had given a great thump; and then nothing more to do with it; and the other, being three-quarters drunk, had followed his leader (as one might say) but feebly, and making two of it. Whereupon up jumped Lorna, and declared that her John was there.

All this Gwenny told me shortly, between the whiles of eating, and even while she licked the spoon: and then there came a message for me, that my love was sensible, and was seeking all around for me. Then I told Gwenny to hold her tongue (whatever she did, among us), and not to trust to women's words; and she told me they all were liars, as she had found out long ago; and the only thing to believe in was an honest man, when found. Thereupon I could have kissed her, as a sort of tribute, liking to be appreciated; yet the peas upon her lips made me think about it; and thought is fatal to action. So I went to see my dear.

That sight I shall not forget; till my dying head falls back, and my breast can lift no more. I know not whether I were then more blessed, or harrowed by it. For in the settle was my Lorna, propped with pillows round her, and her clear hands spread sometimes to the blazing fireplace. In her eyes no knowledge was of any thing around her, neither in her neck the sense of leaning towards any thing. Only both her lovely hands were entreating something, to spare her or to love her; and the lines of supplication quivered in her sad white face.

'All go away except my mother,' I said very quietly, but so that I would be obeyed; and everybody knew it. Then mother came to me alone; and she said, 'The frost is in her brain: I have heard of this before, John.' 'Mother, I will have it out,' was all that I could answer her; 'leave her to me altogether: only you sit there and watch.' For I felt that Lorna knew me, and no other soul but me; and that if not interfered with, she would soon come home to me. Therefore I sat gently by her, leaving nature, as it were, to her own good time and will. And presently the glance that watched me, as at distance and in doubt, began to flutter and to brighten, and to deepen into kindness, then to beam with trust and love, and then with gathering tears to falter, and in shame to turn away. But the small entreating hands found their way, as if by instinct, to my great protecting palms; and trembled there, and rested there.

For a little while we lingered thus, neither wishing to move away, neither caring to look beyond the presence of the other; both alike so full of hope, and comfort, and true happiness; if only the world would let us be. And then a little sob disturbed us, and mother tried to make believe that she was only coughing. But Lorna, guessing who she was, jumped up so very rashly that she almost set her frock on fire from the great ash-log; and away she ran to the old oak chair, where mother was by the clock-case pretending to be knitting, and she took the work from mother's hands, and laid them both upon her head, kneeling humbly, and looking up.

'God bless you, my fair mistress!' said mother, bending nearer, and then as Lorna's gaze prevailed, 'God bless you, my sweet child!'

And so she went to mother's heart, by the very nearest road, even as she had come to mine; I mean the road of pity, smoothed by grace, and youth, and gentleness.

HARRIET'S HAIRLOOM

Joan Aiken

'Oh, Mother,' Harriet said as she did every year. 'Can't I open my birthday presents at breakfast?'

And as she did every year, Mrs Armitage replied,

'Certainly not! You know perfectly well that you weren't born till half past four. You get your birthday presents at tea-time, not before.'

'We could change the custom now we're in our teens,' Harriet suggested cunningly. 'You know you hate having to get up at half past two in the morning for Mark's presents.'

But Mark objected strongly to any change, and Mrs Armitage added,

'In any case, don't forget that as it's your thirteenth birthday you have to be shown into the Closed Room; there'd never be time to do that before school. Go and collect your schoolbooks now, and, Mark, wash the soot from behind your ears; if you must hunt for Lady Anne's pearls in the chimney, I wish you'd clean up before coming to breakfast.'

'You'd be as pleased as anyone else if I found them,' Mark grumbled, going off to put sooty marks all over the towels.

'What do you suppose is in the Closed Room?' Mark said later, as he and Harriet walked to the school bus. 'I think it's a rotten swindle that only girls in the family are allowed to go inside when they get to be thirteen. Suppose it's a monster like at Glamis, what'll you do?'

'Tame it,' said Harriet promptly. 'I shall feed it on bread-and-milk and lettuce.'

'That's hedgehogs, dope! Suppose it has huge teeth and tentacles and a poisonous sting three yards long?'

'Shut up! Anyway I don't suppose it is a monster. After all we never see Mother going into the Closed Room with bowls of food. It's probably just some mouldering old great-aunt in her coffin or something boring like that.'

Still, it was nice to have a Closed Room in the family, Harriet reflected, and she sat in the bus happily speculating about what it might contain—jewels, perhaps, rubies as big as tomatoes, or King Arthur's sword Excalibur, left with the Armitage family for safe keeping when he went off to Avalon, or the Welsh bard Taliesin, fallen asleep in the middle of a poem—or a Cockatrice—or the vanished crew of the *Marie Celeste*, playing cards and singing shanties—

Harriet was still in a dreamy state when school began. The first lesson was geography with old Mr Gubbins so there was no need to pay attention; she sat trying to think of suitable pet names for Cockatrices until she heard a stifled sobbing on her left.

'. . . is of course the Cathay of the ancients,' Mr Gubbins was rambling on. 'Marco Polo in his travels . . .'

Harriet looked cautiously round and saw that her best friend, and left-hand neighbour Desiree, or Dizzry as everyone called her, was crying bitterly, hunched over the inkwell on her desk so that the tears ran into it.

Dizzry was the daughter of Ernie Perrow, the village chimney-sweep; the peculiarity of the Perrow family was that none of them ever grew to be more than six inches high. Dizzry travelled to school every day in Harriet's pocket and instead of sitting at her desk in the usual way had a small table and chair, which Mark had obligingly made her out of matchboxes, on the top of it.

'What's the matter?' whispered Harriet. 'Here, don't cry into the ink—you'll make it weaker than it is already. Haven't you a handkerchief?'

She pulled sewing things out of her own desk, snipped a shred off the corner of a tablecloth she was embroidering, and passed it to Dizzry, who gulped, nodded, took a deep breath, and wiped her eyes on it.

'What's the matter?' Harriet asked again.

'It was what Mr Gubbins said that started me off,' Dizzry muttered. 'Talking about Cathay. Our Min always used to say she'd a fancy to go to Cathay. She'd got it muddled up with café. She thought she'd get cake and raspberryade and ice-cream there.'

'Well, so what?' said Harriet, who saw nothing to cry about in that.

'Haven't you heard? We've lost her—we've lost our Min!'

'Oh, my goodness! You mean she's dead?'

'No, not died. Just lost. Nobody's seen her since yesterday breakfast time!'

Harriet privately thought this ought to have been rather a relief for the family but was too polite to say so. Min, the youngest of the Perrow children, was a perfect little fiend, always in trouble of one kind or another. When not engaged in entering sweet jars in the village shop and stealing Butter Kernels or Quince Drops, she was probably worming her way through keyholes and listening to people's secrets, or hitching a free lift round the houses in her enemy the postman's pocket and jabbing him with a darning needle as a reward for the ride, or sculling about the pond on Farmer Beezeley's ducks and driving them frantic by tickling them under their wings, or galloping down the street on somebody's furious collie, or climbing into the vicar's TV and frightening him half to death by shouting 'Time is short!' through the screen. She frequently ran fearful risks but seemed to have a charmed life. Everybody in the village heartily detested Min Perrow, but her elder brothers and sisters were devoted to her and rather proud of her exploits.

Poor Dizzry continued to cry, on and off, for the rest of the day. Harriet tried to console her but it seemed horribly probable that Min had at last gone too far and had been swallowed by a cow or drowned in a sump or rolled into a Swiss roll at the bakery while stealing jam—so many ill fates might easily have befallen her that it was hard to guess the likeliest.

'I'll help you hunt for her this evening,' Harriet promised, however, 'and so will Mark. As soon as my birthday tea's finished.'

Dizzry came home with Harriet for the birthday tea and was a little cheered by the cake made in the shape of a penguin with blackcurrant

A powerful leap lifted his short legs off the ground, and he aimed straight for the white of Boomer's trembling throat. *(p.88)*

In a moment I had him round the waist, and he went out of the window with a mighty crash of glass. *(p.129)*

icing and an orange beak, and Harriet's presents, which included a do-it-yourself water-divining kit from Mark (a hazel twig and a bucket of water), an electronic guitar which could sing as well as play, a little pocket computer for working out sums and, from Harriet's fairy godmother, a tube of everlasting toothpaste. Harriet was not particularly grateful for this last; the thought of toothpaste supplied for the rest of her life left her unmoved.

'I'd rather have had an endless stick of liquorice,' she said crossly. 'Probably I shan't have any teeth left by the time I'm ninety; what use will toothpaste be then?'

Her presents from Dizzry were by far the nicest: a pink-and-orange necklace of spindleberries, beautifully carved, and a starling named Alastair whom Dizzry had trained to take messages, answer the telephone or the front door, and carry home small quantities of shopping.

'Now,' said Mrs Armitage rather nervously when the presents had been admired, 'I'd better show Harriet the Closed Room.'

Mr Armitage hurriedly retired to his study while Mark, controlling some natural feelings of envy, kindly said he would help Dizzry hunt for Min, and carried her off to inspect all the reapers and binders in Mr Beezeley's farmyard.

Harriet and Mrs Armitage went up to the attic floor and Mrs Armitage paused before a cobweb-shrouded door and pulled a rusty old key out of her pocket.

'Now you must say "I, Harriet Armitage, solemnly swear not to reveal the secret of this room to any other soul in the world."'

'But when I grow up and have a daughter,' objected Harriet, 'won't I have to tell her, just as Granny told you and you're telling me?'

'Well, yes, I suppose so,' Mrs Armitage said uncertainly. 'I've rather forgotten how the oath went, to tell you the truth.'

'Why do we have to promise not to tell?'

'To be honest, I haven't the faintest idea.'

'Let's skip that bit—there doesn't seem much point to it—and just go in,' Harriet suggested. So they opened the door (it was very stiff, for it had been shut at least twenty years) and went in.

The attic was dim, lit only by a patch of green glass tiles in the roof; it was quite empty except for a small, dusty loom, made of black wood, with a stool to match.

'A loom?' said Harriet, very disappointed. 'Is that all?'

'It isn't an ordinary loom,' her mother corrected her. 'It's a hairloom. For weaving human hair.'

'Who wants to weave human hair? What can you make?'

'I suppose you make a human hair mat. You must only use hair that's never been cut since birth.'

'Haven't you ever tried?'

'Oh, my dear, I never seemed to get a chance. When I was your age and Granny first showed me the loom everyone wore their hair short; you couldn't get a bit long enough to weave for love or money. And then you children came along—somehow I never found time.'

'Well I jolly well shall,' Harriet said. 'I'll try and get hold of some hair. I wonder if Miss Pring would let me have hers? I bet it's never been cut—she must have yards. Maybe you can make a cloak of invisibility, or the sort that turns swans into humans.'

She was so pleased with this notion that only as they went downstairs did she think to ask, 'How did the loom get into the family?'

'I'm a bit vague about that,' Mrs Armitage admitted. 'I believe it belonged to a Greek ancestress that one of the crusading Armitages married and brought back to England. She's the one I'm called Penelope after.'

Without paying much attention, Harriet went off to find Mark and Dizzry. Her father said they were along at the church, so she followed, pausing at the post office to ask elderly Miss Pring the postmistress if she would sell her long grey hair to be woven into a rug.

'It would look very pretty,' she coaxed. 'I could dye some of it pink or blue.'

Miss Pring was not keen.

'Sell my hair? Cut it off? The idea! Dye it? What impertinence! Get along with you, sauce-box!'

So Harriet had to abandon that scheme, but she stuck up a postcard on the notice-board: HUMAN HAIR REQUIRED, UNCUT: BEST PRICES PAID, and posted off another to the local paper. Then she joined Mark and Dizzry, who were searching the church organ pipes, but without success.

Harriet had met several other members of the Perrow family on her way: Ernie, Min's father, driving an old dolls' push-chair which he had fitted with an engine and turned into a convertible like a Model T Ford; old Gran Perrow, stomping along and gloomily shouting 'Min!' down all the drain-holes; and Sid, one of the boys, riding a bike made from cocoa tins and poking out nests from the hedge with a bamboo in case Min had been abducted.

When it was too dark to go on searching Harriet and Mark left Dizzry at Rose Cottage, where the Perrows lived.

'We'll go on looking tomorrow!' they called. And Harriet said, 'Don't worry too much.'

'I expect she'll be all right wherever she is,' Mark said. 'I'd back Min against a mad bull any day.'

As they walked home he asked Harriet,

'What about the Closed Room, then? Any monster?'

'No, very dull—just a hairloom.'

'I say, you shouldn't tell me, should you?'

'It's all right—we agreed to skip the promise to keep it secret.'

'What a let-down,' Mark said. 'Who wants an old loom?'

They arrived home to trouble. Their father was complaining, as he did every day, about soot on the carpets and black tide-marks on the bathroom basin and towels.

'Well, if you don't want me to find Lady Anne's necklace—' Mark said aggrievedly. 'If it was worth a thousand pounds when she lost it in 1660, think what it would fetch now.'

'Why in heaven's name would it be up the chimney? Stop arguing and go to bed. And brush your teeth!'

'I'll lend you some of my toothpaste,' Harriet said.

'Just the same,' Mark grumbled, brushing his teeth with yards of toothpaste so that the foam stood out on either side of his face like Dundreary whiskers and flew all over the bathroom, 'Ernie Perrow definitely told me that his great-great-great-grandfather Oliver Perrow had a row with Lady Anne Armitage because she ticked him off for catching field-mice in her orchard; Oliver was the village sweep, and her pearls vanished just after; Ernie thinks old Oliver stuck them in the chimney to teach her a lesson, and then he died, eaten by a fox before he had a chance to tell anyone. But Ernie's sure that's where the pearls are.'

'Perhaps Min's up there looking for them too.'

'Not her! She'd never do anything as useful as that.'

Harriet had asked Alastair the starling to call her at seven; in fact she was roused at half past six by loud bangs on the front door.

'For heaven's sake, somebody, tell that maniac to go away!' shouted Mr Armitage from under his pillow.

Harriet flung on a dressing-gown and ran downstairs. What was her surprise to find at the door a little old man in a white duffel-coat with the hood up. He carried a very large parcel, wrapped in sacking. Harriet found the sharp look he gave her curiously disconcerting.

'Would it be Miss Armitage now, the young lady who put the advertisement in the paper then?'

'About hair?' Harriet said eagerly. 'Yes, I did. Have you got some, Mr—?'

'Mr Thomas Jones, the Druid, I am. Beautiful hair I have then, look you—finer than any lady's in the land. Only see now till I get this old parcel undone!' And he dumped the bundle down at her feet and started un-knotting the cords. Harriet helped. When the last half-hitch twanged apart a great springy mass of hair came boiling out. It was soft and fine, dazzlingly white with just a few strands of black, and smelt slightly of tobacco.

'There, now indeed to goodness! Did you ever see finer?'

'But,' said Harriet, 'has it ever been cut short?' She very much hoped that it had not; it seemed impossible that they would ever be able to parcel it up again.

'Never has a scissor-blade been laid to it, till I cut it all off last night,' the old man declared.

Harriet wondered whose it was; something slightly malicious and self-satisfied about the old man's grin as he said, 'I cut it all off' prevented her from asking.

'Er—how much would you want for it?' she inquired cautiously.

'Well, indeed,' he said. 'It would be hard to put a price on such beautiful hair, whatever.'

At this moment there came an interruption. A large van drew up in front of the Armitage house. On its sides iridescent bubbles were painted, and, in rainbow colours, the words SUGDEN'S SOAP.

A uniformed driver jumped out, consulting a piece of paper.

'Mr Mark Armitage live here?' he asked Harriet. She nodded.

'Will he take delivery of one bathroom, complete with shower, tub, footbath, de-luxe basin, plastic curtains, turkish towelling, chrome sponge-holder, steel-and-enamel hair drier, and a six years' supply of Sugden's Soap?'

'I suppose so,' Harriet said doubtfully. 'You're sure there's no mistake?'

The delivery note certainly had Mark's name and address.

'Mark!' Harriet yelled up the stairs, forgetting it was still only seven a.m. 'Did you order a bathroom? Because it's come.'

'Merciful goodness!' groaned the voice of Mr Armitage. 'Has no one any consideration for my hours of rest?'

Mark came running down, looking slightly embarrassed.

'Darn it,' he said as he signed the delivery note, 'I never expected I'd get a bathroom; I was hoping for the free cruise to Saposoa.'

'Where shall we put it, guv?' said the driver, who was plainly longing to be away and get some breakfast at the nearest carmen's pull-in.

Mark looked about him vaguely. At this moment Mr Armitage came downstairs in pyjamas and a very troublesome frame of mind.

'Bathroom? Bathroom?' he said. 'You've bought a bathroom? What the blazes did you want to go and get a bathroom for? Isn't the one we have good enough for you, pray? You leave it dirty enough. Who's going to pay for this? And why has nobody put the kettle on?'

'I won it,' Mark explained, blushing. 'It was the second prize in the Sugden's Soap Competition. In the *Radio Times*, you know.'

'What did you have to do?' Harriet asked.

'Ten uses for soap in correct order of importance.'

'I bet washing came right at the bottom,' growled his father. 'Greased stairs and fake soft-centres are more your mark.'

'Anyway he won!' Harriet pointed out. 'Was that all you had to do?'

'You had to write a couplet too.'

'What was yours?'

Mark blushed even pinker. 'Rose or White or Heliotrope, Where there's life there's Sugden's Soap.'

'Come on now,' said the van driver patiently, 'we don't want to be here all day, do we? Where shall we put it, guv? In the garden?'

'Certainly not,' snapped Mr Armitage. He was proud of his garden.

'How about in the field?' suggested Harriet diplomatically. 'Then

Mark and I can wash in it, and you needn't be upset by soot on the towels.'

'That's true,' her father said, brightening a little. 'All right, stick it in the field. And now will somebody please put on a kettle and make a cup of tea, is that too much to ask?' And he stomped back to bed, leaving Mark and the driver to organize the erection of the bathroom in the field beside the house. Harriet put a kettle on the stove and went back to Mr Jones the Druid who was sunning himself in the front porch.

'Have you decided what you want for your hair?' she asked.

'Oh,' he said. 'There is a grand new bathroom you have with you! Lucky that is, indeed. Now I am thinking I do not want any money at all for my fine bundle of hair, but only to strike a bargain with you.'

'Very well,' Harriet said cautiously.

'No bathroom I have at my place, see? Hard it is to wash the old beard, and chilly of a winter morning in the stream. But if you and your brother, that I can see is a kind-hearted obliging young gentleman, would let me come and give it a bit of a lather now and again in your bathroom—'

'Why yes, of course,' Harriet said. 'I'm sure Mark won't mind at all.'

'So it shall be, then. Handy that will be, indeed. Terrible deal of the old beard there is, look you, and grubby she do get.'

'With that he undid his duffel-coat and pulled back the hood. All round his head and wound about his body like an Indian Sari was a prodigiously long white beard which he proceeded to untwine until it trailed on the ground. It was similar to the white hair in the bundle, but not so clean.

'Is that somebody's beard, then?' Harriet asked, pointing to the bundle.

'My twin brother, Dai Jones the Bard. Bathroom he has by him, the lucky old cythryblwr! But soon I will be getting a bigger one. Made a will, my Dad did, see, leaving all his money to the one of us who has the longest and whitest beard on our ninetieth birthday, that falls tomorrow on Midsummer Day. So I crept into his house last night and cut his beard off while he slept; hard he'll find it now to grow another in time! All Dada's money I will be getting, he, he, he!'

Mr Jones the Druid chuckled maliciously.

Harriet could not help thinking he was rather a wicked old man, but a bargain was a bargain, so she picked up the bundle of beard, with difficulty, and was about to say goodbye when he stopped her.

'Weaving the hair into a mat, you would be, isn't it?' he said wheedlingly. 'There is a fine bath-mat it would make! Towels and curtains there are in that grand new bathroom of yours but no bath-mat—pity that is, indeed.' He gave her a cunning look out of the corners of his eyes, but Harriet would not commit herself.

'Come along this evening, then, I will, for a good old wash-up before my birthday,' Mr Jones said. He wound himself in his beard again and went off with many nods and bows. Harriet ran to the field to see how the bathroom was getting on. Mark had it nearly finished. True enough, there was no bath-mat. It struck Harriet that Mr Jones's suggestion was not a bad one.

'I'll start weaving a mat as soon as we've had another thorough hunt for Min Perrow,' she said. 'Saturday, thank goodness, no school.'

However during breakfast (which was late, owing to these various events) Ernie Perrow drove along in the push-chair with Lily and Dizzry to show the Armitages an air letter which had arrived from the British Consul in Cathay.

Dear Sir or Madam,

Kindly make earliest arrangements to send passage money back to England for your daughter Hermione who has had herself posted here, stowed away in a box of Health Biscuits. Please forward without delay fare and expenses totalling £1,093 7*s*. 1*d*.

A postscript, scrawled by Min, read: 'Dun it at last! Sux to silly old postmun!'

'Oh, what shall we do?' wept Mrs Perrow. 'A thousand pounds! How can we ever find it?'

While the grown-ups discussed ways and means, Mark went back to his daily search for Lady Anne's pearls, and Harriet took the woebegone Dizzry up to the attic, hoping to distract her by a look at the hairloom.

Dizzry was delighted with it. 'Do let's do some weaving!' she said. 'I like weaving better than anything.'

So Harriet lugged in the great bundle of beard and they set up the loom. Dizzry was an expert weaver. She had been making beautiful scarves for years on a child's toy loom—she could nip to and fro with the shuttle almost faster than Harriet's eyes could follow. By tea-time they had woven a handsome thick white mat with the words BATH MA across the middle (there had not been quite enough black for the final T).

'Anyway you can see what it's meant to be,' Harriet said. They took the new mat and spread it in their elegant bathroom.

'Tell you what,' Mark said, 'we'd better hide the bath and basin plugs when Min gets back or she'll climb in and drown herself.'

'Oh, I do wonder what Dad and Mum are doing about getting her back,' sighed Dizzry, who was sitting on a sponge. She wiped her eyes on a corner of Harriet's face-cloth.

'Let's go along to your house,' Harriet said, 'and find out.'

There was an atmosphere of deep gloom in the Perrow household. Ernie had arranged to sell his Model T push-chair, the apple of his eye, to the Motor Museum at Beaulieu.

'A thousand pounds they say they'll give for it,' he said miserably. 'With that and what I've saved from the chimney sweeping, we can just about pay the fare. Won't I half clobber young Min when I get her back, the little varmint!'

'Mrs Perrow,' Harriet said, 'may Dizzry come and spend the evening at our house, as Mother and Daddy are going to a dance? And have a bath in our new bathroom? Mother says it's all right and I'll take great care of her.'

'Oh, very well, if your Ma doesn't mind,' sighed Mrs Perrow. 'I'm so distracted I hardly know if I'm coming or going. Don't forget your wash things, Diz, and the bath-salts.'

Harriet was enchanted with the bath-salts, no bigger than hundreds-and-thousands.

On Midsummer Eve the Armitage children were allowed to stay up as late as they liked. Mark, a single-minded boy, said he intended to go on hunting for Lady Anne's necklace in the chimney. The girls had their baths and then went up to Harriet's room with a bagful of apples and the gramophone, intending to have a good gossip.

At half past eleven Harriet, happening to glance out of the window, saw a light in the field.

'That must be Mr Jones,' she said. 'I'd forgotten he was coming to shampoo his beard. It's not Mark, I can still hear him bumping around in the chimney.'

There was indeed an excited banging to be heard from the chimney-breast, but it was as nothing compared with the terrible racket that suddenly broke out in the field. They heard shouts and cries of rage, thuds, crashes, and the tinkle of smashed glass.

'Heavens, what can be going on?' cried Harriet. She flung up the sash and prepared to climb out of the window.

'Wait for me!' said Dizzry.

'Here, jump into my pocket. Hold tight!'

Harriet slid down the wisteria and dashed across the garden. A moment later they arrived at the bathroom door and witnessed a wild scene.

Evidently Mr Jones the Druid had finished washing his beard and been about to leave when he saw his doom waiting for him outside the door in the form of another, very angry, old man who was trying to batter his way in.

'It must be his brother!' Harriet whispered. 'Mr Jones the Bard!'

The second old man had no beard, only a ragged white frill cut short round his chin. He was shouting.

'Wait till I catch you, you hocsdwr, you herwhaliwr, you ffrawd-dunio, you wicked old llechwr! A snake would think shame to spit on you! Cutting off your brother's beard, indeed! Just let me get at you and I'll trim you to spillikins I'll shave your beard round your eyebrows!' And he beat on the door with a huge pair of shears. A pane of glass fell in and broke on the bathroom tiles; then the whole door gave way.

Dizzry left Harriet's pocket and swarmed up on to her head to see what was happening. They heard a fearful bellow from inside the bathroom, a stamping and crashing, fierce grunts, the hiss of the shower and more breaking glass.

'Hey!' Harriet shouted. 'Stop wrecking our bathroom!'

No answer. The noise of battle went on.

Then the bathroom window flew open and Jones the Druid shot out, all tangled in his beard which was snowy white now, but still damp. He had the bath-mat rolled up under his arm. As soon as he was out he flung it down, leapt on it, and shouted, 'Take me out of here!'

The mat took off vertically and hovered, about seven feet up, while Mr Jones began hauling in his damp beard, hand over hand. 'Come back!' Harriet cried. 'You've no right to go off with our bath-mat.'

Jones the Bard came roaring out of the window, waving his shears.

'Come back, ystraffaldiach! Will you come down off there and let me mince you into macaroni! Oh, you wicked old weasel, I'll trim your beard shorter than an earwig's toe-nails!'

He made a grab for the bath-mat but it was just out of reach.

'He, he, he!' cackled Jones the Druid up above. 'You didn't know your fine beard would make up so nice into a flying carpet, did you, brother? Has to be woven on a hair-loom on Midsummer Eve and then it'll carry you faster than the Aberdovey Flyer.'

'Just let me get at you, rheibiwr!' snarled Jones the Bard, making another vain grab.

But Dizzry, who was now jumping up and down on the top of Harriet's head, made a tremendous spring, grabbed hold of a trailing strand of Mr Jones's beard, and hauled herself up on to a corner of the flying bath-mat.

'Oh dammo!' gasped the Druid at the sight of her. He was so taken aback that he lost his balance, staggered, and fell headlong on top of his brother. There was a windmill confusion of arms and legs, all swamped by the foaming mass of beard. Then Jones the Bard grabbed his shears with a shout of triumph and began chopping away great sways of white hair.

Harriet, however, paid no heed to these goings-on.

'Dizzry!' she shouted, cupping her hands round her mouth. 'It's a wishing-mat. Make it take you—'

Dizzry nodded. She needed no telling. 'Take me to Cathay!' she cried, and the mat soared away through the milky air of midsummer night.

At this moment Mark came running across the field.

'Oh, Mark!' Harriet burst out. 'Look what those old fiends have done to our bathroom! It's ruined. They ought to be made to pay for it.'

Mark glanced through the broken window. The place was certainly a shambles: bath and basin were both smashed, the sponge-rack was wrapped round the hair-drier, the towels were trodden into a soggy pulp and the curtains were in ribbons.

The Jones brothers were in equally bad shape. Jones the Bard was kneeling on Jones the Druid's stomach; he had managed to trim every shred of hair off his brother's head, but he himself was as bald as a coot.

Both had black eyes and swollen lips.

'Oh, well,' Mark said. 'They seem to have trouble of their own. I bet neither of them comes into that legacy now. And I never did care much for washing anyway. Look, here comes Dizzry back.'

The bath-mat swooped to a three-point landing, Dizzry and Min rolled off it laughing and crying.

'You wicked, wicked, bad little girl,' Dizzry cried, shaking and hugging her small sister at the same time. 'Don't you ever dare do such a thing again.'

'Now I will take my own property which is my lawful beard,' said Mr Jones the Bard, and he jumped off his brother's stomach on to the mat and addressed it in a flood of Welsh, which it evidently understood, for it rose into the air and flew off in a westerly direction. Mr Jones the Druid slunk away across the field looking, Dizzry said, as hangdog as a cat that has fallen into the milk.

'Now we've lost our bath-mat,' Harriet sighed.

'I'll help you make another,' Dizzry said. 'There's plenty of hair lying about. And at least we've got Min back.'

'Was it nice in Cathay, Min?' Mark said.

'Smashing. I had rice-cake and cherry ice and Coca-Cola.'

At this point Mr and Mrs Armitage returned from their dance and kindly drove Dizzry and Min to break the joyful news to their parents.

Harriet and Mark had a try at putting the bathroom to rights, but it was really past hope.

'I must say, trouble certainly haunts this household,' remarked Mr Armitage, when he came back and found them at it. 'Hurry up and get to bed, you two. Do you realize it's four o'clock on midsummer morning? Oh, Lord, I suppose now we have to go back to the old regime of sooty footmarks all over the bathroom.'

'Certainly not,' said Mark. 'I'd forgotten to tell you. I found Lady Anne's pearls.'

He pulled them out and dangled them: a soot-black, six-foot double strand of pearls as big as cobnuts, probably worth a king's ransom.

'Won't Ernie Perrow be pleased to know they really were in the chimney?' he said.

'Oh, get to bed!' snapped his father. 'I'm fed up with hearing about the Perrows.'

THE TAMING OF PERCY

Gerald Durrell

As a young man in 1950 the famous naturalist Gerald Durrell went to British Guiana (modern Guyana, in northern South America) to bring back for zoological gardens in Britain a living collection of the birds, mammals, reptiles and fish that inhabit that country. In this extract from his book Three Singles to Adventure *he is exploring the creek lands to the north-west with two companions, Ivan and Bob, and a local guide, Kahn, who has become rather tiresome with stories of his prowess as a hunter.*

At the end of the valley the creek waters dutifully re-entered their appointed bed and flowed through a section of thickly wooded countryside The trees grew closer and closer, until we were travelling in green twilight under a tunnel of branches and shimmering leaves, on water that was as black as ebony, touched in places with silver smears of light where there were gaps in the branches overhead. Suddenly a bird flew from a tree opposite to us and sped up the dim tunnel, to alight on the trunk of another tree that was spotlighted with sunshine. It was a great black woodpecker with a long, curling wine-red crest and an ivory-coloured beak.

As it clung to the bark, peering at us, it was joined by its mate, and together they started to scuttle up and down the tree trunk, tapping it importantly with their beaks and listening with their heads on one side. occasionally they would utter a short burst of shrill, metallic laughter, tittering weirdly over some private joke between themselves. They looked like a couple of mad, red-headed doctors, sounding the chest of the great tree and giggling delightedly over the diseases they found, the worm-holes, the tubercular patches of dry rot, and the army of larvae steadily eating their hosts to pieces. The woodpeckers thought it a rich jest.

They were exotic, fantastic-looking birds, and I was determined to try and add some of them to our collection. I pointed them out to Ivan.

'What do they call those, Ivan?'

'Carpenter birds, sir.'

'We must try and get some.'

'I will get you some,' said Mr Kahn. 'Don't you worry, Chief, I will get you anything you want.'

I watched the woodpeckers as they flew from tree to tree, but they were eventually lost to sight in the tangled forest. I hoped that Mr Kahn was right, but I doubted it.

Towards evening we were nearing our destination, an Amerindian village with a tiny mission school, hidden away among the backwaters of the creek lands. We left the main creek and entered an even narrower tributary, and here the growth of aquatic plants was so thick that it covered the water from bank to bank. This green lawn was studded with hundreds of miniature flowers in mauve, yellow and pink, each thimble-sized bloom growing on a stem half an inch high. It seemed when I sat in the bows that the boat was drifting smoothly up some weed-grown drive, for only the ripples of our wash undulating the plants as we passed gave indication of the water beneath. We followed this enchanting path for miles as it twisted through woodland and grassfields, and eventually it led us to a small white beach fringed with palm trees. We could see a few shacks, half hidden among the trees, and a cluster of canoes lying on the clean sand.

As we switched off the engine and drifted shorewards a host of chattering, laughing Amerindian children ran down to meet us, all stark naked, their bodies glistening in the sun. Following them came a tall African who, as soon as we landed, introduced himself as the schoolmaster. He led us, surrounded by the noisy, laughing children, up the white beach to one of the huts, and then he left us, promising to return when we had unpacked and settled down. Our ears had got used to hearing the throb of the boat's engine all day, so the peace and quiet of that little hut among the palms was delightfully soothing. We unpacked and ate a meal in a contented silence; even Mr Kahn seemed to be affected by the place, and remained unusually quiet.

Presently the schoolmaster returned, and with him was one of his small Amerindian pupils.

'This boy wants to know if you will buy this,' said the schoolmaster.

'This' turned out to be a baby crab-eating raccoon, a tiny ball of fluff with sparkling eyes, that looked just like a chow puppy. There was no trace of the mournful expression that it was to wear in later life; instead it was full of good spirits, rolling and gambolling and pretending to bite with its tiny milk teeth, waving its bushy tail like a flag. Even if I had not wanted him I would have found it difficult to resist buying such a charming creature. I felt that he was too young to share a cage with the adult, so I set to work and built him a special one of his own; we installed him in this, his tummy bulging with the meal of milk and fish I had given him, and he curled up in a pile of dry grass, belched triumphantly and then went to sleep.

The schoolmaster suggested that we should attend his class the next morning and show the children pictures of the various animals we wanted. He said that he knew many of his pupils had pets that they would be willing to part with. He also promised to find us some good hunters who would take us out into the creeks in search of specimens.

So the next morning Bob and I attended the school and explained to forty young Amerindians why we had come there, what animals we wanted and the prices we were willing to pay. With great enthusiasm they all promised to bring their pets that afternoon, all, that is, except one small boy, who looked very worried and conversed rapidly with the schoolmaster in a whisper.

'He says,' explained the master, 'he has a very fine animal, but it is too big for him to bring by canoe.'

'What sort of animal is it?'

'He says it is a wild pig.'

I turned to Bob.

'Could you go and fetch it in the boat this afternoon, d'you think?'

Bob sighed.

'I suppose so,' he said, 'as long as it's well tied up.'

That afternoon Bob set off in the boat, accompanied by the little Amerindian boy, to bring back the peccary. I had impressed upon him to buy any other worthwhile specimens he might see in the Amerindian village, and so I awaited his return hopefully. Shortly after the boat had left the first children arrived, carrying their pets, and soon I was deeply engrossed in the thrilling and exciting job of buying specimens, surrounded on all sides by grinning Amerindians and a weird assortment of animals.

Perhaps the commonest ones were agoutis, golden-brown creatures with long, slim legs and rabbit-like faces. They are really not very intelligent creatures, and are so nervous that they have hysterics if you so much as breathe in their direction. Then there were pacas, plump as young pigs, chocolate-coloured beasts decorated with longitudinal lines of cream-coloured blotches. Four or five squirrel and capuchin monkeys capered and chattered on the end of long strings, scrambling up and down the children's bodies as if they were so many bushes.

Many of the children produced young boa-constrictors, beautifully coloured in pink and silver and fawn, coiled round their owners' waists or wrists. They may seem a rather unusual choice of pet for a child, but the Amerindians don't seem to suffer from the European's ridiculous fear of snakes. They keep the boas in their huts and allow the reptiles the run of the place; in return the snake discharges the function usually fulfilled by a cat in more civilized communities, that is to say it keeps the place free from rats, mice and other edible vermin. I cannot think of a better arrangement, for not only is the boa a better ratter than a cat could ever be, but it is much more decorative and beautiful to look at; to have one draped over the beams of your house in the graceful manner that only snakes can achieve would be as good as having a rare and lovely tapestry for decoration, with the individual advantage that your decoration works for its living.

Just as I had finished with the last of the children there came a wild, ringing laugh and one of the red-headed woodpeckers swooped across the clearing and disappeared into the forest.

'Ah!' I yelped, pointing, 'I want one of those.'

The children could not understand my words, but my gesture combined with my pleading, imploring expression told them what they wanted to know. They all burst into roars of laughter, stamping and spluttering and nodding their heads, and I began to feel more hopeful of getting a specimen of the woodpecker. When the Amerindians had gone I set to work to build cages for the varied assortment of wildlife I had bought. It was a long job, and by the time I had finished I could hear in the distance the faint chugging of the returning boat, so I walked down the beach to meet Bob and the peccary.

As the boat came into view I could see Bob and Ivan on the flat roof, sitting back to back on a large box, with strained expression on their faces. The boat nosed into the shallows, and Bob glared at me from his seat on the box.

'Did you get it?' I enquired hopefully.

'Yes, thank you,' said Bob, 'and we've been trying to keep it in this blasted box ever since we left the village. Apparently it doesn't like being shut up. I thought it was meant to be tame. In fact I *remember* you telling me it was a tame one. That was the only reason I agreed to go and fetch it.'

'Well, the boy said it was tame.'

'The boy, bless him, was mistaken,' said Bob coldly; 'the brute appears to be suffering from claustrophobia.'

Gingerly we carried the box from the boat to the beach.

'You'd better watch out,' warned Bob, 'it's already got some of the slats loose on top.'

As he spoke the peccary leapt inside the box and hit the top like a sledge-hammer; the slats flew off like rockets, and the next minute a bristling and enraged pig had hauled himself out and was galloping up the beach, snorting savagely.

'There!' said Bob, 'I knew that would happen.'

Halfway up the beach the peccary met a small group of Amerindians. He rushed among them, squealing with rage, trying to bite their legs; his sharp, half-inch tusks clicked together at each bite. The Amerindians fled back to the village, hotly pursued by the pig, who was in turn being chased by Ivan and myself. When we reached the huts the inhabitants appeared to have vanished, and the peccary was having a quick snack off some mess he had found under a palm tree. We had rounded the corner of a hut and come upon him rather unexpectedly, but he did not hestitate for a minute. Leaving his meal he charged straight towards us with champing mouth, uttering a bloodcurdling squeal. The next few moments were crowded, with the peccary twirling round and round, chopping and squealing, while Ivan and I leapt madly about with the speed and precision of a well-trained *corps de ballet*. At last the pig decided that we were too agile for him, and he retreated into a gap

When the last half-hitch twanged apart, a great springy mass of hair came boiling out. (p.132)

The next minute, a bristling and enraged pig had hauled himself out. (p.145)

between two of the huts and stood there grunting derisively at us.

'You go round and guard the other end, Ivan,' I panted. 'I'll see he doesn't get away this side.'

Ivan disappeared round the other side of the huts, and I saw Mr Kahn waddling over the sand towards me. I was filled with an unholy glee.

'Mr Kahn,' I called. 'Can you come and help for a minute?'

'Surely, Chief,' he said, beaming. 'What you want?'

'Just stand here and guard this opening, will you? There's a peccary in there and I don't want him to get out. I'll be back in a second.'

Leaving Mr Kahn peering doubtfully at the peccary, I rushed over to our hut and unearthed a thick canvas bag, which I wrapped carefully round my left hand. Thus armed I returned to the scene of the fray. To my delight I was just in time to see Mr Kahn panting flatfootedly round the palm trees with the peccary close behind. To my disappointment the pig stopped chasing Mr Kahn as soon as he saw me and retreated once more between the huts.

'Golly!' said Mr Kahn. 'That pig's plenty fierce, Chief.'

He sat down in the shade and fanned himself with a large red handkerchief, while I squeezed my way between the huts and moved slowly towards the peccary. He stood quite still, watching me, champing his jaws occasionally and giving subdued grunts. He let me get within six feet of him, and then he charged. As he reached me I grabbed the bristly scruff of his neck with my right hand and plunged my left, encased in canvas, straight into his mouth. He champed his jaws desperately, but his tusks made no impression through the canvas. I shifted my grip, got my arm firmly round his fat body and lifted him off the ground. As soon as he felt himself hoisted into the air his confidence seemed to evaporate, he stopped biting my hand and started squeaking in the most plaintive manner, kicking out with his fat little hind legs. I carried him over to our hut and deposited him in a box that was strong enough to hold him.

Soon he had his snout buried in a dish full of chopped bananas and milk and was snorting and squelching with satisfaction. Never again did he show off and try to be the Terror of the Jungle; in fact he became absurdly tame. A glimpse of his feeding dish would send him into squealing transports of delight, a frightful song that would only end when his nose was deep in the dish and his mouth full of food. He adored being scratched, and if you continued this treatment for long enough he would heel over and fall flat on his side, lying motionless, with his eyes tighly closed and giving tiny grunts of pleasure. We christened him Percy, and even Bob grew quite fond of him, though I suspect that the chief reason for this was that he had seen him chasing Mr Kahn round the palm trees.

MIRACLE NEEDED

Dodie Smith

In Dodie Smith's story of The Hundred and One Dalmatians *the pups of the Dalmatian Pongo and his Missis are abducted from their London home with the Dearly family by the wicked Cruella de Vil, who aims to make furs for herself out of their skins. They are taken to a remote country house called Hell Hall where they meet other Dalmatians destined for the same fate. But Pongo and Missis, after many adventures, manage to track them down and, soon afterwards, all make their escape. On their way back to London, hotly pursued by Cruella, they have camouflaged themselves by rolling in some soot at the back of the sweep's house. But now serious dangers threaten.*

'Last lap before supper,' said Pongo, as they started off again across the moonlit fields.

It was the most cheering thing he could have said, for the ninety-seven puppies were now extremely hungry. He had guessed this because he was hungry himself. And so was Missis. But she was feeling too peaceful to mind.

They went on for nearly two miles, then Pongo saw a long row of cottage roofs ahead across the fields.

'This should be it,' he said.

'What is that glow in the sky beyond the roof-tops?' asked Missis.

Pongo was puzzled. He had seen such a glow in the sky over towns which had many lights, but never over a village. And this was a very bright glow. 'Perhaps it's a larger place than we expected it to be,' he said, and did not feel it would be safe to go any nearer until some dog came to meet them. He called a halt and barked news of their arrival.

He was answered at once, by a bark that said: 'Wait where you are. I am coming.' And though he did not tell Missis, Pongo felt there was something odd about this bark that answered his. For one thing, there were no cheerful words of welcome.

Soon a graceful red setter came dashing towards them. They guessed, even before she spoke, that something was very wrong.

'The bakery's on fire!' she gasped.

The blaze, due to a faulty chimney, had begun only a few minutes before—the fire-engine had not yet arrived. No one had been hurt, but the bakehouse was full of flames and smoke—all the food spread out for the Dalmatians was burned.

'There's nothing for you to eat and nowhere for you to sleep,' moaned the poor setter—she was hysterical. 'And the village street's full of people.' She looked pitifully at Missis. 'All your poor hungry puppies!'

The strange thing was that Missis felt quite calm. She tried to comfort the setter, saying they would go to some barn.

'But no arrangements are made,' wailed the setter. 'And there's no spare food anywhere. All the village dogs brought what they could to the bakery.'

Just then came a shrill whistle.

'My pet is calling me,' said the setter. 'He's the doctor here. There's no dog at the bakery, so I was chosen to arrange everything—because I took first prize in a dog show. And now I've failed you.'

'You have *not* failed,' said Missis. 'No one could say the fire was act of dog. Go back to your pet and don't worry. We shall simply go on to the next village.'

'*Really?*' said the setter, gasping again—but with relief.

Missis kissed her on the nose. 'Off with you, my dear, and don't give the matter another thought. And thank you for all you did.'

The whistle came again and the setter ran off, wildly waving her feathered tail.

'Feather-brained as well as feather-tailed,' said Pongo.

'Just very young,' said Missis, gently. 'I doubt if she's had a family yet. Well, on to the next village.'

'Thank you for being so brave, dear Missis,' said Pongo. 'But where *is* the next village?'

'In the country, there are villages in *every* direction,' said Missis, brightly.

Desperately worried though he was, Pongo smiled lovingly at her. Then he said: 'We will go to the road now.'

'But what about traffic, Pongo?'

'We shall not be very long on the road,' said Pongo.

Then he told her what he had decided. Even if the next village should only be a few miles away, many of the pups were too tired and too hungry to get there—some of them were already asleep on the frozen ground. And every minute it got colder.

'And even if we could get to the next village, where should we sleep, Missis, what should we eat, with no plans made ahead? We must give in, my dear. Come, wake the pups! Quick march, everyone!'

The waking pups whimpered and shivered, and Missis saw that even the strongest pups were now wretchedly cold. So she helped Pongo to make them all march briskly. Then she whispered:

'But *how* do we give in, Pongo?'

Pongo said: 'We must go into the village and find the police station.'

Missis stared at him in horror. 'No, Pongo, no! The police will take the puppies from us!'

'But they will feed them, Missis. And perhaps we shall be kept together until Mr Dearly has been told about us. They will have read the papers. They will know we are the missing Dalmatians.'

'But we are not Dalmatians any more, Pongo,' cried Missis. 'We are black. They will think we are ordinary stray dogs. And we are illegal—ninety-nine dogs without collars. We shall be put in prison.'

'No, Missis!' But Pongo was shaken. He had forgotten they were now black dogs. Suppose the police did *not* recognize them? Suppose the Dearlys were never told about them. What happened to stray dogs that no one claimed?

'Please, Pongo, I beg you!' cried Missis. 'Let us go on with our journey! I *know* it will be all right.'

They had now reached the road and were on the edge of the village. Pongo was faced with a terrible choice. But it still seemed to him wiser to trust the police than to lead the hungry, exhausted puppies into the bitter winter night.

'Missis, dear Missis, we *must* go to the police station,' he said, and turned towards the village. They could now see the burning bakery and at that moment a huge flame leapt up through the roof. By its light Pongo saw the whole village street, with the villagers making a human chain to hand along buckets of water. And he also saw something else

—something which made him stop dead, shouting 'Halt!' at the top of his bark.

In front of the burning bakery was a great striped black-and-white car. And with it was Cruella de Vil—standing right up on the roof of the car, where she had climbed so as to get a good view of the fire. Her white face and absolutely simple white mink cloak no longer looked white. From head to foot she was bathed in the red-gold flicker of the flames. And as they leapt higher and higher she clapped her hands in delight.

The next instant there was a wild clamour of bells as the fire-engine arrived at last. The noise, the flames and, above all, the sight of Cruella were too much for many of the puppies. Squealing in terror, they turned and fled, with Pongo, Missis and Lucky desperately trying to call them to order.

Fortunately, the clamour from the fire-engine prevented anyone in the village hearing the barking and yapping. And after a little while, the terrified pups obeyed Pongo's orders and stopped their headlong flight. They were very shame-faced as Pongo told them that, though he quite understood how they had felt, they must never, never behave in such a panic-stricken way and must always, always obey orders instantly. Then he praised the pups who had stuck to the Cadpig's cart, praised Patch for staying close to the Cadpig, rescued Roly Poly from a ditch and counted the pups carefully. He did all this as hurriedly as possible for he knew now that they must press on with their journey. There was no way they could get to the police station without passing Cruella de Vil.

Their plight was now worse than ever. They not only had to face the dangers of hunger and cold; there was the added danger of Cruella. They knew from the direction her car was facing that their enemy must have already been to Hell Hall, learned that they had escaped, and now be on her way back to London. At any moment, she might leave the fire and overtake them.

If only they could have left the road and travelled by the fields again! But there were now woods on either side of the road, woods so thick that the army could not have kept together.

'But we can hide in there, if we see the car's headlights,' said Pongo, and explained to the puppies. Then the army was on the march again.

'At least the pups are warm now,' said Missis. 'And they have forgotten how tired and hungry they are. It will be all right, Pongo.'

The pace was certainly good for a couple of miles, then it got slower and slower.

'The puppies will have to rest,' said Missis. 'And this is a good place for it.'

There was now a wide, grassy verge to the road. The moment Pongo called a halt the pups sank down on the frosty grass. Many of them at once fell asleep.

'They ought not to sleep,' said Pongo, anxiously.

'Let them, for a little while,' said Missis.

The Cadpig was not asleep. She sat up in her cart and said: 'Will there be a barn soon, with kind cows and warm milk?'

'I'm sure there will be *something* nice,' said Missis. 'Snuggle down in your hay, my darling. Pongo, how strangely quiet it is.'

They could no longer hear any sounds from the village. No breath of wind rustled the grass or stirred the trees. The world seemed frozen into a silvery, silent stillness.

Something soft and fluffy touched Pongo's head, something that puzzled him. Then, as he realized what it was, Missis whispered:

'Look, Pongo! Look at the puppies!'

Tiny white dots were appearing on the sooty black coats. Snow had begun to fall.

Missis said, smiling: 'Instead of being white pups with black spots they are turning into black pups with white spots—only soon, they will be all white. How soft and gentle the snow is!'

Pongo was not smiling. He cried: 'If they sleep on until it has covered them, they will never wake—they will freeze to death beneath that soft, gentle snow! Wake up, pups! Wake up!

By now, every pup but Lucky and the Cadpig had fallen into a deep, exhausted sleep. Lucky helped his parents to rouse them, and the Cadpig helped, too, sitting up in her cart and yapping piercingly. The poor pups begged to be left to sleep, and those who tottered on to their feet soon tottered off them again.

'We shall never get them going,' said Pongo despairingly.

For a moment, the Cadpig stopped yapping and there was a sudden silence. Then, from the village behind them, came the strident blare of the loudest motor-horn in England.

The pups sprang up, their exhaustion driven away by terror.

'To the woods!' cried Pongo. Then he saw that the woods were now protected by wire netting, through which not even the smallest pup could squeeze. And there was no ditch to hide in. But he could see that the woods ended, not very far ahead. 'We must go on,' he cried. 'There may be fields, there may be a ditch.'

The horn sounded again, repeatedly. Pongo guessed that the fire-engine had put out the fire and now Cruella was scattering the villagers as she drove on her way. Already she would be less than two miles behind them—and the great striped car could travel two miles in less than two minutes. But the woods were ending, there were fields ahead!

'To the fields!' cried Pongo. 'Faster, faster!'

The pups made a great spurt forward, then fell back in dismay. For though the woods ended, the wire netting still continued, on both sides of them. There was still no way off the road. And the horn sounded again—louder and nearer.

'Nothing but a miracle can save us now,' said Pongo.

'Then we must find a miracle,' said Missis, firmly. 'Pongo, what *is* a miracle?'

It was at that moment that they suddenly saw, through the swirling snow, a very large van drawn up on the road ahead of them. The tail-board was down and the inside of the van was lit by electric light. And sitting there, on a newspaper, was a Staffordshire terrier with a short clay pipe in his mouth. That is, it looked like a clay pipe. It was really made of sugar and had once had a fine long stem. Now the Staffordshire drew the bowl of the pipe into his mouth and ate it. Then he looked up from the newspaper—which he was reading as well as sitting on—and stared in astonishment at the army of pups rushing helter-skelter towards him.

'Help, help, help!' barked Pongo. 'We are being pursued. How soon can we get off this road?'

'I don't know, mate,' barked back the Staffordshire. 'You'd better hide in my van.'

'The miracle, the miracle!' gasped Pongo to Missis.

'Quickly, pups! Jump into the nice miracle,' said Missis, who now thought 'miracle' was another name for a removal van.

A swarm of pups surged up the tailboard. Up went the Cadpig's cart, pulled from the front and pushed from behind. Then more and more pups jumped or scrambled up until the entire army was in.

'Golly, there are a lot of you,' said the Staffordshire, who had flattened himself against the side of the van. 'Lucky the van was empty. Who's after you, mates? Old Nick?'

'Some relation of his, I think,' said Pongo. The strident horn sounded again and now two strong headlights could be seen in the distance. 'And she's in that car.'

'Then I'd better put the light off,' said the Staffordshire, neatly working the switch with his teeth. 'That's better.'

Pongo's heart seem to miss a beat. Suddenly he knew that letting the pups get into the van had been a terrible mistake.

'But the car's headlights will shine in,' he gasped. 'Our enemy will see the pups.'

'Not black pups in a black-van,' said the Staffordshire. 'Not if they close their eyes.'

Oh, excellent suggestion! Quickly Pongo gave the command:

'Pups, close your eyes—or they will reflect the car's headlights and shine like jewels in the darkness. Close them and do not open them, however frightened you are, until I give the word. Remember, your lives may depend on your obedience now. Close your eyes and keep them closed!'

Instantly all the puppies closed their eyes tight. And now the car's headlights were less than a quarter of a mile away.

'Close your eyes, Missis,' said Pongo.

'And don't forget to close your own, mate,' said the Staffordshire.

Now the car's powerful engine could be heard. The strident horn blared again and again, as if telling the van to get out of the way. Louder and louder grew the noise from the engine. The glare from the headlights was now so intense that Pongo was conscious of it through his tightly shut eyelids. Would the pups obey orders? Or would terror make them look towards the oncoming car? Pongo, himself, had a wild desire to do so and a wild fear that the car was going to crash into the van. The noise of horn and engine grew deafening, the glare seemed blinding, even to closed eyes. Then, with a roar, the great striped car was on them—and past them, roaring on and on into the night!

'You may open your eyes now, my brave, obedient pups,' cried Pongo. And indeed they deserved praise, for not one eye had been opened.

'That was quite a car, mate,' said the Staffordshire to Pongo. 'You must have quite an enemy. Who are you, anyway? The local pack of soot-hounds?' Then he suddenly stared very hard at Pongo's nose. 'Well, swelp me if it *isn't* soot! And it doesn't fool me. You're the missing Dalmatians. Want a lift back to London?'

A lift? A lift all the way in this wonderful van! Pongo and Missis could hardly believe it. Swiftly the pups settled to sleep on the rugs and blankets used for wrapping around furniture.

'But why are there so many pups?' said the Staffordshire. 'The newspapers don't know the half of it, not the quarter, neither. They think there are only fifteen missing.'

Pongo started to explain but the Staffordshire said they would talk during the drive to London. 'My pets will be out of that house there any minute. Fancy us doing a removal on a Sunday—*and* Christmas Eve. But the van broke down yesterday and we had to finish the job.'

'How many days will the journey to London take?' asked Missis.

'Days?' said the Staffordshire. 'It won't take much more than a couple of hours, if *I* know my pets. They want to get home to finish decorating their kids' Christmas trees. Sssh, now! Pipe down, both of you.'

A large man in a rough apron was coming out of a nearby house. Missis thought: 'As soon as one danger is past, another threatens.' Would they all be turned out of the miracle?

The Staffordshire, wagging his tail enthusiastically, hurled himself at the man's chest, nearly knocking him down.

'Look out, Bill!' said the man, over his shoulder. 'The canine cannonball's feeling frisky.'

Bill was an even larger man, but even he was shaken by the Staffordshire's loving welcome.

'Get down, you self-launched bomb,' he shouted, with great affection.

The two men and the Staffordshire came back to the van and the Staffordshire jumped inside. The sooty Dalmatians, huddled together, were invisible in the darkness.

'Want to ride inside, do you?' said Bill. 'Well, it *is* cold.' He put the tailboard up and shouted: 'Next stop, St John's Wood.' A moment later, the huge van took the road.

St John's Wood! Surely, that was where the splendid vet lived—quite close to Regent's Park! What wonderful, wonderful luck, thought Pongo. Just then he heard a clock strike. It was still only eight o'clock.

'Missis!' he cried. 'We shall get home tonight! We shall be home for Christmas!'

'Yes, Pongo,' said Missis, gaily. But she did not feel as gay as she sounded. For Missis, who had been so brave, so confident up to the moment they had found the miracle, had suddenly been smitten by a great fear. Suppose the Dearlys did not recognize them now they were black dogs? Suppose the dear, dear Dearlys turned them away?

She kept her fears to herself. Why should she frighten Pongo with them? How fast the miracle was travelling! She thought of the days it had taken her and Pongo to reach Suffolk on foot. Why, it seemed like weeks since they had left London! Yet it was only—how long? Could it be only *four* days? They'd slept one day in the stable at the inn, one day at the dear spaniel's, one day in the Folly, part of a night in the barn after the escape from Hell Hall, then a day at the bakery. So much had happened in so short a time. And now, would it be all right when they got home? Would it? Would it?

Meanwhile, Pongo had his own worries. He had been telling the Staffordshire all about Cruella and had remembered what she had said, that night at Hell Hall—how she intended to wait until people had forgotten about the stolen puppies, and then start her Dalmatian fur farm again. Surely he and Missis would get this lot of puppies safely home (it had never occurred to *him* that the Dearlys might not let them in) but what of the future? How could he make sure that other puppies did not end up as fur-coats later on? He asked the Staffordshire's advice.

'Why not kill this Cruella?' said the Staffordshire. 'And I'll help you. Let's make a date for it now.'

Pongo shook his head. He had come to believe that Cruella was not an ordinary human but some kind of devil. If so, could one kill her? In any case, he didn't want his pups to have a killer-dog for a father. He would have sprung at Cruella if she had attacked any pup, but he didn't fancy cold-blooded murder. He told the Staffordshire so.

'Your blood would soon warm up once you started the job,' said the Staffordshire. 'Well, let me know if you change your mind. And now you take a nap, mate. You've still got quite a job ahead of you.'

The Staffordshire, like Missis, wondered if the Dearlys would recognize these black Dalmatians—and if even the kindest pets would take in so many pups. But he said nothing of this to Pongo.

Missis, lulled by the movement of the van, had fallen asleep. Soon Pongo slept, too. But their dreams were haunted by their separate anxieties.

On and on through the dark went the mile-eating miracle.

JOAN OF ARC

Mollie Hardwick

The slim, dark-haired girl lifted her head with a puzzled frown on her almost boyish face, and looked everywhere around. She was quite alone in the garden, and yet she could hear a voice—as clearly as though someone were standing right beside her.

She listened more intently. There it was again! She had heard it before, telling her then that her mother wanted her to go indoors; but when she had obeyed she found that she had not been summoned at all.

Where could the voice be coming from? Perhaps she had been working too long in the sun and was getting dizzy from the heat? She dropped the hoe she had been using and walked towards the shade of her father's farmhouse. The disembodied voice followed her, a soothing, peaceful, melodic sound repeating her name over and over—'Joan . . . Joan . . .'

The girl was Joan of Arc, and she was now thirteen years old. She had lived all her life in the village of Domrémy, in the province of Lorraine in eastern France. Although her father was quite a prosperous farmer she could not read or write; but she could cook and sew and spin, and help in the fields. She was strong-minded and intelligent, and differed from the other village children in that instead of playing games she liked to sit alone in the peace of the little church.

Joan soon grew used to hearing the strange voice. Sometimes there seemed to be others, and all had the same message: that she must be good, take care of herself, and attend church regularly. She decided they must be angels speaking to her, and began to wonder if she had been specially chosen to fulfil an ancient prophesy she knew of—that France would one day be saved by a girl from Lorraine.

At this time, 1425, France had been at war with England for years. Large areas of the country were occupied by English soldiers. Villages were continually being raided and destroyed, causing widespread misery and suffering. The more Joan listened to her 'voices', as she called them, the more she became convinced that she was the girl destined to save France.

No one believed her when she first told her family and friends. And when strange visions started appearing to her no one believed her account of them, either. This was when she was sixteen. They were misty and indistinct at first, she said, but later she recognized one of the figures as the Archangel Michael. He was dressed in a suit of gleaming armour, and beside him stood the two patron saints of Lorraine, St Margaret and St Catherine.

Joan's family could not decide whether she was ill, or trying to frighten them with such fanciful stories—particularly when, one day, she told them that her voices had given her a new message. She had been chosen by God to drive the English from France, to lead the army to victory and secure the throne for the Dauphin—the title borne by the eldest son of the kings of France. This one, Charles, had actually succeeded to the throne in 1416, when he was only thirteen, but the war with England and civil strife in the provinces had so far prevented his coronation as Charles VII.

'Daughter of God,' Joan claimed she had been told, 'go to the town of Vaucouleurs and seek out the commander, Robert de Baudricourt. He will provide you with soldiers to take you to the Dauphin.'

Joan was now seventeen years old, a small girl, only five feet two inches tall, but strong and healthy and quite used to walking the distance it took to reach the neighbouring town of Vaucouleurs. Here she enlisted the help of an uncle and, through him, arranged an interview with Robert de Baudricourt. In her patched red dress she stood before the powerful commander and told him her story. At first he was furious at having his valuable time wasted with such 'nonsense'. He said her father should box her ears to knock a little sense into her.

Undeterred, Joan persisted in her request for his help, and her obvious sincerity impressed the tough, professional soldier. He began to wonder whether she might not, after all, be telling the truth. This was an age of deep superstition and credulity, when people believed in all kinds of miracles and wonders. If Joan really had been sent by God to save France, reasoned de Baudricourt, it would be wrong to hinder her. Besides, the army had just suffered another defeat and morale among the soldiers was very low. The message brought by this simple country girl might put fresh heart into them.

So, just as her voices had told her, Joan set out to see the Dauphin with an escort provided by the commander. She had changed her appearance for the journey: in place of the red gown she wore trousers and shirt, and her dark hair had been cropped short, so that she looked even more like a boy.

'God told me to wear a man's clothing because I am to carry a man's weapons. If I am dressed as a man among men, they will treat me as one of themselves and thus I will be able to preserve my chastity, both of spirit and body.'

The journey was a long and dangerous one, covering more than two hundred miles across battle territory. Joan's destination was the city of Chinon, near Tours, where the Dauphin had set up his court. Charles was a sickly, timid young man who relied heavily on the advice of his counsellors, only rousing himself by fits and starts. But he was extremely pious, and very superstitious, and when he learned of Joan's arrival in Chinon and the purpose of her journey he was only too ready to grant her an audience.

But to test her, he disguised himself as a courtier while another man took his place on the throne. It is part of the legend surrounding Joan of Arc that when she arrived in the audience chamber—a slight, travel-stained figure in contrast with the jewel-encrusted noblemen surrounding her—she turned from the throne and immediately singled out the Dauphin. Kneeling before him she cried out, 'Sire, I have been sent by God to bring help to the kingdom and to tell you that you are the true heir to France!'

Charles believed her. His counsellors advised him to be cautious until they had questioned this strange girl, but in the end they too were convinced. Joan told them that her first task was to drive the English from the besieged city of Orléans. Two months earlier, in February 1429, the enemy had encircled it, and if they succeeded in capturing it the whole of southern France would be soon overrun. Joan was placed at the head of an army of three thousand men. By this time rumour of her mission, of her voices and visions of saints, had spread among the soldiers. They hailed her as the saviour of France, calling her *La Pucelle*—The Maid.

Before beginning the expedition she sent a message to the English, ordering them to withdraw from the towns they had captured. 'If you do not,' she warned, 'know that I am military leader and wherever I find your soldiers I shall chase them out of France whether they wish to go or not.'

There was no reply. The English leaders could not believe that a mere girl of seventeen could be appointed head of an army—unless she had used witchcraft to enchant the Dauphin and his counsellors. They had already heard how she had apparently been led to the lost sword of the

She rode at the head of the army towards Orléans and the English soldiers . . .

old French hero, Charles Martel, discovered where Joan said it would be, buried behind the altar of a small church. When her battle steed, one of the massively powerful horses used at that time, had reared up and refused to let her mount, she led him to the market cross and the horse had quietened immediately.

To the English these stories sounded like sorcery. The French soldiers were inspired by them and their devotion to The Maid deepened with each fresh account of her power. To them she appeared 'a thing wholly divine' as she rode at the head of the army towards Orléans. The Dauphin had presented her with a suit of white armour, over which she wore a surcoat of scarlet and silver, and at her side fluttered her personal banner embroidered with the figure of Christ.

The army commanders were not so easily impressed. They were still smarting from the humiliation of having to take orders from a mere girl, and plotted to sabotage her plans by leading her to the wrong side of the River Loire. The soldiers could not cross over because the wind was blowing against them; yet no sooner had Joan arrived than it changed direction and the entire army was able to reach the city. The

French saw this as yet another sign of her holy power; the English interpreted it as further proof of diabolical witchcraft.

The battle to drive the enemy from Orléans lasted over two days of bitter fighting. Wherever the fray was thickest Joan's banner could be seen as she encouraged her soldiers forward. They fought with such ferocity that the English were finally forced to retreat. Her victory was regarded as nothing less than a miracle, and the legends about her redoubled. A white dove carrying a crown of gold was said to have alighted on her banner; angelic warriors were seen galloping across the sky; divine signs were rumoured to have been observed at the moment of her birth.

The English called her 'disciple and bloodhound of the Devil' and 'the fiend of France'. Their hatred and fear of her increased even more after she won a further resounding victory against them at Patay and captured some of their leading knights. Within a short time they had been driven from all the towns they had taken in the Loire district, and were forced to retreat to Paris.

Joan was now able to fulfil her promise to place the Dauphin on the throne. She rode at his side on the long journey to Rheims, and stood by the high altar in the cathedral as he knelt to receive the crown and be declared Charles VII of France. Her job was done, her mission completed. Her father had come to fetch her, and now she could go home.

But it was not to be. The new king still wanted her to lead his forces, and reluctantly Joan had to obey him. But she no longer heard voices, no longer saw visions of the saints. Although during the months that followed she took part in many skirmishes against the English, her inspiration seemed to have gone. She was beginning to show signs of fatigue. An attempt to drive the English out of Paris failed miserably. As she lay wounded by an arrow, her soldiers scattering before the overwhelming forces of the enemy, she felt intuitively that it would not be long before she was taken prisoner. Her intuition was right.

In May 1430, during an attack on Compiègne, Joan was captured by soldiers of the Duke of Burgundy, an ally of the English. In exchange for ten thousand livres she was handed over to her enemies to stand trial for witchcraft and heresy. She was taken to the English-held city of Rouen, where, during a long and arduous interrogation, she was treated with great cruelty by her captors. She was not allowed to attend

Mass, and was kept chained to a wooden stake in an underground cell.

At the end of March 1431, Joan was found guilty of the charges made against her. She was condemned to be burned to death. Her king, Charles VII, for whom her inspired deeds had won his throne, did nothing to intercede for her. She was only nineteen years old when, on 30 May, she died agonizingly at the stake in the market-place of Rouen. As the flames were lit around her an English soldier thrust a rough wooden cross into her hands. When it was all over, her ashes were thrown into the River Seine.

In 1456 Pope Calixtus III formally pronounced Joan to be innocent of all the charges made against her. In 1920 she was canonized as St Joan of Arc and became the national saint of France. Each year, on the anniversary of her death, young girls in white garments strew flowers on the waters of the Seine at Rouen, at the spot where her ashes were scattered so unceremoniously by her enemies.

Whatever the truth of her seemingly mystic gifts, her story has always served as the inspiration for French patriotism. She did not win that long war—the Hundred Years War—but her countrymen gained new heart from her example and fought at last as one nation, undivided by old feuds and jealousies. To Napoleon and others since she has been the symbol of France's ability to survive threat and even defeat.

THE LUCKY ORPHAN

Jean Webster

Jerusha Abbott is the oldest girl in an orphanage. From it she is sent to college by an anonymous benefactor. In Daddy-Long-Legs, *from which this extract comes, she tells her benefactor in a series of letters about her life as a student. (In the end she marries him).*

The first Wednesday in every month was a Perfectly Awful Day—a day to be awaited with dread, endured with courage and forgotten with haste. Every floor must be spotless, every chair dustless, and every bed without a wrinkle. Ninety-seven squirming little orphans must be scrubbed and combed and buttoned into freshly starched ginghams; and all ninety-seven reminded of their manners, and told to say, 'Yes, sir', 'No, sir', whenever a Trustee spoke.

It was a distressing time; and poor Jerusha Abbott, being the oldest orphan, had to bear the brunt of it. But this particular first Wednesday, like its predecessors, finally dragged itself to a close. Jerusha escaped from the pantry where she had been making sandwiches for the asylum's guests, and turned upstairs to accomplish her regular work. Her special care was room F, where eleven little tots, from four to seven, occupied eleven little cots set in a row. Jerusha assembled her charges, straightened their rumpled frocks, wiped their noses, and started them in an orderly and willing line towards the dining-room to engage themselves for a blessed half-hour with bread and milk and prune pudding.

Then she dropped down on the window-seat and leaned throbbing temples against the cool glass. She had been on her feet since five that morning, doing everybody's bidding, scolded and hurried by a nervous matron. Mrs Lippett, behind the scenes, did not always maintain that calm and pompous dignity with which she faced an audience of Trustees and lady visitors. Jerusha gazed out across a broad stretch of frozen lawn, beyond the tall iron paling that marked the confines of the asylum, down undulating ridges sprinkled with country estates, to the spires of the village rising from the midst of bare trees.

The day was ended—quite successfully, so far as she knew. The Trustees and the visiting committee had made their rounds, and read their reports and drunk their tea, and now were hurrying home to their own cheerful firesides, to forget their bothersome little charges for another month. Jerusha leaned forward watching with curiosity—and a touch of wistfulness—the stream of carriages and automobiles that rolled out of the asylum gates. In imagination she followed first one equipage, then another, to the big houses dotted along the hillside. She pictured herself in a fur coat and a velvet hat trimmed with feathers leaning back in the seat and nonchalantly murmuring 'Home' to the driver. But on the door-sill of her home the picture grew blurred.

Jerusha had an imagination—an imagination, Mrs Lippett told her, that would get her into trouble if she didn't take care—but keen as it was, it could not carry her beyond the front porch of the houses she would enter. Poor, eager, adventurous little Jerusha, in all her seventeen years, had never stepped inside an ordinary house; she could not picture the daily routine of those other human beings who carried on their lives undiscommoded by orphans.

Je-ru-sha Ab-bott
You are wan-ted
In the of-fice,
And I think you'd
Better hurry up!

Tommy Dillon, who had joined the choir, came singing up the stairs and down the corridor, his chant growing louder as he approached room F. Jerusha wrenched herself from the window and refaced the troubles of life.

'Who wants me?' she cut into Tommy's chant with a note of sharp anxiety.

Mrs Lippett in the office,
And I think she's mad.
Ah-a-men!

Tommy piously intoned, but his accent was not entirely malicious. Even the most hardened little orphan felt sympathy for an erring sister who was summoned to the office to face an annoyed matron; and Tommy liked Jerusha even if she did sometimes jerk him by the arm and nearly scrub his nose off.

Jerusha went without comment, but with two parallel lines on her brow. What could have gone wrong, she wondered. Were the sandwiches not thin enough? Were there shells in the nut cakes? Had a lady visitor seen the hole in Susie Hawthorn's stocking? Had—O horrors!—one of the cherubic little babes in her own room F 'sauced' a Trustee?

The long lower hall had not been lighted, and as she came downstairs, a last Trustee stood, on the point of departure, in the open door that led to the porte-cochère. Jerusha caught only a fleeting impression of the man—and the impression consisted entirely of tallness. He was waving his arm towards an automobile waiting in the curved drive. As it sprang into motion and approached, head-on for an instant, the glaring headlights threw his shadow sharply against the wall inside. The shadow pictured grotesquely elongated legs and arms that ran along the floor and up the wall of the corridor. It looked, for all the world, like a huge, wavering daddy-long-legs.

Jerusha's anxious frown gave place to quick laughter. She was by nature a sunny soul, and had always snatched the tiniest excuse to be amused. If one could derive any sort of entertainment out of the oppressive fact of a Trustee, it was something unexpected to the good. She advanced to the office quite cheered by the tiny episode, and presented a smiling face to Mrs Lippett. To her surprise the matron was also, if not exactly smiling, at least appreciably affable; she wore an expression almost as pleasant as the one she donned for visitors.

'Sit down, Jerusha. I have something to say to you.'

Jerusha dropped into the nearest chair and waited with a touch of breathlessness. An automobile flashed past the window; Mrs Lippett glanced after it.

'Did you notice the gentleman who has just gone?'

'I saw his back.'

'He is one of our most affluential Trustees, and has given large sums of money towards the asylum's support. I am not at liberty to mention his name; he expressly stipulated that he was to remain unknown.'

Jerusha's eyes widened slightly; she was not accustomed to being summoned to the office to discuss the eccentricities of Trustees with the matron.

'This gentleman has taken an interest in several of our boys. You remember Charles Benton and Henry Freize? They were both sent through college by Mr—er—this Trustee, and both have repaid with hard work and success the money that was so generously expended. Other payment the gentleman does not wish. Heretofore his philanthropies have been directed solely towards the boys; I have never been able to interest him in the slightest degree in any of the girls in the institution, no matter how deserving. He does not, I may tell you, care for girls.'

'No, ma'am,' Jerusha murmured, since some reply seemed to be expected at this point.

'Today, at the regular meeting, the question of your future was brought up.'

Mrs Lippett allowed a moment of silence to fall, then resumed in a slow, placid manner extremely trying to her hearer's suddenly tightened nerves.

'Usually, as you know, the children are not kept after they are sixteen, but an exception was made in your case. You had finished our school at fourteen, and having done so well in your studies—not always, I must say, in your conduct—it was determined to let you go on in the village high school. Now you are finishing that, and of course the asylum cannot be responsible any longer for your support. As it is, you have had two years more than most.'

Mrs Lippett overlooked the fact that Jerusha had worked hard for her board during those two years; that the convenience of the asylum had come first and her education second; that on days like the present she was kept at home to scrub.

'As I say, the question of your future was brought up and your record was discussed—thoroughly discussed.'

Mrs Lippett brought accusing eyes to bear upon the prisoner in the dock, and the prisoner looked guilty because it seemed to be expected—not because she could remember any strikingly black pages in her record.

'Of course the usual disposition of one in your place would be to put you in a position where you could begin to work, but you have done well in school in certain branches; it seems that your work in English has even been brilliant. Miss Pritchard, who is on our visiting committee, is also on the school board; she has been talking with your rhetoric teacher, and made a speech in your favour. She also read aloud an essay that you had written entitled, 'Blue Wednesday'.

Jerusha's guilty expression this time was not assumed.

'It seemed to me that you showed little gratitude in holding up to ridicule the institution that has done so much for you. Had you not managed to be funny I doubt if you would have been forgiven. But fortunately for you, Mr—that is, the gentleman who has just gone—appears to have an immoderate sense of humour. On the strength of that impertinent paper, he has offered to send you to college.'

'To college?' Jerusha's eyes grew big.

Mrs Lippett nodded.

'He waited to discuss the terms with me. They are unusual. The gentleman, I may say, is erratic. He believes that you have originality, and he is planning to educate you to become a writer.'

'A writer?' Jerusha's mind was numbed. She could only repeat Mrs Lippett's words.

'That is his wish. Whether anything will come of it, the future will show. He is giving you a very liberal allowance, almost, for a girl who has never had any experience in taking care of money, too liberal. But he planned the matter in detail, and I did not feel free to make any suggestions. You are to remain here through the summer, and Miss Pritchard has kindly offered to superintend your outfit. Your board and tuition will be paid directly to the college, and you will receive in addition during the four years you are there, an allowance of thirty-five dollars a month. This will enable you to enter on the same standing as the other students. The money will be sent to you by the gentleman's private secretary once a month, and in return, you will write a letter of acknowledgment once a month. That is, you are not to thank him for the money; he doesn't care to have that mentioned, but you are to write a letter telling of the progress in your studies and the details of your daily life. Just such a letter as you would write to your parents if they were living.

'These letters will be addressed to Mr John Smith and will be sent in care of the secretary. The gentleman's name is not John Smith, but he prefers to remain unknown. To you he will never be anything but John Smith. His reason in requiring the letters is that he thinks nothing so fosters facility in literary expression as letter-writing. Since you have no family with whom to correspond, he desires you to write in this way; also, he wishes to keep track of your progress. He will never answer your letters, nor in the slightest particular take any notice of them. He detests letter-writing and does not wish you to become a burden. If any point should ever arise where an answer would seem to be imperative—such as in the event of your being expelled, which I trust will not occur—you may correspond with Mr Griggs, his secretary. These monthly letters are absolutely obligatory on your part; they are the only payment that Mr Smith requires, so you must be as punctilious in sending them as though it were a bill that you were paying. I hope that they will always be respectful in tone and will reflect credit on your training. You must remember that you are writing to a Trustee of the John Grier Home.'

Jerusha's eyes longingly sought the door. Her head was in a whirl of excitement, and she wished only to escape from Mrs Lippett's platitudes, and think. She rose and took a tentative step backwards. Mrs Lippett detained her with a gesture; it was an oratorical opportunity not to be slighted.

'I trust that you are properly grateful for this very rare good fortune that has befallen you? Not many girls in your position ever have such an opportunity to rise in the world. You must always remember—'

'I—yes, ma'am, thank you. I think, if that's all, I must go and sew a patch on Freddie Perkins's trousers.'

The door closed behind her, and Mrs Lippett watched it with dropped jaw, her peroration in mid air.

★ ★ ★ ★

215 FERGUSSEN HALL
September 24th.

Dear Kind-Trustee-Who-Sends-Orphans-to-College,

Here I am! I travelled yesterday for four hours in a train. It's a funny sensation, isn't it? I never rode in one before.

College is the biggest, most bewildering place—I get lost whenever I leave my room. I will write you a description later when I'm feeling less muddled; also I will tell you about my lessons. Classes don't begin until Monday morning, and this is Saturday night. But I wanted to write a letter first just to get acquainted.

It seems queer to be writing letters to somebody you don't know. It seems queer to me to be writing letters at all—I've never written more than three or four in my life, so please overlook it if these are not a model kind.

Before leaving yesterday morning, Mrs Lippett and I had a very serious talk. She told me how to behave all the rest of my life, and especially how to behave towards the kind gentleman who is doing so much for me. I must take care to be Very Respectful.

But how can one be very respectful to a person who wishes to be called John Smith? Why couldn't you have picked out a name with a little personality? I might as well write letters to Dear Hitching-Post or Dear Clothes-Prop.

I have been thinking about you a great deal this summer; having somebody take an interest in me after all these years makes me feel as though I had found a sort of family. It seems as though I belong to somebody now, and it's a very comfortable sensation. I must say, however, that when I think about you, my imagination has very little to work upon. There are just three things that I know:

I. You are tall.
II. You are rich.
III. You hate girls.

I suppose I might call you Dear Mr Girl-Hater. Only that's rather insulting to me. Or Dear Mr Rich-Man, but that's insulting to you, as though money were the only important thing about you. Besides, being rich is such a very external quality. Maybe you won't stay rich all your life; lots of very clever men get smashed up in Wall Street. But at last you will stay tall all your life! So I've decided to call you dear Daddy-Long-Legs. I hope you won't mind. It's just a private pet name—we won't tell Mrs Lippett.

The ten o'clock bell is going to ring in two minutes. Our day is divided into sections by bells. We eat and sleep and study by bells. It's very enlivening; I feel like a fire-horse all of the time. There it goes! Lights out. Good night.

Observe with what precision I obey rules—due to my training in the John Grier Home.

Yours most respectfully,
JERUSHA ABBOTT

To Mr Daddy-Long-Legs Smith.

October 1st

Dear Daddy-Long-Legs,

I love college and I love you for sending me—I'm very, *very* happy, and so excited every moment of the time that I can scarcely sleep. You can't imagine how different it is from the John Grier Home. I never dreamed there was such a place in the world. I'm feeling sorry for everybody who isn't a girl and who can't come here; I am sure the college you attended when you were a boy couldn't have been so nice.

My room is up in a tower that used to be the contagious ward before they built the new infirmary. There are three other girls on the same floor of the tower—a Senior who wears spectacles and is always asking us please to be a little more quiet, and two freshmen named Sallie McBride and Julia Rutledge Pendleton. Sallie has red hair and a turn-up nose and is quite friendly; Julia comes from one of the first families in New York and hasn't noticed me yet. They room together and the Senior and I have singles. Usually Freshmen can't get singles; they are very scarce, but I got one without even asking. I suppose the registrar didn't think it would be right to ask a properly brought-up girl to room with a foundling. You see there are advantages!

My room is on the north-west corner with two windows and a view. After you've lived in a ward for eighteen years with twenty room-mates, it is restful to be alone. This is the first chance I've ever had to get acquainted with Jerusha Abbott. I think I'm going to like her.

Do you think you are?

Tuesday.

They are organizing the Freshman basket-ball team and there's just a chance that I shall get in it. I'm little of course, but terribly quick and wiry and tough. While the others are hopping about in the air, I can dodge under their feet and grab the ball. It's loads of fun practising—out in the athletic field in the afternoon with the trees all red and yellow and the air full of the smell of burning leaves, and everybody laughing and shouting. These are the happiest girls I ever saw—and I am the happiest of all!

I meant to write a long letter and tell you all the things I'm learning (Mrs Lippett said you wanted to know), but 7th hour has just rung, and in ten minutes I'm due at the athletic field in gymnasium clothes. Don't you hope I'll get in the team?

Yours always,
JERUSHA ABBOTT.

PS. (9 o'clock.)

Sallie McBride just poked her head in at my door. This is what she said:

'I'm so homesick that I simply can't stand it. Do you feel that way?'

I smiled a little and said no, I thought I could pull through. At least homesickness is one disease that I've escaped! I never heard of anybody being asylum-sick, did you?

THE ESCAPE OF PRINCESS CLEMENTINA

John Buchan

In the year 1718 the Chevalier de St George, or, as some called him, the Old Pretender, after the defeat of his hopes in Scotland, had retired to Rome. At the age of thirty he was still a bachelor, but the unhappiness of his condition was due not to his celibacy but to his misfortunes. The Jacobite campaign of 1715 had proved a disastrous failure; and although he still retained the courtesy title of James III, he was a king without a realm. While the royal exile was twiddling his thumbs in the Italian capital, waiting for a better turn of luck, his friends, seeing that nothing further was to be gained by the pursuit of Mars, sought the aid of Cupid. They laid before the Chevalier the flattering proposal of a marriage with a princess of beauty and race. This move was inspired less by romance than by politics, for a suitable marriage would not only encourage the waning Jacobite hopes, but might also raise up an heir to their cause.

The Chevalier readily concurred in the scheme, and a certain Mr Charles Wogan was dispatched to the various European courts to report on a suitable bride for the Chevalier. Wogan's choice fell on the little Polish Princess Clementina Sobiesky, daughter of James Sobiesky of Poland and Edwige Elizabeth Amelia of the house of Newburgh, and grand-daughter of the famous John Sobiesky, the 'deliverer of Christendom'.

The chronicles of the time are loud in the praises of this lady, her illustrious birth, her qualities of heart and mind, 'her Goodness, Sweetness of Temper, and other Beauties of a valuable character'. She is said to have been 'happy in all the Charms, both of Mind and Body, her Sex can boast of'; 'the Agreeableness of Seventeen and the Solidity of Thirty'. Her accomplishments included Polish, High Dutch, French, Italian, and English, all of which she spoke so well that it was difficult to distinguish which of these languages was the most familiar to her. She was also a young woman of exemplary piety, and therefore a suitable bride for a king in exile. Princess Clementina was only sixteen when the Chevalier and his friends laid siege to her affections.

It was no ordinary business, for there were many hazards and difficulties in the way. The Chevalier had given his consent to the proposed alliance; it was for his friends to see it brought to a successful issue, and the plan of campaign was left entirely in their hands. The bridegroom was a mere pawn—a willing pawn—in the game. The real difficulty was the House of Hanover, the inveterate enemy of the Stuart cause, which was by no means inclined to look with indulgence on the proposed alliance. Although the affair was kept a profound secret, the matter gradually leaked out; and George I of England protested with such vigour to the Emperor on the folly and danger of the impending marriage, threatening among other things to break up the Quadruple Alliance, that Princess Clementina was arrested at Innsbruck with her mother and kept there under strict surveillance.

The Chevalier and his friends were in a quandary. Obviously a man built in the heroic mould was necessary to extricate them from the dilemma. They bethought them of Wogan, who had been recalled from his delicate mission on the pretext that it was impolitic to entrust the matter further to an Irish Catholic. Wogan was well adapted for this sort of adventure. He was, besides being something of a poet, a cavalier and a courtier. He had shared the hard fortunes of the Chevalier in Scotland, and had suffered imprisonment for his devotion to the Stuart cause. Once more the soldier of fortune was called upon to prove his devotion in a cause no less hazardous.

The Pope, who had been taken into the secret, had provided Wogan with a passport in the name of the Comte de Cernes, and forth he fared like a fairy-tale knight to rescue a distressed princess. Never had d'Artagnan and his Musketeers a more difficult task. Wogan duly arrived at Innsbruck in the disguise of a merchant, and obtained an interview with the Princess and her mother, who heartily concurred in the proposed plan of a secret 'elopement'. We next find him at Ohlau in quest of the Prince Sobiesky, the lady's father. Here he met with a rebuff. Prince Sobiesky, a practical man of the world, viewed the whole affair as midsummer madness, and absolutely refused to lend his aid or consent to Wogan's scheme.

Wogan was in a quandary, but he did not lose heart. He had nothing to complain of during his stay with Prince Sobiesky, for he was well lodged and treated with the most flattering attentions, but the real business of the mission hung fire. Still he waited—he had long learned the game of patience—and, being a courtier, was used to waiting.

At length a happy accident turned the scale in his favour. On New Year's Day, Prince Sobiesky, as a mark of his esteem, presented his guest with a magnificent snuff-box, formed of a single turquoise set in gold, a family heirloom, and part of the treasure found by John Sobiesky in the famous scarlet pavilion of Kara Mustapha. Wogan, with a charming gesture, declined the gift on the plea that, although he was sensible of the high honour shown him by the Prince, he could not think of returning to Italy with a present for himself and a refusal for his master. The Prince was so touched that he finally yielded, and furnished Wogan with the necessary instructions to his wife and daughter. Wogan set out once more on his adventures in high spirits, carrying not only the precious instructions, but the snuff-box, which Prince Sobiesky had pressed on him as a parting gift.

The next thing was to establish secret communication with the Princess. This was more easily said than done. The garrulity of Prince Sobiesky, who in his parental agitation had babbled the whole story to a certain German baron, and the suspicions of the Countess de Berg, a noted *intriguante* and spy of the Austrian court, almost brought Wogan's mission to an inglorious end. The baron was brought over at 'considerable expenditure', but the Countess was a more difficult matter. While Wogan was the guest of honour of Prince Sobiesky she had been puzzled at the attentions shown to him, which she argued could be for no good end, and set her spies on his track. Wogan escaped by the skin of his teeth, and only evaded capture by ostentatiously announcing his departure for Prague. Then by a skilful detour he gave his pursuers the slip and posted on to Vienna, where he vainly tried to enlist the sympathy of the Papal Nuncio, Monseigneur Spinola.

Then came a thunderbolt, for suddenly Prince Sobiesky changed his mind. He dispatched an urgent message to Wogan saying that both the Princess and her mother, alarmed at the dangers that encompassed them, had resolved to proceed no further in the business, and that he forthwith cancelled his previous instructions.

Here was a pretty kettle of fish! Wogan was a stout-hearted fellow, but this new blow almost unmanned him. In his dilemma he wrote to the Chevalier and told the whole story, asking him at the same time to send a confidential servant to obtain fresh powers from Prince Sobiesky. The Chevalier promptly dispatched one of his valets, a Florentine called Michael Vezzosi, who, when attached to the Venetian Embassy in London, had been instrumental in aiding the escape of Lord Nithsdale from the Tower. The Chevalier reminded Prince Sobiesky that by his foolish behaviour he was not only needlessly endangering the lives of Wogan and his friends, but adding to the difficulties of the captives at Innsbruck. He also gave the most explicit instructions to Wogan to proceed with the enterprise.

Wogan accordingly set out for Schlettstadt, where he met his three kinsmen, Major Gaydon and Captains Misset and O'Toole, who were to lend their aid in the now difficult mission. Mrs Misset accompanied her husband, together with her maid Jeanneton, but neither of the women was told the real nature of the undertaking. Jeanneton was to play a conspicuous part in the escape of Clementina. Wogan's plan was that the maid should change places with the Princess and generally impersonate her till she had made good her escape. The light-headed girl was told a cock-and-bull story about O'Toole having fallen violently in love with a beautiful heiress, and Wogan played to such a tune on her sense of the romantic that she gleefully entered into the plot of the 'elopement'.

Wogan, however, was not yet out of the wood. So far he had succeeded, but he had now to deal with the whims and caprice of the ladies who had been pressed into the enterprise. Jeanneton, whose importance to the success of the venture was paramount, proved especially troublesome. First of all she refused point-blank to wear the low-heeled shoes which had been specially ordered for her, so as to reduce her height to conformity with that of the Princess; and not only screamed and swore, but went so far in her tantrums as to knock the shoemaker down. She had once been a camp-follower, and her manners were those of the tented field. It was not until Mrs Misset, in an excess of despair, had thrown herself imploringly at her feet, a ceremony in which the gentlemen of the party were constrained to join, that the maid relented, and the party set forth at last in a ramshackle berline for Innsbruck.

So far so good. At an inn between Nassereith and Innsbruck, while the other members of the party regaled themselves with a banquet of wild boar and sauerkraut, Wogan stole out in the rain to keep an important appointment with a certain M. Châteaudoux, gentleman-usher to the Princess Sobiesky. This gentleman had not Wogan's spirit, and proposed to defer the matter of the escape till the weather had cleared and the roads were in better condition for travel.

Wogan firmly waived aside his objections, and succeeded so well in convincing him that now or never was the time, that at half-past eleven that same night he and the precious Jeanneton made their way in the storm to the *schloss* where the Princess was confined. Fortune smiled on the enterprise, and even the tempest was propitious, for the sentry, heedless of danger on such a night, had sought refuge in the inn.

Meanwhile within the prison walls the Princess Clementina, in order to assist the plan of escape, was playing the part of an invalid. Jeanneton's role was simple: the Princess having regained her freedom, all that the maid had to do was to keep her bed on the plea that her migraines were no better, refusing to see any one but her mother. The secret was well kept; not even the governess was told, lest her grief at the sudden departure of the Princess might arouse suspicions.

At midnight, according to plan, Châteaudoux was in readiness, and Jeanneton, clad in a shabby riding-hood and female surtout, was successfully smuggled into the sleeping chamber of the Princess. Wogan and O'Toole waited at the street corner ready to convoy the Princess to the inn. There was a lengthy farewell scene between the Princess and her mother. The two having wept and embraced each other, Clemen-

Princess Clementina followed Châteaudoux down the winding stairs and out into the night. . .

tina excused herself for her hurried departure on the plea that nothing in heaven or earth must stand in the way between her and her husband. Then she hastily dressed herself in Jeanneton's clothes, and followed Châteaudoux down the winding stairs and out into the night.

The Princess was no longer a captive. The tempest, which had increased, favoured the escape. Once more successfully evading the sentry, they quickly gained the street corner where Wogan and O'Toole were kicking their heels, consumed with fear and anxiety. They reached the inn, drenched to the skin, with but one slight misadventure. Clementina, mistaking a floating wisp of hay for a solid log of wood, slipped and plunged over the ankles into a channel of half-melted snow. At the inn she eagerly swallowed a cup of hot spiced wine and changed her soaking garments. Konski, her mother's page, had followed meanwhile with what the chronicles of the period call 'inside apparel' and a casket containing her jewels, said to be valued at about 150,000 pistoles. The foolish Konski, no doubt scared out of his wits at his share in the adventure, had thrown the precious packet behind the door and taken ignominiously to his heels.

They were now ready for the road. Captain Misset, who had gone out to reconnoitre, having returned with a favourable report, off they started. The inn was silent and shuttered, everybody having retired for the night, including the landlady; so they stole off unobserved. As the ancient coach lumbered past the dismal *schloss* where the Princess had been so recently a prisoner, she could not restrain some natural emotion at the thought of her mother; and then suddenly she discovered the loss of the precious packet. Here was a nice to-do! There was nothing for it but to return to the inn and fetch the packet. O'Toole was entrusted with this anxious mission. By one more stroke of good fortune he succeeded in retrieving it from behind the door where the careless Konski had thrown it, but he had first to prise the door off its hinges.

At sunset the party reached the village of Brenner, where the Princess, who had so far borne up nobly, had a slight attack of the vapours. She was speedily revived, however, by a dose of eau de Carmes, and, having had a meal, soon regained her accustomed gaiety, and began to ply Wogan with all sorts of innocent questions about the manners and customs of the English and his adventures with the Chevalier in Scotland. One by one the party dropped off to sleep, all but Wogan, who as the Master of Ceremonies, managed to keep himself awake by the expedient of taking prodigious pinches of snuff. At last even he, overcome by the ardours of the night, began to show signs of drowsiness. While dropping off to sleep, his snuff-box accidentally slipped from his lap and fell on to the curls of the Princess, who with her head resting against his knees was reposing at the bottom of the carriage.

Verona was still a journey of forty-six hours, and the party were much inconvenienced by the lack of post-horses. To their horror they discovered that they were travelling in the wake of the Princess of Baden and her son, one of the husbands who had been proposed for Clementina, and whom she had been actually bribed to marry! At another stage of the journey the coackman was drunk, and they were saved only by a miracle from being dashed to pieces at the foot of one of the precipitous gorges of the Adige.

They were now approaching the most difficult part of the journey, and it was arranged before they passed the frontier of the Venetian States that O'Toole and Misset should remain behind to intercept any messengers from Innsbruck and guard the retreat. This prescience was amply rewarded. O'Toole had soon the satisfaction of waylaying a courier who had been dispatched in hot pursuit of the fugitive. The fellow was not only put entirely off the scent, but at supper was plied so generously with old brandy he had to be carried drunk to bed. Having relieved him of his documents the cavaliers rode on to rejoin the party in the berline.

One or two trials had still to be overcome. At Trent there was some delay owing to the behaviour of a surly governor who put every obstacle in their way. There was besides the continual fear of Clementina being detected by her Highness of Baden, who had installed herself in state at the inn. The poor little Princess had perforce to remain hidden at the bottom of the coach in the public square until such time as they could obtain fresh relays. The best they could find was a couple of tired screws taken from a neighbouring field. At Roveredo things were even worse, as no horses were to be had at all; and to crown their misfortunes they had not proceeded six miles with their weary beasts when the axle of the ramshackle old berline broke!

But at length they reached the great white wall that denoted the boundary between the Venetian States and the dominions of the

Emperor. At half-past three in the morning they stole across the frontier and solemnly offered up a *Te Deum* for their safe deliverance. They reached Pery with the bells merrily ringing for Mass, and narrowly missed being recognized by the Princess of Baden, who with her son was just entering the church when the berline drew up at the church door.

Verona was reached at dusk, and here for the first time during the three days' journey the Princess had her hair dressed. They came to Bologna on 2 May, where the Princess sent a message to the Cardinal Origo announcing her arrival. The Cardinal speedily repaired to pay his respects, bringing the present of a 'toyley, artificial flowers, and other little things', and the offer of a box at the opera. More welcome and important than the courtesies of the Cardinal was the arrival of Mr Murray, the Chevalier's agent, with messages from his royal master.

The drama of the royal elopement draws to its close. On 9 May Clementina was married by proxy. The little Princess, all agog with excitement, rose at 5 a.m., and having attired herself in a white dress and a pearl necklace went to Mass and received the Holy Communion. The marriage ceremony was performed by an English priest. The Chevalier was represented by Mr Murray, with Wogan as witness, and Prince Sobiesky by the Marquis of Monte-Boularois, a loyal friend of the Stuart cause. The 'powers' of the Chevalier were read publicly on conclusion of the Mass, setting forth his willingness to marry the Princess Clementina Sobiesky, and the ceremony was forthwith performed with the ring which he had sent expressly for the purpose.

The Princess entered Rome on 15 May, amid general rejoicings; and on 2 September a public marriage was celebrated at Montefiascone.

The daring flight and escape of the Princess Clementina caused some sensation at the time, and a medal was struck to commemorate the event. The Chevalier created Wogan a baronet, as well as his three kinsmen, and Wogan had the further distinction of being made a Roman Senator by Pope Clement XI. Jeanneton, who had played her part well, apart from the regrettable incident of the low-heeled shoes, duly escaped from Innsbruck and was sent to Rome as the maid of the Duchess of Parma. Prince Sobiesky was exiled to Passau by the Emperor for his complicity in the business, and was also deprived of a couple of valuable duchies. Wogan, who had always been something of a poet, devoted the remainder of his life to the cultivation of the Muse, his efforts drawing encomiums from so severe a critic as Dean Swift, to whom he had sent a copy of his verses in 'a bag of green velvet embroidered in gold'. He died in 1747.

As for the Princess, her wedded life did not fulfil the romantic promise of its beginnings. Married to a worthy but doleful husband, she never sat on the throne which she had been promised. She was the mother of Prince Charles Edward, and seems to have fallen into delicate health, for in one of his boyish letters, the little Prince promises not to jump or make a noise so as to 'disturb mamma'.

THE TREASURE HUNT

Robert Louis Stevenson

Jim Hawkins, whose father kept the Admiral Benbow Inn*, discovers a map in the sea-chest of old Billy Bones and takes it to Squire Trelawney. It turns out to be a map giving details of the buried treasure of Captain Flint, a pirate with whom Bones has served. Squire Trelawney, taking with him Dr Livesey and Jim, fits out the* Hispaniola *at Bristol to find the treasure. The squire's careless talk, however, attracts the scheming Long John Silver, who persuades Trelawney to enrol him as ship's cook and to crew the schooner with his nominees. The latter are all cut-throats and mutineers, and Silver himself Flint's old quartermaster.*

Immediately on landing at Treasure Island the trouble starts. The squire, the doctor and Jim, together with a few loyal seamen, escape from the ship and shift for themselves on the island.

Jim discovers Ben Gunn, who has been marooned for three years; but returning from a hazardous journey round the island on the Hispaniola, *which he has secured in North Islet, he falls into the hands of Silver and his gang. Silver now has possession of the map through a deal with the doctor, but the lack of success of his plans to this point has put him in danger from his unruly followers. The pirates, taking Jim with them, start on the treasure hunt and stumble across a skeleton.*

Partly from the damping influence of this alarm, partly to rest Silver and the sick folk, the whole party sat down as soon as they had gained the brow of the ascent.

The plateau being somewhat tilted toward the west, this spot on which we had paused commanded a wide prospect on either hand. Before us, over the treetops, we beheld the Cape of the Woods fringed with surf; behind, we not only looked down upon the anchorage and Skeleton Island, but saw—clear across the spit and the eastern lowlands

—a great field of open sea upon the east. Sheer above us rose the Spyglass, here dotted with single pines, there black with precipices. There was no sound but that of the distant breakers, mounting from all round, and the chirp of countless insects in the brush. Not a man, not a sail upon the sea; the very largeness of the view increased the sense of solitude.

Silver, as he sat, took certain bearings with his compass.

'There are three "tall trees",' said he, 'about in the right line from Skeleton Island. "Spyglass shoulder", I take it, means that lower p'int there. It's child's play to find the stuff now. I've half a mind to dine first.'

'I don't feel sharp,' growled Morgan. 'Thinkin' o' Flint—I think it were—has done me.'

'Ah, well, my son, you praise your stars he's dead,' said Silver.

'He were an ugly devil,' cried a third pirate, with a shudder; 'that blue in the face, too!'

'That was how the rum took him,' added Merry.

'Blue! well, I reckon he was blue. That's a true word.'

Ever since they had found the skeleton and got upon this train of thought they had spoken lower and lower, and they had almost got to whispering by now, so that the sound of their talk hardly interrupted the silence of the wood. All of a sudden, out of the middle of the trees in front of us, a thin, high, trembling voice struck up the well-known air and words:

'Fifteen men on the dead man's chest—Yo-ho-ho, and a bottle of rum!'

I never have seen men more dreadfully affected than the pirates. The colour went from their six faces like enchantment; some leaped to their feet, some clawed hold of others; Morgan grovelled on the ground.

'It's Flint, by——!' cried Merry.

The song had stopped as suddenly as it began—broken off, you would have said, in the middle of a note, as though someone had laid his hand upon the singer's mouth. Coming so far through the clear, sunny atmosphere among the green treetops, I thought it had sounded airily and sweetly; and the effect on my companions was the stranger.

'Come,' said Silver, struggling with his ashen lips to get the word out, 'this won't do. Stand by to go about. This is a rum start, and I can't name the voice: but it's someone skylarking—someone that's flesh and blood, and you may lay to that.'

His courage had come back as he spoke, and some of the colour to his face along with it. Already the others had begun to lend an ear to this encouragement, and were coming a little to themselves, when the same voice broke out again—not this time singing, but in a faint, distant hail, that echoed yet fainter among the clefts of the Spyglass.

'Darby M'Graw,' it wailed—for that is the word that best describes the sound—'Darby M'Graw! Darby M'Graw!' again and again and again; and then rising a little higher, and with an oath that I leave out, 'Fetch aft the rum, Darby!'

The buccaneers remained rooted to the ground, their eyes starting from their heads. Long after the voice had died away they still stared in silence, dreadfully, before them.

'That fixes it!' gasped one. 'Let's go.'

'They was his last words,' moaned Morgan, 'his last words above-board.'

Dick had his Bible out and was praying volubly. He had been well brought up, had Dick, before he came to sea and fell among bad companions.

Still, Silver was unconquered. I could hear his teeth rattle in his head; but he had not yet surrendered.

'Nobody in this here island ever heard of Darby,' he muttered; 'not one but us that's here.' And then, making a great effort, 'Shipmates,' he cried, 'I'm here to get that stuff, and I'll not be beat by man nor devil. I never was feared of Flint in his life and, by the powers, I'll face him dead. There's seven hundred thousand pound not a quarter of a mile from here. When did ever a gentleman o' fortune show his stern to that much dollars, for a boozy old seaman with a blue mug—and him dead, too?'

But there was no sign of reawakening courage in his followers; rather, indeed, of growing terror at the irreverence of his words.

'Belay there, John!' said Merry. 'Don't you cross a sperrit.'

And the rest were all too terrified to reply. They would have run away severally had they dared, but fear kept them together, and kept them close by John, as if his daring helped them. He, on his part, had pretty well fought his weakness down.

'Sperrit! Well, maybe,' he said. 'But there's one thing not clear to me. There was an echo. Now, no man ever seen a sperrit with a shadow; well, then, what's he doing with an echo to him, I should like to know? That ain't in natur', surely?'

This argument seemed weak enough to me. But you can never tell what will affect the superstitious, and, to my wonder, George Merry was greatly relieved.

'Well, that's so,' he said. 'You've a head upon your shoulders, John, and no mistake. 'Bout ship, mates! This here crew is on a wrong tack, I do believe. And come to think on it, it was like Flint's voice, I grant you, but not just so clear-away like it, after all. It was liker somebody else's voice now—it was liker——'

'By the powers, Ben Gunn!' roared Silver.

'Aye, and so it were,' cried Morgan, springing on his knees. 'Ben Gunn it were!'

'It don't make much odds, do it, now?' asked Dick. 'Ben Gunn's not here in the body, any more'n Flint.'

But the older hands greeted this remark with scorn.

'Why, nobody minds Ben Gunn,' cried Merry; 'dead or alive, nobody minds him.'

It was extraordinary how their spirits had returned and how the natural colour had revived in their faces. Soon they were chatting together, with intervals of listening: and not long after, hearing no further sound, they shouldered the tools and set forth again, Merry walking first with Silver's compass to keep them on the right line with Skeleton Island. He had said the truth: dead or alive, nobody minded Ben Gunn.

Dick alone still held his Bible, and looked around him as he went, with fearful glances: but he found no sympathy, and Silver even joked him on his precautions.

'I told you,' said he, 'I told you you had sp'iled your Bible. If it ain't no good to swear by, what do you suppose a sperrit would give for it? Not that!' and he snapped his big fingers, halting a moment on his crutch.

But Dick was not to be comforted; indeed, it was soon plain to me that the lad was falling sick; hastened by heat, exhaustion, and the shock of his alarm, the fever predicted by Dr Livesey was evidently growing swiftly higher.

It was fine open walking here, upon the summit; our way lay a little downhill, for, as I have said, the plateau tilted toward the west. The pines, great and small, grew wide apart; and even between the clumps of nutmeg and azalea wide-open spaces baked in the hot sunshine. Striking, as we did, pretty near north-west across the island, we drew, on the one hand, ever nearer under the shoulders of the Spyglass and, on the other, looked ever wider over that western bay where I had once tossed and trembled in the coracle.

The first of the tall trees was reached, and by the bearing proved the wrong one. So with the second. The third rose nearly two hundred feet into the air above a clump of underwood; a giant of a vegetable, with a red column as big as a cottage, and a wide shadow around in which a company could have manoeuvred. It was conspicuous far to sea on both the east and west, and might have been entered as a sailing mark upon the chart.

But it was not its size that now impressed my companions; it was the knowledge that seven hundred thousand pounds in gold lay somewhere buried below its spreading shadow. The thought of the money, as they drew nearer, swallowed up their previous terrors. Their eyes burned in their heads; their feet grew speedier and lighter; their whole soul was bound up in that fortune, that whole lifetime of extravagance and pleasure, that lay waiting for each of them.

Silver hobbled, grunting, on his crutch; his nostrils stood out and quivered; he cursed like a madman when the flies settled on his hot and shiny countenance; he plucked furiously at the line that held me to him and, from time to time, turned his eyes upon me with a deadly look. Certainly he took no pains to hide his thoughts; and certainly I read them like print. In the immediate nearness of the gold, all else had been forgotten; his promise and the doctor's warning were both things of the past; and I could not doubt that he hoped to seize upon the treasure, find and board the *Hispaniola* under cover of night, cut every honest throat about that island, and sail away as he had at first intended, laden with crimes and riches.

Shaken as I was with these alarms, it was hard for me to keep up with the rapid pace of the treasure hunters. Now and again I stumbled, and it was then that Silver plucked so roughly at the rope and launched at me his murderous glances. Dick, who had dropped behind us and now brought up the rear, was babbling to himself both prayers and curses, as his fever kept rising. This also added to my wretchedness, and, to crown all, I was haunted by the thought of the tragedy that had once been acted on that plateau, when that ungodly buccaneer with the blue face—he who died at Savannah, singing and shouting for drink—had there, with his own hand, cut down his six accomplices. This grove, that was now so peaceful, must then have rung with cries, I thought; and even with the thought I could believe I heard it ringing still.

We were now at the margin of the thicket and more light shone through the trees.

'Huzza, mates, all together!' shouted Merry, and the foremost broke into a run.

And suddenly, not ten yards farther, we beheld them stop. A low cry arose. Silver doubled his pace, digging away with the foot of his crutch like one possessed; and next moment he and I came to a dead halt.

Before us was a great excavation, not very recent, for the sides had fallen in and grass had sprouted on the bottom. In this were the shaft of a pick broken in two and the boards of several packing cases strewn around. On one of these boards I saw, branded with a hot iron, the name *Walrus*—the name of Flint's ship.

All was clear to probation. The cache had been found and rifled: the seven hundred thousand pounds were gone!

There never was such an overturn in this world. Each of these six men was as though he had been struck. But with Silver the blow passed almost instantly. Every thought of his soul had been set full-stretch, like a racer, on that money. Well, he was brought up in a single second, dead; and he kept his head, found his temper, and changed his plan before the others had had time to realize the disappointment.

'Jim', he whispered, 'take that, and stand by for trouble.'

And he passed me a double-barrelled pistol.

At the same time he began quietly moving northward, and in a few steps had put the hollow between us two and the other five. Then he looked at me and nodded, as much as to say, 'Here is a narrow corner,' as, indeed, I thought it was. His looks were now quite friendly; and I was so revolted at these constant changes that I could not forbear whispering, 'So you've changed sides again.'

There was no time left for him to answer in. The buccaneers, with oaths and cries, began to leap, one after another, into the pit, and to dig with their fingers, throwing the boards aside as they did so. Morgan found a piece of gold. He held it up with a spout of oaths. It was a two-guinea piece, and it went from hand to hand among them for a quarter of a minute.

'Two guineas!' roared Merry, shaking it at Silver. 'That's your seven hundred thousand pounds, is it? You're the man for bargains, ain't you? You're him that never bungled nothing, you wooden-headed lubber!'

'Dig away, boys,' said Silver, with the coolest insolence, 'you'll find some pignuts and I shouldn't wonder.'

'Pignuts!' repeated Merry in a scream. 'Mates, do you hear that? I tell you, now, that man there knew it all along. Look in the face of him, and you'll see it wrote there.'

'Ah, Merry,' remarked Silver, 'standing for cap'n again? You're a pushing lad, to be sure.'

But this time everyone was entirely in Merry's favour. They began to scramble out of the excavation, darting furious glances behind them. One thing I observed, which looked well for us: they all got out upon the opposite side from Silver.

Well, there we stood, two on one side, five on the other, the pit between us, and nobody screwed up high enough to offer the first blow. Silver never moved; he watched them, very upright on his crutch, and looked as cool as ever I saw him. He was brave, and no mistake.

At last Merry seemed to think a speech might help matters.

'Mates', says he, 'there's two of them alone there: one's the old cripple that brought us all here and blundered us down to this; the other's that cub that I mean to have the heart of. Now, mates——'

He was raising his arm and his voice, and plainly meant to lead a charge. But jest then—*crack! crack! crack!*—three muskets shots flashed out of the thicket. Merry tumbled head foremost into the excavation; the man with the bandage spun round like a teetotum and fell all his length upon his side, where he lay dead, but still twitching; and the other three turned and ran for it with all their might.

Before you could wink, Long John had fired two barrels of a pistol into the struggling Merry; and as the man rolled up his eyes at him in the last agony, 'George,' said he, 'I reckon I settled you.'

At the same moment, the doctor, Gray and Ben Gunn joined us, with smoking muskets, from among the nutmeg trees.

'Forward!' cried the doctor. 'Double quick, my lads. We must head 'em off the boats.'

And we set off at a great pace, sometimes plunging through the bushes to the chest.

I tell you, but Silver was anxious to keep up with us. The work that man went through, leaping on his crutch till the muscles of his chest were fit to burst, was work no sound man ever equalled; and so thinks the doctor. As it was, he was already thirty yards behind us, and on the verge of strangling, when we reached the brow of the slope.

'Doctor,' he hailed, 'see there! No hurry!'

Sure enough there was no hurry. In a more open part of the plateau we could see the three survivors still running in the same direction as they had started, right for Mizzenmast Hill. We were already between them and the boats, and so we four sat down to breathe, while Long John, mopping his face, came slowly up with us.

'Thank ye kindly, doctor,' says he. 'You came in in about the nick, I guess, for me and Hawkins. And so it's you, Ben Gunn!' he added. 'Well, you're a nice one, to be sure.'

'I'm Ben Gunn, I am,' replied the maroon, wriggling like an eel in his embarrassment. 'And,' he added, after a long pause, 'how do, Mr Silver? Pretty well, I thank ye, says you.'

'Ben, Ben,' murmured Silver, 'to think as you've done me!'

The doctor sent back Gray for one of the pickaxes, deserted, in their flight, by the mutineers; and then as we proceeded leisurely downhill to where the boats were lying, related, in a few words, what had taken place. It was a story that interested Silver; and Ben Gunn, the half-idiot maroon, was the hero from beginning to end.

Ben, in his long, lonely wanderings about the island, had found the skeleton—it was he that had rifled it; he had found the treasure; he had dug it up (it was the haft of his pickaxe that lay broken in the excavation); he had carried it on his back, in many weary journeys, from the foot of the tall pine to a cave he had on the two-pointed hill at the north-east angle of the island, and there it had lain stored in safety since two months before the arrival of the *Hispaniola*.

When the doctor had wormed this secret from him, on the afternoon of the attack, and when next morning he saw the anchorage deserted, he had gone to Silver, given him the chart, which was now useless—

given him the stores, for Ben Gunn's cave was well supplied with goats' meat salted by himself—given anything and everything to get a chance of moving in safety from the stockade to the two-pointed hill, there to be clear of malaria and keep a guard on the money.

'As for you, Jim,' he said, 'it went against my heart, but I did what I thought best for those who had stood by their duty. And if you were not one of these, whose fault was it?'

That morning, finding that I was to be involved in the horrid disappointment he had prepared for the mutineers, he had run all the way to the cave and, leaving the squire to guard the captain, had taken Gray and the maroon, and started, making the diagonal across the island, to be at hand beside the pine. Soon, however, he saw that our party had the start of him; and Ben Gunn, being fleet of foot, had been dispatched in front to do his best alone. Then it had occurred to him to work upon the superstitions of his former shipmates; and he was so far successful that Gray and the doctor had come up and were already ambushed before the arrival of the treasure hunters.

'Ah,' said Silver, 'it were fortunate for me that I had Hawkins here. You would have let old John be cut to bits, and never given it a thought, doctor.'

'Not a thought,' replied Dr Livesey cheerily.

And by this time we had reached the gigs. The doctor, with the pickaxe, demolished one of them, and then we all got aboard the other, and set out to go round by sea for North Inlet.

This was a run of eight or nine miles. Silver, though he was almost killed already with fatigue, was set to an oar, like the rest of us, and we were soon skimming swiftly over a smooth sea. Soon we passed out of the straits and doubled the south-east corner of the island, round which, four days ago, we had towed the *Hispaniola*.

As we passed the two-pointed hill we could see the black mouth of Ben Gunn's cave, and a figure standing by it, leaning on a musket. It was the squire, and we waved a handkerchief and gave him three cheers, in which the voice of Silver joined as heartily as any.

Three miles farther, just inside the mouth of North Inlet, what should we meet but the *Hispaniola*, cruising by herself. The last flood had lifted her, and had there been much wind, or a strong tide current, as in the southern anchorage, we should never have found her more, or found her stranded beyond help. As it was, there was little amiss beyond the wreck of the mainsail. Another anchor was got ready, and dropped in a fathom and a half of water. We all pulled round again to Rum Cove, the nearest point for Ben Gunn's treasure house; and then Gray, single-handed, returned with the gig to the *Hispaniola*, where he was to pass the night on guard.

A gentle slope ran up from the beach to the entrance of the cave. At the top the squire met us. To me he was cordial and kind, saying nothing of my escapade, either in the way of blame or praise. At Silver's polite salute he somewhat flushed.

'John Silver,' he said, 'you're a prodigious villain and impostor—a monstrous impostor, sir. I am told I am not to prosecute you. Well, then, I will not. But the dead men, sir, hang about your neck like mill-stones.'

'Thank you kindly, sir,' replied Long John, again saluting.

'I dare you to thank me!' cried the squire. 'It is a gross dereliction of my duty. Stand back.'

And thereupon we all entered the cave. It was a large, airy place, with a little spring and a pool of clear water, overhung with ferns. The floor was sand. Before a big fire lay Captain Smollett, and in a far corner, only duskily flickered over by the blaze, I beheld great heaps of coin and quadrilaterals built of bars of gold. That was Flint's treasure that we had come so far to seek, and that had cost already the lives of seventeen men from the *Hispaniola*. How many it had cost in the amassing, what blood and sorrow, what good ships scuttled on the deep, what brave men walking the plank blindfold, what shot of cannon, what shame and lies and cruelty, perhaps no man alive could tell. Yet there were still three upon that island—Silver, and old Morgan, and Ben Gunn—who had each taken his share in these crimes, as each had hoped in vain to share in the reward.

'Come in, Jim,' said the captain. 'You're a good boy in your line, Jim, but I don't think you and me'll go to sea again. You're too much of the born favourite for me. Is that you, John Silver? What brings you here, man?'

'Come back to my dooty, sir,' returned Silver.

'Ah!' said the captain; and that was all he said.

What a supper I had of it that night, with all my friends around me;

and what a meal it was, with Ben Gunn's salted goat, and some delicacies and a bottle of old wine from the *Hispaniola*. Never, I am sure, were people gayer or happier. And there was Silver, sitting back almost out of the firelight, but eating heartily, prompt to spring forward when anything was wanted, even joining quietly in our laughter—the same bland, polite, obsequious seaman of the voyage out.

HIS FIRST FLIGHT

Liam O'Flaherty

The young seagull was alone on his ledge. His two brothers and sister had already flown away the day before. He had been afraid to fly with them. Somehow when he had taken a little run forward to the brink of the ledge and attempted to flap his wings he became afraid. The great expanse of sea stretched down beneath, and it was such a long way down —miles down. He felt certain that his wings would never support him, so he bent his head and ran away back to the little hole under the ledge where he slept at night.

Even when each of his brothers and his little sister, whose wings were far shorter than his own, ran to the brink, flapped their wings, and flew away he failed to muster up courage to take that plunge which appeared to him so desperate. His father and mother had come around calling to him shrilly, upbraiding him, threatening to let him starve on his ledge unless he flew away. But for the life of him he could not move.

That was twenty-four hours ago. Since then nobody had come near him. The day before, all day long he had watched his parents flying about with his brothers and sister, perfecting them in the art of flight, teaching them how to skim the waves and how to dive for fish. He had, in fact, seen his older brother catch his first herring and devour it, standing on a rock, while his parents circled around raising a proud cackle. And all the morning the whole family had walked about on the big plateau midway down the opposite cliff, taunting him with his cowardice.

The sun was now ascending the sky, blazing warmly on his ledge that faced south. He felt the heat because he had not eaten since the previous nightfall. Then he had found a dried piece of mackerel's tail at the far end of his ledge. Now there was not a single scrap of food left. He had searched every inch, rooting among the rough, dirt-caked straw nest where he and his brothers and sister had been hatched. He even gnawed at the dried pieces of spotted eggshell. It was like eating part of himself.

He had then trotted back and forth from one end of the ledge to the other, his grey body the colour of the cliff, his long grey legs stepping daintily, trying to find some means of reaching his parents without having to fly. But on each side of him the ledge ended in a sheer fall of precipice, with the sea beneath. And between him and his parents there was a deep, wide chasm.

Surely he could reach them without flying if he would only move northwards along the cliff face? But then on what could he walk? There was no ledge, and he was not a fly. And above him he could see nothing. The precipice was sheer, and the top of it was perhaps farther away than the sea beneath him.

He stepped slowly out to the brink of the ledge, and, standing on one leg with the other leg hidden under his wing, he closed one eye, then the other, and pretended to be falling asleep. Still they took no notice of him. He saw his two brothers and his sister lying on the plateau dozing, with their heads sunk into their necks. His father was preening the feathers on his white back. Only his mother was looking at him.

She was standing on a little high hump on the plateau, her white breast thrust forward. Now and again she tore at a piece of fish that lay at her feet, and then scraped each side of her beak on the rock. The sight of the food maddened him. How he loved to tear food that way, scraping his beak now and again to whet it! He uttered a low cackle. His mother cackled too, and looked over at him.

Ga, ga, ga, he cried, begging her to bring him over some food.

With a loud scream the young gull fell outwards into space . . .

Gawl-ool-ah, she screamed back derisively. But he kept calling plaintively, and after a minute or so he uttered a joyful scream. His mother had picked up a piece of the fish and was flying across to him with it. He leaned out eagerly, tapping the rock with his feet, trying to get nearer to her as she flew across. But when she was just opposite to him, abreast of the ledge, she halted, her legs hanging limp, her wings motionless, the piece of fish in her beak almost within reach of his beak.

He waited a moment in surprise, wondering why she did not come nearer, and then maddened by hunger, he dived at the fish. With a loud scream he fell outwards and downwards into space. His mother had swooped upwards. As he passed beneath her he heard the swish of her wings.

Then a monstrous terror seized him and his heart stood still. He could hear nothing. But it only lasted a moment. The next moment he felt his wings spread outwards. The wind rushed against his breast feathers, then under his stomach and against his wings. He could feel the tips of his wings cutting through the air. He was not falling headlong now. He was soaring gradually downwards and outwards. He was no longer afraid. He just felt a bit dizzy. Then he flapped his wings once and he soared upwards.

He uttered a joyous scream and flapped them again. He soared higher. He raised his breast and banked against the wind. *Ga, ga, ga. Ga, ga, ga. Gawl-ool-ah.* His mother swooped past him, her wings making a loud noise. He answered her with another scream. Then his father flew over him screaming. Then he saw his two brothers and sister flying around him, curvetting and banking and soaring and diving.

Then he completely forgot that he had not always been able to fly, and commenced himself to dive and soar and curvet, shrieking shrilly.

He was near the sea now, flying straight over it, facing out over the ocean. He saw a vast green sea beneath him, with little ridges moving over it, and he turned his beak sideways and crowed amusedly. His parents and his brothers and sister had landed on this green floor in front of him. They were beckoning to him, calling shrilly. He dropped his legs to stand on the green sea. His legs sank into it. He screamed with fright and attempted to rise again, flapping his wings. But he was tired and weak with hunger and he could not rise, exhausted by the strange exercise. His feet sank into the green sea, and then his belly touched it and he sank no farther.

He was floating on it. And around him his family was screaming, praising him, and their beaks were offering him scraps of dogfish.

He had made his first flight.

THE MAN WHO COULD WORK MIRACLES

H. G. Wells

It is doubtful whether the gift was innate. For my own part, I think it came to him suddenly. Indeed, until he was thirty he was a sceptic, and did not believe in miraculous powers. And here, since it is the most convenient place, I must mention that he was a little man, and had eyes of a hot brown, very erect red hair, a moustache with ends that he twisted up, and freckles. His name was George McWhirter Fotheringay—not the sort of name by any means to lead to any expectation of miracles—and he was clerk at Gomshott's. He was greatly addicted to assertive argument. It was while he was asserting the impossibility of miracles that he had his first intimation of his extraordinary powers. This particular argument was being held in the bar of the Long Dragon, and Toddy Beamish was conducting the opposition by a monotonous but effective 'So *you* say', that drove Mr Fotheringay to the very limit of his patience.

There were present, besides these two, a very dusty cyclist, landlord Cox, and Miss Maybridge, the perfectly respectable and rather portly barmaid of the Dragon. Miss Maybridge was standing with her back to Mr Fotheringay, washing glasses; the others were watching him, more or less amused by the present ineffectiveness of the assertive method. Goaded by the Torres Vedras tactics of Mr Beamish, Mr Fotheringay determined to make an unusual rhetorical effort. 'Looky here, Mr Beamish,' said Mr Fotheringay. 'Let us clearly understand what a miracle is. It's something contrariwise to the course of nature done by power of will, something what couldn't happen without being specially willed.'

'So *you* say,' said Mr Beamish, repulsing him.

Mr Fotheringay appealed to the cyclist, who had hitherto been a silent auditor, and received his assent—given with a hesitating cough and a glance at Mr Beamish. The landlord would express no opinion, and Mr Fotheringay, returning to Mr Beamish, received the unexpected concession of a qualified assent to his definition of a miracle.

'For instance,' said Mr Fotheringay, greatly encouraged. 'Here would be a miracle. That lamp, in the natural course of nature, couldn't burn like that upsy-down, could it, Beamish?'

'*You* say it couldn't,' said Beamish.

'And you?' said Fotheringay. 'You don't mean to say—eh?'

'No,' said Beamish reluctantly. 'No, it couldn't.'

'Very well,' said Mr Fotheringay. 'Then here comes someone, as it might be me, along here, and stands as it might be here, and says to that lamp, as I might do, collecting all my will—"Turn upsy-down without breaking, and go on burning steady," and——Hullo!'

It was enough to make anyone say 'Hullo!' The impossible, the incredible, was visible to them all. The lamp hung inverted in the air, burning quietly with its flame pointing down. It was as solid, as indisputable as ever a lamp was, the prosaic common lamp of the Long Dragon bar.

Mr Fotheringay stood with an extended forefinger and the knitted brows of one anticipating a catastrophic smash. The cyclist, who was sitting next to the lamp, ducked and jumped across the bar. Everybody jumped, more or less. Miss Maybridge turned and screamed. For nearly three seconds the lamp remained still. A faint cry of mental distress came from Mr Fotheringay. 'I can't keep it up,' he said, 'any longer.' He staggered back, and the inverted lamp suddenly flared, fell against the corner of the bar, smashed upon the floor, and went out.

It was lucky it had a metal receiver, or the whole place would have been in a blaze. Mr Cox was the first to speak, and his remark, shorn of needless excrescences, was to the effect that Fotheringay was a fool. Fotheringay was beyond disputing even so fundamental a proposition as that! He was astonished beyond measure at the thing that had occurred. The subsequent conversation threw absolutely no light on the matter so far as Fotheringay was concerned; the general opinion not only followed Mr Cox very closely but very vehemently. Everyone accused Fotheringay of a silly trick, and presented him to himself as a foolish destroyer of comfort and security. His mind was in a tornado of perplexity, he was himself inclined to agree with them, and he made a remarkably ineffectual opposition to the proposal of his departure.

He went home flushed and heated, coat-collar crumpled, eyes smarting and ears red. He watched each of the ten street-lamps nervously as he passed it. It was only when he found himself alone in his little bedroom in Church Row that he was able to grapple seriously with his memories of the occurrence, and ask, 'What on earth happened?'

He had removed his coat and boots, and was sitting on the bed with his hands in his pockets repeating the text of his defence for the seventeenth time, '*I* didn't want the confounded thing to upset,' when it occurred to him that at the precise moment he had said the commanding words he had inadvertently willed the thing he said, and that when he had seen the lamp in the air he had felt that it depended on him to maintain it there without being clear how this was to be done. He had not a particularly complex mind, or he might have stuck for a time at that 'inadvertently willed', embracing, as it does, the abstrusest problems of voluntary action; but as it was, the idea came to him with a quite acceptable haziness. And from that, following, as I must admit, no clear logical path, he came to the test of experiment.

He pointed resolutely to his candle and collected his mind, though he felt he did a foolish thing. 'Be raised up,' he said. But in a second that feeling vanished. The candle was raised, hung in the air one giddy moment, and as Mr Fotheringay gasped, fell with a smash on his toilet-table, leaving him in darkness save for the expiring glow of its wick.

For a time Mr Fotheringay sat in the darkness, perfectly still. 'It did happen, after all,' he said. 'And 'ow I'm to explain it I *don't* know.' He sighed heavily, and began feeling in his pockets for a match. He could find none, and he rose and groped about the toilet-table. 'I wish I had a match,' he said. He resorted to his coat, and there were none there, and then it dawned upon him that miracles were possible even with matches. He extended a hand and scowled at it in the dark. 'Let there be a match in that hand,' he said. He felt some light object fall across his palm, and his fingers closed upon a match.

After several ineffectual attempts to light this, he discovered it was a safety-match. He threw it down, and then it occurred to him that he might have willed it lit. He did, and perceived it burning in the midst of his toilet-table mat. He caught it up hastily, and it went out. His perception of possibilities enlarged, and he felt for and replaced the candle in its candlestick. 'Here! *You* be lit,' said Mr Fotheringay, and forthwith the candle was flaring, and he saw a little black hole in the toilet-cover with a wisp of smoke rising from it. For a time he stared from this to the little flame and back, and then looked up and met his own gaze in the looking-glass. By this he communed with himself in silence for a time.

'How about miracles now?' said Mr Fotheringay at last, addressing his reflection.

The subsequent meditations of Mr Fotheringay were of a severe but confused description. So far as he could see, it was a case of pure willing with him. The nature of his first experiences disinclined him for any further experiments except of the most cautious type. But he lifted a sheet of paper, and turned a glass of water pink and then green, and he created a snail, which he miraculously annihilated, and got himself a miraculous new toothbrush. Sometime in the small hours he had reached the fact that his will-power must be of a particularly rare and pungent quality, a fact of which he had certainly had inklings before, but no certain assurance. The scare and perplexity of his first discovery was now qualified by pride in this evidence of singularity and by vague intimations of advantage. He became aware that the church clock was striking one, and as it did not occur to him that his daily duties at Gomshott's might be miraculously dispensed with, he resumed undressing, in order to get to bed without further delay. As he struggled to get his shirt over his head, he was struck with a brilliant idea. 'Let me be in bed,' he said, and found himself so. 'Undressed,' he stipulated; and, finding the sheets cold, added hastily, 'and in my nightshirt—no, in a nice soft woollen nightshirt. Ah!' he said with immense enjoyment. 'And now let me be comfortably asleep . . .'

He awoke at his usual hour and was pensive all through breakfast-time, wondering whether his overnight experience might not be a particularly vivid dream. At length his mind turned again to cautious experiments. For instance, he had three eggs for breakfast; two his landlady had supplied, good, but shoppy, and one was a delicious fresh goose-egg, laid, cooked, and served by his extraordinary will. He hurried off to Gomshott's in a state of profound but carefully concealed excitement, and only remembered the shell of the third egg when his landlady spoke of it that night. All day he could do no work because of this astonishing new self-knowledge, but this caused him no inconvenience, because he made up for it miraculously in his last ten minutes.

As the day wore on his state of mind passed from wonder to elation, albeit the circumstances of his dismissal from the Long Dragon were still disagreeable to recall, and a garbled account of the matter that had reached his colleagues led to some badinage. It was evident he must be careful how he lifted breakable articles, but in other ways his gift promised more and more as he turned it over in his mind. He intended among other things to increase his personal property by unostentatious acts of creation. He called into existence a pair of very splendid diamond studs, and hastily annihilated them again as young Gomshott came across the counting-house to his desk. He was afraid young Gomshott might wonder how he had come by them. He saw quite clearly the gift required caution and watchfulness in its exercise, but so far as he could judge the difficulties attending its mastery would be no greater than those he had already faced in the study of cycling. It was that analogy, perhaps, quite as much as the feeling that he would be unwelcome in the Long Dragon, that drove him out after supper into the lane beyond the gas-works, to rehearse a few miracles in private.

There was possibly a certain want of originality in his attempts, for apart from his will-power Mr Fotheringay was not a very exceptional man. The miracle of Moses' rod came to his mind, but the night was dark and unfavourable to the proper control of large miraculous snakes. Then he recollected the story of 'Tannhäuser' that he had read in the back of the Philharmonic programme. That seemed to him singularly attractive and harmless. He struck his walking-stick—a very nice Poona-Penang lawyer—into the turf that edged the footpath, and commanded the dry wood to blossom. The air was immediately full of the scent of roses, and by means of a match he saw for himself that this beautiful miracle was indeed accomplished. His satisfaction was ended by advancing footsteps. Afraid of a premature discovery of his powers, he addressed the blossoming stick hastily: 'Go back.' What he meant was 'Change back'; but of course he was confused. The stick receded at a considerable velocity, and incontinently came a cry of anger and a bad word from the approaching person. 'Who are you throwing brambles at, you fool?' cried a voice. 'That got me on the shin.'

'I'm sorry, old chap,' said Mr Fotheringay, and then realizing the awkward nature of the explanation, caught nervously at his moustache. He saw Winch, one of the three Immering constables, advancing.

'What d'yer mean by it?' asked the constable. 'Hullo! It's you, is it? The gent that broke the lamp at the Long Dragon!'

'I don't mean anything by it,' said Mr Fotheringay. 'Nothing at all.'

'What d'yer do it for then?'

'Oh, bother!' said Mr Fotheringay.

'Bother indeed! D'yer know that stick hurt? What d'yer do it for, eh?'

For the moment Mr Fotheringay could not think what he had done it for. His silence seemed to irritate Mr Winch. 'You've been assaulting the police, young man, this time. That's what *you* done.'

'Look here, Mr Winch,' said Mr Fotheringay, annoyed and confused. 'I'm very sorry. The fact is——'

'Well?'

He could think of no way but the truth. 'I was working a miracle.' He tried to speak in an off-hand way, but try as he would he couldn't.

'Working a——! 'Ere, don't you talk rot. Working a miracle, indeed! Miracle! Well, that's downright funny! Why, you's the chap that don't believe in miracles . . . Fact is, this is another of your silly conjuring tricks—that's what this is. Now, I tell you——'

But Mr Fotheringay never heard what Mr Winch was going to tell him. He realized he had given himself away, flung his valuable secret to all the winds of heaven. A violent gust of irritation swept him to action. He turned on the constable swiftly and fiercely. 'Here,' he said, 'I've had enough of this, I have! I'll show you a silly conjuring trick, I will! Go to Hades! Go, now!'

He was alone!

Mr Fotheringay performed no more miracles that night, nor did he trouble to see what had become of his flowering stick. He returned to the town, scared and very quiet, and went to his bedroom. 'Lord!' he said, 'it's a powerful gift—an extremely powerful gift. I didn't hardly mean as much as that. Not really . . . I wonder what Hades is like!'

He sat on the bed taking off his boots. Struck by a happy thought he transferred the constable to San Francisco, and without any more interference with normal causation went soberly to bed. In the night he dreamt of the anger of Winch.

The next day Mr Fotheringay heard two interesting items of news. Someone had planted a most beautiful climbing rose against the elder Mr Gomshott's private house in the Lullaborough Road, and the river as far as Rawling's Mill was to be dragged for Constable Winch.

Mr Fotheringay was abstracted and thoughtful all that day, and performed no miracles except certain provisions for Winch, and the miracle of completing his day's work with punctual perfection in spite of all the bee-swarm of thoughts that hummed through his mind. And the extraordinary abstraction and meekness of his manner was remarked by several people, and made a matter for jesting. For the most part he was thinking of Winch.

On Sunday evening he went to chapel, and oddly enough, Mr Maydig, who took a certain interest in occult matters, preached about 'things that are not lawful'. Mr Fotheringay was not a regular chapel-goer, but the system of assertive scepticism, to which I have already alluded, was now very much shaken. The tenor of the sermon threw an entirely new light on these novel gifts, and he suddenly decided to consult Mr Maydig immediately after the service. So soon as that was determined, he found himself wondering why he had not done so before.

Mr Maydig, a lean, excitable man with quite remarkably long wrists and neck, was gratified at a request for a private conversation from a young man whose carelessness in religious matters was a subject for general remark in the town. After a few necessary delays, he conducted him to the study of the Manse, which was contiguous to the chapel, seated him comfortably, and, standing in front of a cheerful fire—his legs threw a Rhodian arch of shadow on the opposite wall—requested Mr Fotheringay to state his business.

At first Mr Fotheringay was a little abashed, and found some difficulty in opening the matter. 'You will scarcely believe me, Mr Maydig, I am afraid'—and so forth for some time. He tried a question at last, and asked Mr Maydig his opinion of miracles.

Mr Maydig was still saying 'Well' in an extremely judicial tone, when Mr Fotheringay interrupted again: 'You don't believe, I suppose, that some common sort of person—like myself, for instance—as it might be sitting here now, might have some sort of twist inside him that made him able to do things by his will.'

'It's possible,' said Mr Maydig. 'Something of the sort is possible.'

'If I might make free with something here, I think I might show you by a sort of experiment,' said Mr Fotheringay. 'Now, take that tobacco-jar on the table, for instance. What I want to know is whether what I am going to do with it is a miracle or not. Just half a minute, Mr Maydig, please.'

He knitted his brows, pointed to the tobacco-jar and said: 'Be a bowl of vi'lets.'

The tobacco-jar did as it was ordered.

Mr Maydig started violently at the change, and stood looking from the miracle-worker to the bowl of flowers. He said nothing. Presently he ventured to lean over the table and smell the violets; they were fresh-picked and very fine ones. Then he stared at Mr Fotheringay again.

'How did you do that?' he asked.

Mr Fotheringay pulled his moustache. 'Just told it—and there you are. Is that a miracle, or is it black art, or what is it? And what do you think's the matter with me? That's what I want to ask.'

'It's a most extraordinary occurrence.'

'And this day last week I knew no more that I could do things like that than you did. It came quite sudden. It's something odd about my will, I suppose, and that's as far as I can see.'

'Is *that*—the only thing? Could you do other things besides that?'

'Lord, yes!' said Mr Fotheringay. 'Just anything.' He thought, and suddenly recalled a conjuring entertainment he had seen. 'Here!' He pointed. 'Change into a bowl of fish—no, not that—change into a glass bowl full of water with goldfish swimming in it. That's better. You see that, Mr Maydig?'

'It's astonishing. It's incredible. You are either a most extraordinary . . . But no——'

'Stop there!' said Mr Fotheringay, and the pigeon hung motionless in the air.

'I could change it into anything,' said Mr Fotheringay. 'Just anything. Here! be a pigeon, will you?'

In another moment a blue pigeon was fluttering round the room and making Mr Maydig duck every time it came near him. 'Stop there, will you,' said Mr Fotheringay; and the pigeon hung motionless in the air. 'I could change it back to a bowl of flowers,' he said, and after replacing the pigeon on the table worked that miracle. 'I expect you will want your pipe in a bit,' he said, and restored the tobacco-jar.

Mr Maydig had followed all these later changes in a sort of ejaculatory silence. He stared at Mr Fotheringay and, in a very gingerly manner, picked up the tobacco-jar, examined it, replaced it on the table. '*Well!*' was the only expression of his feelings.

'Now, after that it's easier to explain what I came about,' said Mr Fotheringay; and proceeded to a lengthy and involved narrative of his strange experience, beginning with the affair of the lamp in the Long Dragon and complicated by persistent allusions to Winch. As he went on, the transient pride Mr Maydig's consternation had caused passed away; he became the very ordinary Mr Fotheringay of everyday again. Mr Maydig listened intently, the tobacco-jar in his hand, and his bearing changed also with the course of the narrative. Presently, while Mr Fotheringay was dealing with the miracle of the third egg, the minister interrupted with a fluttering extended hand——

'It is possible,' he said. 'It is credible. It is amazing, of course, but it reconciles a number of difficulties. The power to work miracles is a gift—a peculiar quality like genius or second sight—hitherto it has come very rarely and to exceptional people. But in this case . . . I have always wondered at the miracles of Mahomet, and at yogis' miracles, and the miracles of Madame Blavatsky. But, of course! Yes, it is simply a gift! It carries out so beautifully the arguments of that great thinker'—Mr Maydig's voice sank—'his Grace the Duke of Argyll. Here we plumb some profounder law—deeper than the ordinary laws of nature. Yes—yes. Go on. Go on!'

Mr Fotheringay proceeded to tell of his misadventure with Winch, and Mr Maydig, no longer overawed or scared, began to jerk his limbs about and interject astonishment. 'It's this what troubled me most,' proceeded Mr Fotheringay; 'it's this I'm most mightily in want of advice for; of course he's at San Francisco—wherever San Francisco may be—

'Quickly pups! Jump into the nice miracle,' said Missis. (p.153)

It looked, for all the world, like a huge daddy-long-legs. (p.166)

but of course it's awkward for both of us, as you'll see, Mr Maydig. I don't see how he can understand what has happened, and I dare say he's scared and exasperated something tremendous, and trying to get at me. I dare say he keeps on starting off to come here. I send him back, by a miracle, every few hours, when I think of it. And of course, that's a thing he won't be able to understand, and it's bound to annoy him; and, of course, if he takes a ticket every time it will cost him a lot of money. I done the best I could for him, but of course it's difficult for him to put himself in my place. I thought afterwards that his clothes might have got scorched, you know—if Hades is all it's supposed to be—before I shifted him. In that case I suppose they'd have locked him up in San Francisco. Of course I willed him a new suit of clothes on him directly I thought of it. But, you see, I'm already in a deuce of a tangle——'

Mr Maydig looked serious. 'I see you are in a tangle. Yes, it's a difficult position. How you are to end it . . .' He became diffuse and inconclusive.

'However, we'll leave Winch for a little and discuss the larger question. I don't think this is a case of the black art or anything of the sort. I don't think there is any taint of criminality about it at all, Mr Fotheringay—none whatever, unless you are suppressing material facts. No, it's miracles—pure miracles—miracles, if I may say so, of the very highest class.'

He began to pace the hearthrug and gesticulate, while Mr Fotheringay sat with his arm on the table and his head on his arm, looking worried. 'I don't see how I'm to manage about Winch,' he said.

'A gift of working miracles—apparently a very powerful gift,' said Mr Maydig, 'will find a way about Winch—never fear. My dear sir, you are a most important man—a man of the most astonishing possibilities. As evidence, for example! And in other ways, the things you may do . . .'

'Yes, *I've* thought of a thing or two,' said Mr Fotheringay. 'But—some of the things came a bit twisty. You saw that fish at first? Wrong sort of bowl and wrong sort of fish. And I thought I'd ask someone.'

'A proper course,' said Mr Maydig, 'a very proper course—altogether the proper course.' He stopped and looked at Mr Fotheringay. 'It's practically an unlimited gift. Let us test your powers, for instance.

If they really *are* . . . If they really are all they seem to be.'

And so, incredible as it may seem, in the study of the little house behind the Congregational Chapel, on the evening of Sunday, 10 November 1896, Mr Fotheringay, egged on and inspired by Mr Maydig, began to work miracles. The reader's attention is specially and definitely called to the date. He will object, probably has already objected that certain points in this story are improbable, that if any things of the sort already described had indeed occurred, they would have been in all the papers a year ago. The details immediately following he will find particularly hard to accept, because among other things they involve the conclusion that he or she, the reader in question, must have been killed in a violent and unprecedented manner more than a year ago.

Now a miracle is nothing if not improbable, and as a matter of fact the reader *was* killed in a violent and unprecedented manner a year ago. In the subsequent course of this story that will become perfectly clear and credible, as every right-minded and reasonable reader will admit. But this is not the place for the end of the story, being but little beyond the hither side of the middle. And at first the miracles worked by Mr Fotheringay were timid little miracles—little things with the cups and parlour fitments, as feeble as the miracles of Theosophists, and, feeble as they were, they were received with awe by his collaborator. He would have preferred to settle the Winch business out of hand, but Mr Maydig would not let him. But after they had worked a dozen of these domestic trivialities, their sense of power grew, their imagination began to show signs of stimulation, and their ambition enlarged. Their first larger enterprise was due to hunger and the negligence of Mrs Minchin, Mr Maydig's housekeeper. The meal to which the minister conducted Mr Fotheringay was certainly ill-laid and uninviting as refreshment for two industrious miracle-workers; but they were seated, and Mr Maydig was descanting in sorrow rather than in anger upon his housekeeper's shortcomings, before it occurred to Mr Fotheringay that an opportunity lay before him. 'Don't you think, Mr Maydig,' he said, 'if it isn't a liberty, I——'

'My dear Mr Fotheringay! Of course! No—I didn't think.'

Mr Fotheringay waved his hand. 'What shall we have?' he said, in a large, inclusive spirit, and, at Mr Maydig's order, revised the supper very thoroughly. 'As for me,' he said, eyeing Mr Maydig's selection,

'I am always particularly fond of a tankard of stout and a nice Welsh rarebit, and I'll order that. I ain't much given to Burgundy,' and forthwith stout and Welsh rarebit promptly appeared at his command. They sat long at their supper, talking like equals, as Mr Fotheringay presently perceived with a glow of surprise and gratification, of all the miracles they would presently do. 'And, by the by, Mr Maydig,' said Mr Fotheringay, 'I might perhaps be able to help you—in a domestic way.'

'Don't quite follow,' said Mr Maydig, pouring out a glass of miraculous old Burgundy.

Mr Fotheringay helped himself to a second Welsh rarebit out of vacancy, and took a mouthful. 'I was thinking,' he said, 'I might be able (*chum chum*) to work (*chum chum*) a miracle with Mrs Minchin (*chum chum*)—make her a better woman.'

Mr Maydig put down the glass and looked doubtful. 'She's—she strongly objects to interference, you know, Mr Fotheringay. And—as a matter of fact—it's well past eleven and she's probably in bed and asleep. Do you think, on the whole——'

Mr Fotheringay considered these objections. 'I don't see that it shouldn't be done in her sleep.'

For a time Mr Maydig opposed the idea, and then he yielded. Mr Fotheringay issued his orders, and a little less at their ease, perhaps, the two gentlemen proceeded with their repast. Mr Maydig was enlarging on the changes he might expect in his housekeeper next day, with an optimism that seemed even to Mr Fotheringay's senses a little forced and hectic, when a series of confused noises from upstairs began. Their eyes exchanged interrogations, and Mr Maydig left the room hastily. Mr Fotheringay heard him calling up to his housekeeper and then his footsteps going softly up to her.

In a minute or so the minister returned, his step light, his face radiant. 'Wonderful!' he said, 'and touching! Most touching!'

He began pacing the hearthrug. 'A repentance—a most touching repentance—through the crack of the door. Poor woman! A most wonderful change! She had got up. She must have got up at once. She had got up out of her sleep to smash a private bottle of brandy in her box. And to confess it too! . . . But this gives us—it opens—a most amazing vista of possibilities. If we can work this miraculous change in *her* . . .'

'The thing's unlimited seemingly,' said Mr Fotheringay. 'And about Mr Winch——'

'Altogether unlimited.' And from the hearthrug Mr Maydig, waving the Winch difficulty aside, unfolded a series of wonderful proposals—proposals he invented as he went along.

Now what those proposals were does not concern the essentials of this story. Suffice it that they were designed in a spirit of infinite benevolence, the sort of benevolence that used to be called post-prandial. Suffice it, too, that the problem of Winch remained unsolved. Nor is it necessary to describe how far that series got to its fulfilment. There were astonishing changes. The small hours found Mr Maydig and Mr Fotheringay careering across the chilly market-square under the still moon, in a sort of ecstasy of thaumaturgy, Mr Maydig all flap and gesture, Mr Fotheringay short and bristling, and no longer abashed at his greatness. They had reformed every drunkard in the parliamentary division, changed all the beer and alcohol to water (Mr Maydig had overruled Mr Fotheringay on this point), they had, further, greatly improved the railway communication of the place, drained Flinders' swamp, improved the soil of One Tree Hill, and cured the vicar's wart. And they were going to see what could be done with the injured pier at South Bridge. 'The place,' gasped Mr Maydig, 'won't be the same place tomorrow! How surprised and thankful everyone will be!' And just at that moment the church clock struck three.

'I say,' said Mr Fotheringay, 'that's three o'clock! I must be getting back. I've got to be at business by eight. And besides, Mrs Wimms——'

'We're only beginning,' said Mr Maydig, full of the sweetness of unlimited power. 'We're only beginning. Think of all the good we're doing. When people wake——'

'But——' said Mr Fotheringay.

Mr Maydig gripped his arm suddenly. His eyes were bright and wild. 'My dear chap,' he said, 'there's no hurry. Look'—he pointed to the moon at the zenith—'Joshua!'

'Joshua?' said Mr Fotheringay.

'Joshua,' said Mr Maydig. 'Why not? Stop it.'

Mr Fotheringay looked at the moon.

'That's a bit tall,' he said after a pause.

'Why not?' said Mr Maydig. 'Of course it doesn't stop. You stop the rotation of the earth, you know. Time stops. It isn't as if we were doing harm.'

'H'm!' said Mr Fotheringay. 'Well,' He sighed. 'I'll try. Here——'

He buttoned up his jacket and addressed himself to the habitable globe, with as good an assumption of confidence as lay in his power. 'Jest stop rotating, will you,' said Mr Fotheringay.

Incontinently he was flying head over heels through the air at the rate of dozens of miles a minute. In spite of the innumerable circles he was describing per second, he thought; for thought is wonderful—sometimes as sluggish as flowing pitch, sometimes as instantaneous as light. He thought in a second, and willed. 'Let me come down safe and sound. Whatever else happens, let me down safe and sound.'

He willed it only just in time, for his clothes, heated by his rapid flight through the air, were already beginning to singe. He came down with a forcible but by no means injurious bump in what appeared to be a mound of fresh-turned earth. A large mass of metal and masonry, extraordinarily like the clock-tower in the middle of the market-square, hit the earth near him, ricochetted over him, and flew into stonework, bricks, and masonry, like a bursting bomb. A hurtling cow hit one of the larger blocks and smashed like an egg. There was a crash that made all the most violent crashes of his past life seem like the sound of falling dust, and this was followed by a descending series of lesser crashes. A vast wind roared throughout earth and heaven, so that he could scarcely lift his head to look. For a while he was too breathless and astonished even to see where he was or what had happened. And his first movement was to feel his head and reassure himself that his streaming hair was still his own.

'Lord!' gasped Mr Fotheringay, scarce able to speak for the gale. 'I've had a squeak! What's gone wrong? Storms and thunder. And only a minute ago a fine night. It's Maydig set me on to this sort of thing. *What* a wind! If I go on fooling in this way I'm bound to have a thundering accident!

'Where's Maydig?'

'What a confounded mess everything's in!'

He looked about him so far as his flapping jacket would permit. The appearance of things was really extremely strange. 'The sky's all right anyhow,' said Mr Fotheringay. 'And that's about all that is all right.

And even there it looks like a terrific gale coming up. But there's the moon overhead. Just as it was just now. Bright as midday. But as for the rest—— Where's the village? Where's—where's anything? And what on earth set this wind a-blowing! *I* didn't order no wind.'

Mr Fotheringay struggled to get to his feet in vain, and after one failure, remained on all fours, holding on. He surveyed the moonlit world to leeward, with the tails of his jacket streaming over his head. 'There's something seriously wrong,' said Mr Fotheringay. 'And what it is—goodness knows.'

Far and wide nothing was visible in the white glare through the haze of dust that drove before a screaming gale but tumbled masses of earth and heaps of inchoate ruins, no trees, no houses, no familiar shapes, only a wilderness of disorder vanishing at last into the darkness beneath the whirling columns and streamers, the lightnings and thunderings of a swiftly rising storm. Near him in the livid glare was something that might once have been an elm-tree, a smashed mass of splinters, shivered from boughs to base, and further a twisted mass of iron girders—only too evidently the viaduct—rose out of the piled confusion.

You see, when Mr Fotheringay had arrested the rotation of the solid globe, he had made no stipulation concerning the trifling movables upon its surface. And the earth spins so fast that the surface at its equator is travelling at rather more than a thousand miles an hour, and in these latitudes at more than half that pace. So that the village, and Mr Maydig, and Mr Fotheringay, and everybody and everything had been jerked violently forward at about nine miles per second—that is to say, much more violently than if they had been fired out of a cannon. And every human being, every living creature, every house, and every tree—all the world as we know it—had been so jerked and smashed and utterly destroyed. That was all.

These things Mr Fotheringay did not, of course, fully appreciate. But he perceived that his miracle had miscarried, and with that a great disgust of miracles came upon him. He was in darkness now, for the clouds had swept together and blotted out his momentary glimpse of the moon, and the air was full of fitful struggling tortured wraiths of hail. A great roaring of wind and waters filled earth and sky, and, peering under his hand through the dust and sleet to windward, he saw by the play of the lightnings a vast wall of water pouring towards him.

'Maydig!' screamed Mr Fotheringay's feeble voice amid the elemental uproar. 'Here!—Maydig!'

'Stop!' cried Mr Fotheringay to the advancing water. 'Oh, for goodness' sake, stop!'

'Just a moment,' said Mr Fotheringay to the lightnings and thunder. 'Stop jest a moment while I collect my thoughts . . . And now what shall I do?' he said. 'What *shall* I do? Lord! I wish Maydig was about.'

'I know,' said Mr Fotheringay. 'And for goodness' sake let's have it right *this time*.'

He remained on all fours, leaning against the wind, very intent to have everything right.

'Ah!' he said. 'Let nothing what I'm going to order happen until I say "Off!" . . . Lord! I wish I'd thought of that before!'

He lifted his little voice against the whirlwind, shouting louder and louder in the vain desire to hear himself speak. 'Now then!—here goes! Mind about that what I said just now. In the first place, when all I've got to say is done, let me lose my miraculous power, let my will become just like anybody else's will, and all these dangerous miracles be stopped. I don't like them. I'd rather I didn't work 'em. Ever so much. That's the first thing. And the second is—let me be back just before the miracles begin; let everything be just as it was before that blessed lamp turned up. It's a big job, but it's the last. Have you got it? No more miracles, everything as it was—me back in the Long Dragon just before I drank my half-pint. That's it! Yes.'

He dug his fingers into the mould, closed his eyes, and said 'Off!'

Everything became perfectly still. He perceived that he was standing erect.

'So *you* say,' said a voice.

He opened his eyes. He was in the bar of the Long Dragon, arguing about miracles with Toddy Beamish. He had a vague sense of some great thing forgotten that instantaneously passed. You see, except for the loss of his miraculous powers, everything was back as it had been; his mind and memory therefore were now just as they had been at the time when this story began. So that he knew absolutely nothing of all that is told here, knows nothing of all that is told here to this day. And among other things, of course, he still did not believe in miracles.

'I tell you that miracles, properly speaking, can't possibly happen,' he said, 'whatever you like to hold. And I'm prepared to prove it up to the hilt.'

'That's what *you* think,' said Toddy Beamish, and 'Prove it if you can.'

'Looky here, Mr Beamish,' said Mr Fotheringay. 'Let us clearly understand what a miracle is. It's something contrariwise to the course of nature done by power of will . . .'

THE HAND

Guy de Maupassant

The whole party had gathered in a circle round Monsieur Bermutier, the magistrate, who was giving his opinion on the mysterious St Cloud affair, an inexplicable crime, which had been distracting Paris for a month. No one could make anything of it. Standing with his back to the fireplace, Monsieur Bermutier was discussing it, marshalling his proofs, analysing theories, but arriving at no conclusion. Some of the ladies had risen from their chairs and had come nearer him. Clustering round him, they kept their eyes on the clean-shaven lips which uttered such weighty words. They shuddered and trembled, thrilled by that strange awe, that eager and insatiable craving for horrors, which haunts the mind of women and tortures them like the pangs of hunger. One of them, paler than the others, ventured to break a sudden silence:

'How ghastly! It has a touch of the supernatural. No one will ever find out the truth about it.'

Monsieur Bermutier turned to her:

'That is likely enough. But as for your word, supernatural, it has no place in this affair. We are confronted with a crime, which was ably conceived and very ably executed. It is wrapped in such profound mystery that we cannot disengage it from the impenetrable circumstances surrounding it. Still, within my own experience, I had once to follow up a case that really appeared to have an element of the supernatural in it. We had eventually to give it up, for lack of means to elucidate it.'

Several ladies exclaimed as with one voice:

'Oh, do tell us about it.'

With the grave smile appropriate to an investigating magistrate, Monsieur Bermutier resumed:

'At all events pray do not imagine that I myself have for one instant attributed anything of the supernatural to this incident. I believe in normal causes only. It would be much better if we used the word "inexplicable" instead of "supernatural" to express things that we did not understand. In any case, what was striking in the affair I am going to tell you about was not so much the event itself as the circumstances that attended and led up to it. Now to the facts.

'At that time I was investigating magistrate at Ajaccio, a little town of white houses, situated on the edge of a wonderful bay surrounded on all sides by lofty mountains. My principal task there was the investigation of vendettas. Some of these vendettas are sublime, savage, heroic, inconceivably dramatic. In them, one comes across the finest themes of revenge imaginable; hatreds that have endured for centuries, lying for a time in abeyance, but never extinguished; detestable stratagems, assassinations that are mere butchery, others that are almost heroic deeds. For two years I had heard nothing discussed there but the price of blood; nothing but this terrible Corsican tradition, which obliges a man who has been wronged to wreak his revenge upon the man who has wronged him, or upon his descendants or his next-of-kin. Old men, children, distant cousins—I had seen them all slaughtered, and my head was full of tales of vengeance.

'One day I was informed that an Englishman had just taken a lease for several years of a little villa at the far end of the bay. He had brought with him a French manservant, whom he had picked up while passing through Marseilles. It was not long before universal curiosity was excited by this eccentric person, who lived alone and never left his house except to go shooting or fishing. He spoke to no one, never came to the town, and practised for an hour or two every morning with his pistol and carbine. All sorts of legends sprang up about him. He was said to be an exalted personage who had fled his country for political reasons; to this succeeded a theory that he was in hiding because he had committed a horrible crime of which the most shocking details were given.

'In my official capacity, I was anxious to learn something about this man, but my inquiries were fruitless. The name he went by was Sir John Rowell. I had to be satisfied with keeping a close watch upon him, but I never really discovered anything suspicious about him. Nonetheless, the rumours never ceased, and they became so widespread that I determined to make an effort to see this stranger with my own eyes. I therefore took to shooting regularly in the neighbourhood of his property.

'My opportunity was long in arriving, but at length it presented itself in the form of a partridge, which I shot under the Englishman's very nose. My dog brought me the bird, but I took it immediately to Sir John Rowell, and begged him to accept it, at the same time making my apologies for my breach of good manners. He was a red-headed, red-bearded man, very tall and massive, a sort of easy-going, well-mannered Hercules. He had none of the so-called British stiffness, and although his accent came from beyond the Channel, he thanked me warmly for my considerate behaviour. Before a month had elapsed we had conversed five or six times. One evening as I was passing his gate, I caught sight of him smoking his pipe. I greeted him and he invited me to come in and have a glass of beer. I accepted his invitation with alacrity. He received me with all the meticulous English courtesy; and although he made shocking mistakes in grammar he was full of the praises of France and Corsica and professed his affection for these countries. Very cautiously, and under the pretext of a lively interest, I began to question him about his life and his plans for the future. His replies were perfectly frank and he told me that he had travelled much in Africa, India and America.

' "Oh, yes, I have had plenty of adventures," he added, laughing.

'Then I turned the conversation on sport and he gave me the most curious details about shooting hippopotamus, tiger, elephant, and even gorilla.

' "These are all formidable brutes," I said.

' "Why no," he said smiling. "Man is the worst of all."

'He laughed heartily, like a big, genial Englishman.

'" I have done lots of man-hunting, too."

'Then he talked about guns and invited me into his house to look at various makes. His drawing-room was hung with black silk, embroidered with golden flowers that shone like fire on the sombre background. It was Japanese work, he said.

'In the middle of the largest panel, a strange object attracted my attention; it stood out clearly against a square of red velvet. I went up to examine it. It was a hand, the hand of a man. Not a clean, white skeleton hand, but a black, dried-up hand, with yellow nails, bared muscles, and showing old traces of blood, black blood, crusted round the bones, which had been cut clean through as with an axe, about the middle of the forearm. Round the wrist of this unclean object was riveted a powerful chain, which was attached to the wall by a ring strong enough to hold an elephant.

'"What is that?" I asked.

'"That is my worst enemy," replied the Englishman calmly. "He was an American. His hand was chopped off with a sabre. Then it was skinned with sharp flints, and after that it was dried in the sun for a week. It was a good job for me."

'I touched this human relic. The man must have been a Colossus. The fingers were abnormally long and were attached by enormous tendons to which fragments of skin still adhered. It was a terrible sight, this hand, all flayed; it could not but suggest some savage act of vengeance.

'"He must have been a stout fellow," I remarked.

'"Oh yes," replied the Englishman in his gentle tones. "He was strong, but I was stronger. I fixed that chain on his hand to keep it from escaping."

'Thinking that he was joking, I replied:

'"The chain is hardly needed now; the hand can't run away.

'Sir John answered gravely:

'"That hand is always trying to get away. The chain is necessary."

'I cast a rapid, questioning glance at him, wondering whether he was mad or making an unpleasant joke. But this face retained its calm, impenetrable, benevolent expression. I changed the subject and began to admire his guns. I noticed, however that, there were three loaded

Round the wrist of the dried-up hand was riveted a powerful chain.

revolvers lying about on the chairs and tables. Apparently this man lived in constant dread of an attack.

'I went to see him several times, and then my visits ceased. People had become accustomed to his presence and took no further interest in him.

'A whole year passed. One morning towards the end of November, my servant woke me with the news that Sir John Rowell had been murdered during the night. Half an hour later I was in the Englishman's house. With me were the Superintendent of Police and the Captain of gendarmes. Sir John's manservant was weeping at the door of the house; he was distraught and desperate. At first I suspected him. He was, however, innocent. Nor was the murderer ever discovered.

'When I entered the drawing-room, the first thing to strike me was the sight of Sir John's corpse lying flat on its back in the middle of the floor. His waistcoat was torn; one sleeve of his coat was ripped off. There was every indication that a terrible struggle had taken place.

'Death had been caused by strangulation. Sir John's face was black, swollen, and terrifying. It bore an expression of hideous dread. His teeth were clenched on some object. In his neck, which was covered with blood, there were five holes, which might have been made by iron fingers. A doctor arrived. After a prolonged examination of the finger-marks in the flesh, he uttered these strange words:

'"It almost looks as if he has been strangled by a skeleton."

'A shudder passed down my spine, and I cast a glance at the wall, at the spot where I had been wont to see that horrible, flayed hand. The hand was no longer there. The chain had been broken and was hanging loose. I bent down close to the corpse and between his clenched teeth I found one of the fingers of that vanished hand. At the second joint it had been cut, or rather bitten, off by the dead man's teeth. An investigation was held, but without result. No door or window had been forced that night, no cupboard or drawer had been broken into. The watchdogs had not been disturbed. The substance of the servant's evidence can be given briefly. For a month past his master had seemed to have something on his mind. He had received many letters, which he had promptly burnt. Often he would snatch up a horse-whip and in a passion of rage, which suggested insanity, lash furiously at that withered hand, which had been riveted to the wall, and had mysteriously vanished at the very hour at which the crime was committed.

'Sir John, said the servant, went late to bed and locked himself carefully in his room. He always had firearms within reach. Often during the night he could be heard speaking in loud tones, as if he were wrangling with someone. On the night in question, however, he had made no sound, and it was only on coming to open the windows the next morning that the servant had discovered the murder. The witness suspected no one.

'I told the magistrates and police officers everything I knew about the deceased, and inquiries were made with scupulous care throughout the whole island, but nothing was ever discovered.

'Well, one night, three months after the murder, I had a frightful nightmare. I thought I saw that hand, that ghastly hand, running like a scorpion or a spider over my curtains and walls. Thrice I awoke, and thrice fell asleep again, and thrice did I see that hideous relic gallop around my room, with its fingers running along like the legs of an insect. The next day the hand itself was brought to me. It had been found in the cemetery on Sir John's tomb. He had been buried there, as no trace of his family was discoverable. The index finger of the hand was missing. Ladies, that is my story. That is all I know about it.'

The ladies were horrified, pale and trembling. One of them protested:

'But the mystery is not solved. There is no explanation. We shall never be able to sleep if you don't tell us what you make of it yourself.'

The magistrate smiled a little grimly:

'Well, ladies, I'm afraid I shall deprive you of your nightmares. My theory is the perfectly simple one that the rightful owner of that hand was not dead at all, and that he came looking for his severed member with the one that was left him. But as for explaining how he managed it, that is beyond me. It was a kind of vendetta.'

Another lady protested:

'No, that can't be the real explanation.'

Still smiling, the narrator rejoined:

'I told you it wouldn't satisfy you.'

ARRIETTY'S FIRST ENCOUNTER

Mary Norton

This is the story of a race of tiny people, the Borrowers, who live under the floor, behind the wainscot. They own nothing and borrow everything from their enemies, the giant humans. Girls are not supposed to go 'borrowing', but as Arrietty is an only child, her father breaks the rule one day. This episode relates Arrietty's first foray into the giant world of humans.

She saw great chair legs rearing up into sunlight; she saw the shadowed undersides of their seats spread above her like canopies; she saw the nails and the strapping and odd tags of silk and string; she saw the terraced cliffs of the stairs, mounting up into the distance, up and up . . . she saw carved table legs and a cavern under the chest. And all the time, in the stillness, the clock spoke—measuring out the seconds, spreading its layers of calm.

And then, turning, Arrietty looked at the garden. She saw a gravelled path, full of coloured stones—the size of walnuts they were, with, here and there, a blade of grass between them, transparent green against the light of the sun. Beyond the path she saw a grassy-bank rising steeply to a tangled hedge; and beyond the hedge she saw fruit trees, bright with blossom.

'Here's a bag,' said Pod in a hoarse whisper; 'better get down to work.'

Obediently Arrietty started pulling fibre; stiff it was and full of dust. Pod worked swiftly and methodically, making small bundles, each of which he put immediately in the bag. 'If you have to run suddenly,' he

Silver plucked furiously at the line that held me to him and, from time to time, turned his eyes upon me. *(p.188)*

The pink stalk felt tender and living in her hands. (p.228)

explained, 'you don't want to leave nothing behind.'

'It hurts your hands,' said Arrietty, 'doesn't it?' and suddenly she sneezed.

'Not my hands it doesn't,' said Pod, 'they're hardened like,' and Arrietty sneezed again.

'Dusty, isn't it?' she said.

Pod straightened his back. 'No good pulling where it's knotted right in,' he said, watching her. 'No wonder it hurts your hands. See here,' he exclaimed after a moment, 'you leave it! It's your first time up like. You sit on the step there and take a peek out of doors.'

'Oh, no—' Arrietty began ('If I don't help,' she thought, 'he won't want me again') but Pod insisted.

'I'm better on me own,' he said. 'I can choose me bits, if you see what I mean, seeing as it's me who's got to make the brush.'

★ ★ ★ ★

The step was warm but very steep.'If I got down on to the path,' Arrietty thought, 'I might not get up again,' so for some moments she sat quietly. After a while she noticed the shoe-scraper.

'Arrietty,' called Pod softly, 'where have you got to?'

'I just climbed down the shoe-scraper,' she called back.

He came along and looked down at her from the top of the step. 'That's all right,' he said after a moment's stare, 'but never climb down anything that isn't fixed like. Supposing one of them came along and moved the shoe-scraper—where would you be then? How would you get up again?'

'It's heavy to move,' said Arrietty.

'Maybe,' said Pod, 'but it's movable. See what I mean? There's rules, my lass, and you got to learn.'

'This path,' Arrietty said, 'goes round the house. And the bank does too.'

'Well,' said Pod, 'what of it?'

Arrietty rubbed one red kid shoe on a rounded stone. 'It's my grating,' she explained. 'I was thinking that my grating must be just round the corner. My grating looks out on to this bank.'

'Your grating!' exclaimed Pod. 'Since when has it been your grating?'

'I was thinking,' Arrietty went on. 'Suppose I just went round the corner and called through the grating to mother?'

'No,' said Pod, 'we're not going to have none of that. Not going round corners.'

'Then,' went on Arrietty, 'she'd see I was all right like.'

'Well,' said Pod, and then he half smiled, 'go quickly then and call. I'll watch for you here. Not loud mind!'

Arrietty ran. The stones in the path were firmly bedded and her light, soft shoes hardly seemed to touch them. How glorious it was to run—you could never run under the floor: you walked, you stooped, you crawled—but you never ran. Arrietty nearly ran past the grating. She saw it just in time after she turned the corner. Yes, there it was quite close to the ground embedded deeply in the old wall of the house; there was moss below it in a spreading, greenish stain.

Arrietty ran up to it. 'Mother!' she called, her nose against the iron grille. 'Mother!' She waited quietly and, after a moment, she called again.

At the third call Homily came. Her hair was coming down and she carried, as though it were heavy, the screw lid of a pickle jar, filled with soapy water. 'Oh,' she said in an annoyed voice, 'you didn't half give me a turn! What do you think you're up to? Where's your father?'

Arrietty jerked her head sideways. 'Just there—by the front door!' She was so full of happiness that, out of Homily's sight, her toes danced on the green moss. Here she was on the other side of the grating—here she was at last, on the outside—looking in!

'Yes,' said Homily, 'they open that door like that—the first day of spring. Well,' she went on briskly, 'you run back to your father. And tell him, if the morning-room door happens to be open that I wouldn't say no to a bit of red blotting-paper. Mind out of my way now—while I throw the water!'

'That's what grows the moss,' thought Arrietty as she sped back to her father, 'all the water we empty through the grating . . .'

Pod looked relieved when he saw her but frowned at the message. 'How's she expect me to climb that desk without me pin? Blotting-paper's a curtain-and-chair job and she should know it. Come on now! Up with you!'

'Let me stay down,' pleaded Arrietty, 'just a bit longer. Just till you finish. They're all out. Except Her. Mother said so.'

'She'd say anything,' grumbled Pod, 'when she wants something quick. How does she know She won't take it into her head to get out of that bed of Hers and come downstairs with a stick? How does she know Mrs Driver ain't stayed at home today—with a headache? How does she know that boy ain't still here?'

'What boy?' asked Arrietty.

Pod looked embarrassed. 'What boy?' he repeated vaguely and then went on: 'Or maybe Crampfurl—'

'Crampfurl isn't a boy,' said Arrietty.

'No, he isn't,' said Pod, 'not in a manner of speaking. No,' he went on as though thinking this out, 'no, you wouldn't call Crampfurl a boy. Not, as you might say, a boy—exactly. Well,' he said, beginning to move away, 'stay down a bit if you like. But stay close!'

Arrietty watched him move away from the step and then she looked about her. Oh, glory! Oh, joy! Oh, freedom! The sunlight, the grasses, the soft, moving air and half-way up the bank, where it curved round the corner, a flowering cherry-tree! Below it on the path lay a stain of pinkish petals and at the tree's foot, pale as butter, a nest of primroses.

Arrietty threw a cautious glance towards the front door-step and then, light and dancey, in her soft red shoes, she ran towards the petals. They were curved like shells and rocked as she touched them. She gathered several up and laid them one inside the other . . . up and up . . . like a card castle. And then she spilled them. Pod came again to the top of the step and looked along the path. 'Don't you go far,' he said after a moment. Seeing his lips move, she smiled back at him: she was too far already to hear the words.

A greenish beetle, shining in the sunlight, came towards her across the stones. She laid her fingers lightly on its shell and it stood still, waiting and watchful, and when she moved her hand the beetle went swiftly on. An ant came hurrying in a busy zig-zag. She danced in front of it to tease it and put out her foot. It stared at her, nonplussed, waving its antennae; then pettishly, as though put out, it swerved away. Two birds came down, quarrelling shrilly, into the grass below the tree. One flew away but Arrietty could see the other among the moving grass stems above her on the slope. Cautiously she moved towards the bank and climbed a little nervously in amongst the green blades. As she parted them gently with her bare hands, drops of water plopped on her skirt and she felt the red shoes become damp. But on she went, pulling herself up now and again by rooty stems into this jungle of moss and wood-violet and creeping leaves of clover. The sharp-seeming grass blades, waist high, were tender to the touch and sprang back lightly behind her as she passed. When at last she reached the foot of the tree, the bird took fright and flew away and she sat down suddenly on a gnarled leaf of primrose. The air was filled with scent. 'But nothing will play with you,' she thought and saw the cracks and furrows of the primrose leaves held crystal beads of dew. If she pressed the leaf these rolled like marbles. The bank was warm, almost too warm here within the shelter of the tall grass, and the sandy earth smelled dry. Standing up, she picked a primrose. The pink stalk felt tender and living in her hands and was covered with silvery hairs, and when she held the flower, like a parasol, between her eyes and the sky, she saw the sun's pale light through the veined petals. On a piece of bark she found a wood-louse and she struck it lightly with her swaying flower. It curled immediately and became a ball, bumping softly away downhill in amongst the grass roots. But she knew about wood-lice. There were plenty of them at home under the floor. Homily always scolded her if she played with them because, she said, they smelled of old knives. She lay back among the stalks of the primroses and they made a coolness between her and the sun, and then, sighing, she turned her head and looked sideways up the bank among the grass stems. Startled, she caught her breath. Something had moved above her on the bank. Something had glittered. Arrietty stared.

* * * *

It was an eye. Or it looked like an eye. Clear and bright like the colour of the sky. An eye like her own but enormous. A glaring eye. Breathless with fear, she sat up. And the eye blinked. A great fringe of lashes came curving down and flew up again out of sight. Cautiously, Arrietty moved her legs: she would slide noiselessly in among the grass stems and slither away down the bank.

'Don't move!' said a voice, and the voice, like the eye, was enormous but, somehow, hushed—and hoarse like a surge of wind through the grating on a stormy night in March.

Arrietty froze. 'So this is it,' she thought, 'the worst and most terrible thing of all: I have been "seen"! Whatever happened to Eggletina will now, almost certainly, happen to me!'

There was a pause and Arrietty, her heart pounding in her ears, heard the breath again drawn swiftly into the vast lungs. 'Or,' said the voice, whispering still, 'I shall hit you with my ash stick.'

Suddenly Arrietty became calm. 'Why?' she asked. How strange her own voice sounded! Crystal thin and harebell clear, it tinkled on the air.

'In case,' came the surprised whisper at last, 'you ran towards me, quickly, through the grass . . . in case,' it went on, trembling a little, 'you scrabbled at me with your nasty little hands.'

Arrietty stared at the eye; she held herself quite still. 'Why?' she asked again, and again the word tinkled—icy cold it sounded this time, and needle sharp.

'Things do,' said the voice. 'I've seen them. In India.'

Arrietty thought of her Gazetteer of the World. 'You're not in India now,' she pointed out.

'Did you come out of the house?'

'Yes,' said Arrietty.

'From whereabouts in the house?'

Arrietty stared at the eye. 'I'm not going to tell you,' she said at last bravely.

'Then I'll hit you with my ash stick!'

'All right,' said Arrietty, 'hit me!'

'I'll pick you up and break you in half!'

Arrietty stood up. 'All right,' she said and took two paces forward.

There was a sharp gasp and an earthquake in the grass: he spun away from her and sat up, a great mountain in a green jersey. He had fair, straight hair and golden eyelashes. 'Stay where you are!' he cried.

Arrietty stared up at him. So this was 'the boy'! Breathless, she felt, and light with fear. 'I guessed you were about nine,' she gasped after a moment.

He flushed. 'Well, you're wrong, I'm ten.' He looked down at her, breathing deeply. 'How old are you?'

'Fourteen,' said Arrietty. 'Next June,' she added, watching him.

There was silence while Arrietty waited, trembling a little. 'Can you read?' the boy said at last.

'Of course,' said Arrietty. 'Can't you?'

'No,' he stammered. 'I mean—yes. I mean I've just come from India.'

'What's that got to do with it?' asked Arrietty.

'Well, if you're born in India, you're bilingual. And if you're bilingual, you can't read. Not so well.'

Arrietty stared up at him: what a monster, she thought, dark against the sky.

'Do you grow out of it?' she asked.

He moved a little and she felt the cold flick of his shadow.

'Oh yes,' he said, 'it wears off. My sisters were bilingual; now they aren't a bit. They could read any of those books upstairs in the schoolroom.'

'So could I,' said Arrietty quickly, 'if someone could hold them, and turn the pages. I'm not a bit bilingual. I can read anything.'

'Could you read out loud?'

'Of course,' said Arrietty.

'Would you wait here while I run upstairs and get a book now?'

'Well,' said Arrietty; she was longing to show off; then a startled look came into her eyes. 'Oh—' she faltered.

'What's the matter?' The boy was standing up now. He towered above her.

'How many doors are there to this house?' She squinted up at him against the bright sunlight. He dropped on one knee.

'Doors?' he said. 'Outside doors?'

'Yes.'

'Well, there's the front door, the back door, the gun-room door, the kitchen door, the scullery door . . . and the french windows in the drawing-room.'

'Well, you see,' said Arrietty, 'my father's in the hall, by the front door, working. He . . . he wouldn't want to be disturbed.'

'Working?' said the boy. 'What at?'

'Getting material,' said Arrietty, 'for a scrubbing-brush.'

'Then I'll go in the side door'; he began to move away but turned suddenly and came back to her. He stood a moment, as though embarrassed, and then he said: 'Can you fly?'

'No,' said Arrietty, surprised; 'can you?'

His face became even redder. 'Of course not,' he said angrily; 'I'm not a fairy!'

'Well, nor am I,' said Arrietty, 'nor is anybody. I don't believe in them.'

He looked at her strangely. 'You don't believe in them?'

'No,' said Arrietty; 'do you?'

'Of course not!'

Really, she thought, he is a very angry kind of boy. 'My mother believes in them,' she said, trying to appease him. 'She thinks she saw one once. It was when she was a girl and lived with her parents behind the sand pile in the potting-shed.'

He squatted down on his heels and she felt his breath on her face. 'What was it like?' he asked.

'About the size of a glow-worm with wings like a butterfly. And it had a tiny little face, she said, all alight and moving like sparks and tiny moving hands. Its face was changing all the time, she said, smiling and sort of shimmering. It seemed to be talking, she said, very quickly—but you couldn't hear a word.'

'Oh,' said the boy, interested. After a moment he asked: 'Where did it go?'

'It just went,' said Arrietty. 'When my mother saw it, it seemed to be caught in a cobweb. It was dark at the time. About five o'clock on a winter's evening. After tea.'

'Oh,' he said again and picked up two petals of cherry-blossom which he folded together like a sandwich and ate slowly. 'Supposing,' he said, staring past her at the wall of the house, 'you saw a little man, about as tall as a pencil, with a blue patch in his trousers, halfway up a window curtain, carrying a doll's tea-cup—would you say it was a fairy?'

'No,' said Arrietty, 'I'd say it was my father.'

'Oh,' said the boy, thinking this out, 'does your father have a blue patch on his trousers?'

'Not on his best trousers. He does on his borrowing ones.'

'Oh,' said the boy again. He seemed to find it a safe sound, as lawyers do. 'Are there many people like you?'

'No,' said Arrietty. 'None. We're all different.'

'I mean as small as you?'

Arrietty laughed. 'Oh, don't be silly!' she said. 'Surely you don't think there are many people in the world your size?'

'There are more my size than yours,' he retorted.

'Honestly—' began Arrietty helplessly and laughed again. 'Do you really think—I mean, whatever sort of a world would it be? Those great chairs . . . I've seen them. Fancy if you had to make chairs that size for everyone? And the stuff for their clothes . . . miles and miles of it . . . tents of it . . . and the sewing! And their great houses, reaching up so you can hardly see the ceilings . . . their great beds . . . the *food* they eat . . . great, smoking mountains of it, huge bogs of stew and soup and stuff.'

'Don't you eat soup?' asked the boy.

'Of course we do,' laughed Arrietty. 'My father had an uncle who had a little boat which he rowed round in the stock-pot picking up flotsam and jetsam. He did bottom-fishing too for bits of marrow until the cook got suspicious through finding bent pins in the soup. Once he was nearly shipwrecked on a chunk of submerged shin-bone. He lost his oars and the boat sprang a leak but he flung a line over the pot handle and pulled himself alongside the rim. But all that stock—fathoms of it! And the size of the stock-pot! I mean, there wouldn't be enough stuff in the world to go round after a bit! That's why my father says it's a good thing they're dying out . . . just a few, my father says, that's all we need—to keep us. Otherwise, he says, the whole thing gets—' Arrietty hesitated trying to remember the word—'exaggerated, he says—'

'What do you mean,' asked the boy, '"to keep us"?'

* * * *

So Arrietty told him about borrowing—how difficult it was and how dangerous. She told him about the store-rooms under the floor; about Pod's early exploits, the skill he had shown and the courage; she described those far-off days, before her birth, when Pod and Homily had been rich; she described the musical snuff-box, of gold filigree, and the little bird which flew out of it made of kingfisher feathers, how it flapped its wings and sang its song; she described the doll's wardrobe and the tiny green glasses; the little silver tea-pot out of the drawing-room case; the satin bedcovers and embroidered sheets . . . 'those we have still,' she told him, 'they're Her handkerchiefs . . .' 'She,' the boy realized gradually was his Great Aunt Sophy upstairs; he heard how Pod would borrow from her bedroom, picking his way—in the firelight—among the trinkets on her dressing-table, even climbing her bed-curtains and walking on her quilt. And of how she would watch him and sometimes talk to him because, Arrietty explained, every day at six o'clock they brought her a decanter of Fine Old Pale Madeira, and how before midnight she would drink the lot. Nobody blamed her, not even Homily, because, as Homily would say, 'She' had so few pleasures, poor soul, but, Arrietty explained, after the first three glasses Great Aunt Sophy never believed in anything she saw. 'She thinks my father comes out of the decanter,' said Arrietty, 'and one day when I'm older he's going to take me there and she'll think I come out of the decanter too. It'll please her, my father thinks, as she's used to him now. Once he took my mother, and Aunt Sophy perked up like anything and kept asking why my mother didn't come any more and saying they'd watered the Madeira because once, she says, she saw a little man *and* a little woman and now she only sees a little man . . .'

'I wish she thought I came out of the decanter,' said the boy. 'She gives me dictation and teaches me to write. I only see her in the mornings when she's cross. She sends for me and looks behind my ears and asks Mrs D. if I've learned my words.'

'What does Mrs D. look like?' asked Arrietty. (How delicious it was to say 'Mrs D.' like that . . . how careless and daring!)

'She's fat and has a moustache and gives me my bath and hurts my bruise and my sore elbow and says she'll take a slipper to me one of these days . . .' The boy pulled up a tuft of grass and stared at it angrily and Arrietty saw his lip tremble. 'My mother's very nice,' he said. 'She lives in India. Why did you lose all your worldly riches?'

'Well,' said Arrietty, 'the kitchen boiler burst and hot water came pouring through the floor into our house and everything was washed away and piled up in front of the grating. My father worked night and day. First hot, then cold. Trying to salvage things. And there's a dreadful draught in March through that grating. He got ill, you see, and couldn't go borrowing. So my Uncle Hendreary had to do it and one or two others and my mother gave them things bit by bit, for all their trouble. But the kingfisher bird was spoilt by the water; all its feathers fell off and a great twirly spring came jumping out of its side. My father used the spring to keep the door shut against draughts from the grating and my mother put the feathers in a little moleskin hat. After a while I got born and my father went borrowing again. But he gets tired now and doesn't like curtains, not when any of the bobbles are off . . .'

'I helped him a bit,' said the boy, 'with the tea-cup. He was shivering all over. I suppose he was frightened.'

'My father frightened!' exclaimed Arrietty angrily. 'Frightened of you!' she added.

'Perhaps he doesn't like heights,' said the boy.

'He loves heights,' said Arrietty. 'The thing he doesn't like is curtains. I've told you. Curtains make him tired.'

The boy sat thoughtfully on his haunches, chewing a blade of grass. 'Borrowing,' he said after a while. 'Is that what you call it?'

'What else could you call it?' asked Arrietty.

'I'd call it stealing.'

Arrietty laughed. She really laughed. 'But we *are* Borrowers,' she explained, 'like you're a—a Human Bean or whatever it's called. We're part of the house. You might as well say that the fire-grate steals the coal from the coal-scuttle.'

'Then what is stealing?'

Arrietty looked grave. 'Supposing my Uncle Hendreary borrowed an emerald watch from Her dressing table and my father took it and hung it up on our wall. That's stealing.'

'An emerald watch!' exclaimed the boy.

'Well, I just said that because we have one on the wall at home, but my father borrowed it himself. It needn't be a watch. It could be anything. A lump of sugar, even. But Borrowers don't steal.'

'Except from human beans,' said the boy.

Arrietty burst out laughing; she laughed so much that she had to hide her face in the primrose. 'Oh dear,' she gasped with tears in her eyes, 'you are funny!' She stared upwards at his puzzled face. 'Human beans are *for* Borrowers—like bread's for butter!'

The boy was silent awhile. A sigh of wind rustled the cherry-tree and shivered among the blossom.

'Well, I don't believe it,' he said at last, watching the falling petals. 'I don't believe that's what we're for at all and I don't believe we're dying out!'

'Oh, goodness!' exclaimed Arrietty impatiently, staring up at his chin. 'Just use your common sense: you're the only real human bean I ever saw (although I do just know of three more—Crampfurl, Her, and Mrs Driver). But I know lots and lots of Borrowers: the Overmantels and the Harpsichords and the Rain-Barrels and the Linen-Presses and the Boot-Racks and the Hon. John Studdingtons and—'

He looked down. 'John Studdington? But he was our grand-uncle—'

'Well, this family lived behind a picture,' went on Arrietty, hardly listening, 'and there were the Stove-Pipes and the Bell-Pulls and the—'

'Yes,' he interrupted, 'but did you see them?'

'I saw the Harpsichords. And my mother was a Bell-Pull. The others were before I was born . . .'

He leaned closer. 'Then where are they now? Tell me that.'

'My Uncle Hendreary has a house in the country,' said Arrietty coldly, edging away from his great lowering face; it was misted over, she noticed, with hairs of palest gold. 'And five children, Harpsichords and Clocks.'

'But where are the others?'

'Oh,' said Arrietty, 'they're somewhere.' But where? she wondered. And she shivered slightly in the boy's cold shadow which lay about her, slant-wise, on the grass.

He drew back again, his fair head blocking out a great piece of sky. 'Well,' he said deliberately after a moment, and his eyes were cold, 'I've only seen two Borrowers but I've seen hundreds and hundreds and hundreds and hundreds and hundreds—'

'Oh no—' whispered Arrietty.

'Of human beans.' And he sat back.

Arrietty stood very still. She did not look at him. After a while she said: 'I don't believe you.'

'All right,' he said, 'then I'll tell you—'

'I still won't believe you,' murmured Arrietty.

'Listen!' he said. And he told her about railway stations and football matches and racecourses and royal processions and Albert Hall concerts. He told her about India and China and North America and the British Commonwealth. He told her about the July sales. 'Not hundreds,' he said, 'but thousands and millions and billions and trillions of great, big, enormous people. Now do you believe me?'

Arrietty stared up at him with frightened eyes: it gave her a crick in the neck. 'I don't know,' she whispered.

there are any more Borrowers anywhere in the world. I believe you're the last three,' he said.

Arrietty dropped her face into the primrose. 'We're not. There's Aunt Lupy and Uncle Hendreary and all the cousins.'

'I bet they're dead,' said the boy. 'And what's more,' he went on, 'no one will ever believe I've seen *you*. And you'll be the very last because you're the youngest. One day,' he told her, smiling triumphantly, 'you'll be the only Borrower left in the world!'

He sat still, waiting, but she did not look up. 'Now you're crying,' he remarked after a moment.

'They're not dead,' said Arrietty in a muffled voice; she was feeling in her little pocket for a handkerchief. 'They live in a badger's set two fields away, beyond the spinney. We don't see them because it's too far. There are weasels and things and cows and foxes . . . and crows . . .'

'Which spinney?' he asked.

'I don't KNOW!' Arrietty almost shouted. 'It's along by the gas-pipe—a field called Parkin's Beck.' She blew her nose. 'I'm going home,' she said.

'Don't go,' he said, 'not yet.'

'Yes, I'm going,' said Arrietty.

His face turned pink. 'Let me just get the book,' he pleaded.

'I'm not going to read to you now,' said Arrietty.

'Why not?'

She looked at him with angry eyes. 'Because—'

'Listen,' he said, 'I'll go to that field. I'll go and find Uncle Hendreary. And the cousins. And Aunt What-ever-she-is. And, if they're alive, I'll tell you. What about that? You could write them a letter and I'd put it down the hole—'

Arrietty gazed up at him: 'Would you?' she breathed.

'Yes, I would. Really I would. Now can I go and get the book? I'll go in by the side door.'

'All right,' said Arrietty absently. Her eyes were shining. 'When can I give you the letter?'

'Any time,' he said, standing above her. 'Where in the house do you live?'

'Well—' began Arrietty and stopped. Why once again did she feel this chill? Could it only be his shadow . . . towering above her, blotting out the sun? 'I'll put it somewhere,' she said hurriedly, 'I'll put it under the hall mat.'

'Which one? The one by the front door?'

'Yes, that one.'

He was gone. And she stood there alone in the sunshine, shoulder deep in grass. What had happened seemed too big for thought; she felt unable to believe it really had happened: not only had she been 'seen' but she had been talked to; not only had she been talked to but she had—

'Arrietty!' said a voice.

She stood up, startled, and spun round: there was Pod, moon-faced, on the path looking up at her. 'Come on down!' he whispered.

She stared at him for a moment as though she did not recognize him; how round his face was, how kind, how familiar!

'Come on!' he said again, more urgently; and obediently because he sounded worried, she slithered quickly towards him off the bank, balancing her primrose. 'Put that thing down,' he said sharply, when she stood at last beside him on the path. 'You can't lug great flowers about—you got to carry a bag. What you want to go up there for?' he grumbled as they moved off across the stones. 'I might never have seen you. Hurry up now. Your mother'll have tea waiting!'

THE DANCING ACADEMY

Charles Dickens

Of all the dancing academies that ever were established, there never was one more popular in its immediate vicinity than Signor Billsmethi's, of the 'King's Theatre'. It was not in Spring Gardens, or Newman Street, or Berners Street, or Gower Street, or Charlotte Street, or Percy Street, or any other of the numerous streets which have been devoted time out of mind to professional people, dispensaries, and boarding-houses; it was not in the West End at all—it rather approximated to the eastern portion of London, being situated in the populous and improving neighbourhood of Gray's Inn Lane.

It was not a dear dancing academy—four-and-sixpence a quarter is decidedly cheap upon the whole. It was *very* select, the number of pupils being strictly limited to seventy-five, and a quarter's payment in advance being rigidly exacted. There was public tuition and private tuition—an assembly-room and a parlour. Signor Billsmethi's family were always thrown in with the parlour, and included in parlour price; that is to say a private pupil had Signor Billsmethi's parlour to dance *in*, and Signor Billsmethi's family to dance *with*; and when he had been broken in in the parlour he ran in couples in the assembly-room.

Such was the dancing academy of Signor Billsmethi when Mr Augustus Cooper, of Fetter Lane, first saw an unstamped advertisement walking leisurely down Holborn Hill, announcing to the world that Signor Billsmethi, of the King's Theatre, intended opening for the season with a grand ball.

Now, Mr Augustus Cooper was in the oil and colour line—just of age with a little money, a little business, and a little mother, who, having managed her husband and his business in his lifetime took to managing her son and *his* business after his decease; and so, somehow or other, he had been cooped up in the little back parlour behind the shop on weekdays, and in a little deal box without a lid (called by courtesy a pew) at Bethel Chapel, on Sundays, and had seen no more of the world than if he had been an infant all his days; whereas Young White, at the gas-fitter's over the way, three years younger than him, had been flaring away like winkin'—going to the theatre—supping at harmonic meetings—eating oysters by the barrel—drinking stout by the gallon—even stopping out all night, and coming home as cool in the morning as if nothing had happened. So Mr Augustus Cooper made up his mind that he would not stand it any longer, and had that very morning expressed to his mother a firm determination to be 'blowed' in the event of his not being instantly provided with a street-door key. And he was walking down Holborn Hill, thinking about all these things, and wondering how he could manage to get introduced into genteel society for the first time, when his eyes rested on Signor Billsmethi's announcement, which it immediately struck him was just the very thing he wanted; for he should not only be able to select a genteel circle of acquaintance at once out of the five-and-seventy pupils at four-and-sixpence a quarter, but should qualify himself at the same time to go through a hornpipe in private society, with perfect ease to himself, and great delight to his friends. So he stopped the unstamped advertisement an animated sandwich, composed of a boy between two boards—and having procured a very small card with the Signor's address indented thereon, walked straight at once to the Signor's house—and very fast he walked too, for fear the list should be filled up, and the five-and-seventy completed before he got there. The Signor was at home, and, what was still more gratifying, he was an Englishman! Such a nice man—and so polite! The list was not full, but it was a most extraordinary circumstance that there was only just one vacancy, and even that one would have been filled up that very morning, only Signor Billsmethi was dissatisfied with the reference, and being very much afraid that the lady wasn't select, wouldn't take her.

'And very much delighted I am, Mr Cooper,' said Signor Billsmethi, 'that I did *not* take her. I assure you; Mr Cooper—I don't say it to flatter you, for I know you're above it—that I consider myself extremely fortunate in having a gentleman of your manners and appearance, sir.'

'I am very glad of it too, sir,' said Augustus Cooper.

'And I hope we shall be better acquainted, sir,' said Signor Billsmethi.

'And I'm sure I hope we shall too, sir,' responded Augustus Cooper. Just then the door opened, and in came a young lady with her hair curled in a crop all over her head, and her shoes tied in sandals all over her legs.

'Don't run away, my dear,' said Signor Billsmethi; for the young lady didn't know Mr Cooper was there when she ran in and was going to run out again in her modesty, all in confusion-like. 'Don't run away, my dear,' said Signor Billsmethi, 'this is Mr Cooper—Mr Cooper, of Fetter Lane. Mr Cooper, my daughter, sir—Miss Billsmethi, sir, who I hope will have the pleasure of dancing many a quadrille, minuet, gavotte, country-dance, fandango, double-hornpipe, and farinagholkajingo with you, sir. She dances them all, sir; and so shall you sir before you're a quarter older sir.'

And Signor Billsmethi slapped Mr Augustus Cooper on the back as if he had known him a dozen years—so friendly; and Mr Cooper bowed to the young lady, and the young lady curtseyed to him, and Signor Billsmethi said they were as handsome a pair as ever he'd wish to see; upon which the young lady exclaimed, 'Lor, pa!' and blushed as red as Mr Cooper himself—you might have thought they were both standing under a red lamp at a chemist's shop; and before Mr Cooper went away it was settled that he should join the family circle that very night—taking them just as they were—no ceremony nor nonsense of that kind—and learn his positions, in order that he might lose no time and be able to come out at the forthcoming ball.

Well; Mr Augustus Cooper went away to one of the cheap shoemakers' shops in Holborn, where gentlemen's dress-pumps are seven-and-sixpence, and men's strong walking, just nothing at all, and bought a pair of the regular seven-and-sixpenny, long-quartered, town mades, in which he astonished himself quite as much as his mother, and sallied forth to Signor Billsmethi's. There were four other private pupils in the parlour: two ladies and two gentlemen. Such nice people! Not a bit of pride about them. One of the ladies in particular, who was in training for a Columbine, was remarkably affable, and she and Miss Billsmethi took such an interest in Mr Augustus Cooper, and joked and smiled, and looked so bewitching, that he got quite at home and learnt his steps in no time. After the practising was over, Signor Billsmethi, and Miss Billsmethi, and Master Billsmethi, and a young lady, and the two ladies, and the two gentlemen, danced a quadrille—none of your slipping and sliding about but regular warm work, flying into corners, and diving among chairs, and shooting out at the door—something like dancing! Signor Billsmethi in particular notwithstanding his having a little fiddle to play all the time, was out on the landing every figure, and Master Billsmethi, when everybody else was breathless, danced a horn-pipe with a cane in his hand, and a cheese-plate on his head, to the unqualified admiration of the whole company.

Then Signor Billsmethi insisted as they were so happy, that they should all stay to supper, and proposed sending Master Billsmethi for the beer and spirits, whereupon the two gentlemen swore, 'strike 'em wulgar if they'd stand that'; and they were just going to quarrel who should pay for it, when Mr Augustus Cooper said he would, if they'd have the kindness to allow him—and they *had* the kindness to allow him; and Master Billsmethi brought the beer in a can, and the rum in a quart-pot. They had a regular night of it; and Miss Billsmethi squeezed Mr Augustus Cooper's hand under the table; and Mr Augustus Cooper returned the squeeze and returned home too, at something to six o'clock in the morning when he was put to bed by main force by the apprentice, after repeatedly expressing an uncontrollable desire to pitch his reverend parent out of the second-floor window, and to throttle the apprentice with his own neck-handkerchief.

Weeks had worn on, and the seven-and-sixpenny town-mades had nearly worn out, when the night arrived for the grand dress-ball at which the whole of the five-and-seventy pupils were to meet together for the first time that season, and to take out some portion of their respective four-and-sixpences in lamp-oil and fiddlers. Mr Augustus

Cooper had ordered a new coat for the occasion—a two-pound-tenner from Turnstile. It was his first appearance in public; and after a grand Sicilian shawl-dance by fourteen young ladies in character, he was to open the quadrille department with Miss Bellsmethi herself, with whom he had become quite intimate since his first introduction.

It *was* a night! Everything was admirably arranged. The sandwich-boy took the hats and bonnets at the street-door; there was a turn-up bedstead in the back parlour, on which Miss Billsmethi made tea and coffee for such of the gentlemen as chose to pay for it, and such of the ladies as the gentlemen treated; red port-wine, negus and lemonade were handed round at eighteen pence a head, and, in pursuance of a previous engagement with the public-house at the corner of the street, an extra potboy was laid on for the occasion. In short, nothing could exceed the arrangements, except the company. Such ladies! Such pink silk stockings! Such artificial flowers! Such a number of cabs! No sooner had one cab set down a couple of ladies, than another cab drove up and set down another couple of ladies, and they all knew, not only one another, but the majority of the gentlemen into the bargain, which made it all as pleasant and lively as could be. Signor Billsmethi in black tights, with a large blue bow in his buttonhole, introduced the ladies to such of the gentlemen as were strangers: and the ladies talked away—and laughed they did—it was delightful to see them.

As to the shawl-dance, it was the most exciting thing that ever was beheld; there was such a whisking, and rustling, and fanning, and getting ladies into a tangle with artificial flowers, and then disentangling them again; and as to Mr Augustus Cooper's share in the quadrille, he got through it admirably. He was missing from his partner now and then certainly, and discovered on such occasions to be either dancing with laudable perseverance in another set, or sliding about in perspective, apparently without any definite object; but, generally speaking, they managed to shove him through the figure, until he turned up in the right place. Be this as it may, when he had finished a great many ladies and gentlemen came up and complimented him very much, and said they had never seen a beginner do any thing like it before; and Mr August Cooper was perfectly satisfied with himself, and everybody else into the bargain, and 'stood' considerable quantities of spirits and water, negus, and compounds, for the use and behoof of two or three

Miss Billsmethi betrayed her jealousy by calling the young lady a 'creeter'.

dozen very particular friends, selected from the select circle of five-and-seventy pupils.

Now, whether it was the strength of the compounds, or the beauty of the ladies, or what not, it did so happen that Mr Augustus Cooper encouraged, rather than repelled, the very flattering attentions of a young lady in brown gauze over white calico who had appeared particularly struck with him from the first; and when the encouragements had been prolonged for some time, Miss Billsmethi betrayed her spite and jealousy thereat by calling the young lady in brown gauze a 'creeter', which induced the young lady in brown gauze to retort in certain sentences containing a taunt founded on the payment of four-and-sixpence a quarter, and some indistinct reference to a 'fancy man'; which reference Mr Augustus Cooper, being then and there in a state of considerable bewilderment, expressed his entire concurrence in. Miss Billsmethi, thus renounced, forthwith began screaming in the loudest key of her voice at the rate of fourteen screams a minute; and being unsuccessful, in an onslaught on the eyes and face, first of the lady in gauze and then of Mr Augustus Cooper, called distractedly on the other three-and-seventy pupils to furnish her with oxalic acid for her own private drinking, and the call not being honoured, made another rush at Mr Cooper, and then had her stay-lace cut and was carried off to bed.

Mr Augustus Cooper, not being remarkable for quickness of apprehension, was at a loss to understand what all this meant, till Signor Billsmethi explained it in a most satisfactory manner by stating to the pupils that Mr Augustus Cooper had made and confirmed diverse promises of marriage to his daughter on diverse occasions, and had now basely deserted her; on which the indignation of the pupils became universal and as several chivalrous gentlemen inquired rather pressingly of Mr Augustus Cooper, whether he required anything for his own use, or, in other words, whether he 'wanted anything for himself', he deemed it prudent to make a precipitate retreat.

And the upshot of the matter was, that a lawyer's letter came the next day, and an action was commenced next week; and that Mr Augustus Cooper, after walking twice to the Serpentine for the purpose of drowning himself, and coming twice back without doing it, made a confidant of his mother, who compromised the matter with twenty pounds from the till, which made twenty pounds four shillings and sixpence paid to Signor Billsmethi, exclusive of treats and pumps; and Mr Augustus Cooper went back and lived with his mother, and there he lives to this day; and as he has lost his ambition for society, and never goes into the world, he will never see this account of himself and will never be any the wiser.

A TERRIBLY STRANGE BED

William Wilkie Collins

Shortly after my education at college was finished I happened to be staying in Paris with an English friend. We were both young men then, and lived, I am afraid, rather a wild life in the delightful city of our sojourn. One night we were idling about the neighbourhood of the Palais Royal, doubtful to what amusement we should next betake ourselves. My friend proposed a visit to Frascati's; but his suggestion was not to my taste. I knew Frascati's, as the French saying is, by heart; had lost and won plenty of five-franc pieces there, merely for amusement's sake, until it was amusement no longer, and was thoroughly tired, in fact, of all the ghastly respectabilities of such a social anomaly as a respectable gambling-house.

'For heaven's sake,' said I to my friend, 'let us go somewhere where we can see a little genuine, blackguard, poverty-stricken gaming, with no false gingerbread glitter thrown over it at all. Let us get away from fashionable Frascati's, to a house where they don't mind letting in a man with a ragged coat, or a man with no coat, ragged or otherwise.'

'Very well,' said my friend, 'we needn't go out of the Palais Royal to find the sort of company you want. Here's the place just before us, as blackguard a place, by all report, as you could possibly wish to see.' In another minute we arrived at the door and entered the house.

When we got upstairs, and had left our hats and sticks with the door-keeper, we were admitted into the chief gambling-room. We did not find many people assembled there. But, few as the men were who looked up at us on our entrance, they were all types—lamentably true types—of their respective classes.

We had come to see blackguards; but these men were something worse. There is a comic side, more or less appreciable, in all 'black-guardism'—here there was nothing but tragedy—mute, weird tragedy. The quiet in the room was horrible. The thin, haggard, long-haired young man, whose sunken eyes fiercely watched the turning up of the cards, never spoke; the flabby, fat-faced, pimply player, who pricked his piece of pasteboard perseveringly to register how often black won and how often red—never spoke; the dirty, wrinkled old man, with the vulture eyes and the darned greatcoat, who had lost his last sou, and still looked on desperately after he could play no longer—never spoke. Even the voice of the croupier sounded as if it were strangely dulled and thickened in the atmosphere of the room.

I had entered the place to laugh, but the spectacle before me was something to weep over. I soon found it necessary to take refuge in excitement from the depression of spirits which was fast stealing on me. Unfortunately I sought the nearest excitement by going to the table and beginning to play. Still more unfortunately, as the event will show, I won—won prodigiously, won incredibly; won at such a rate that the regular players at the table crowded round me; and, staring at my stakes with hungry, superstitious eyes, whispered to one another that the English stranger was going to break the bank.

The game was *rouge-et-noir*. I had played at it in every city in Europe, without, however, the care or the wish to study the 'theory of chances' —that philosopher's stone of all gamblers! And a gambler, in the strict sense of the word, I had never been.

But on this occasion it was very different—now, for the first time in my life, I felt what the passion for play really was. My success first bewildered, and then, in the most literal meaning of the word, intoxicated me. Incredible as it may appear, it is nevertheless true, that I only lost when I attempted to estimate chances, and played according to previous calculation. If I left everything to luck, and staked without any care or consideration, I was sure to win—to win in the face of every recognized probability in favour of the bank. At first, some of the men present ventured their money safely enough on my colour; but I speedily increased my stakes to sums which they dared not risk. One after another they left off playing, and breathlessly looked on at my game.

Still, time after time, I staked higher and higher, and still won. The excitement in the room rose to fever pitch. The silence was interrupted by a deep-muttered chorus of oaths and exclamations in different languages every time the gold was shovelled across to my side of the table—even the imperturbable croupier dashed his rake on the floor in a fury of astonishment at my success. But one man present preserved his self-possession, and that man was my friend. He came to my side, and, whispering in English, begged me to leave the place, satisfied with what I had already gained. I must do him the justice to say that he repeated his warnings and entreaties several times, and only left me and went away after I had rejected his advice (I was to all intents and purposes gambling-drunk) in terms which rendered it impossible for him to address me again that night.

Shortly after he had gone a hoarse voice behind me cried, 'Permit me, my dear sir!—permit me to restore to their proper place two Napoleons which you have dropped. Wonderful luck, sir! I pledge you my word of honour, as an old soldier, in the course of my long experience in this sort of thing, I never saw such luck as yours!—never! Go on, sir—*Sacré mille bombes!* Go on boldly, and break the bank!'

I turned round and saw, nodding and smiling at me with inveterate civility, a tall man, dressed in a frogged and braided coat.

If I had been in my senses I should have considered him, personally, as being rather a suspicious specimen of an old soldier. He had goggling bloodshot eyes, mangy mustachios, and a broken nose. His voice betrayed a barrack-room intonation of the worst order, and he had the dirtiest pair of hands I ever saw—even in France. These little personal peculiarities exercised, however, no repelling influence on me. In the mad excitement, the reckless triumph of that moment, I was ready to 'fraternize' with anybody who encouraged me in my game. I accepted the old soldier's offered pinch of snuff, clapped him on the back, and swore he was the most honest fellow in the world, the most glorious relic of the Grand Army that I had ever met with. 'Go on!' cried my military friend, snapping his fingers in ecstasy. 'Go on, and win! Break the bank —*Mille tonnerres!* my gallant English comrade, break the bank!'

And I *did* go on—went on at such a rate that in another quarter of an hour the croupier called out, 'Gentlemen! the bank has discontinued for tonight.' All the notes and all the gold in that 'bank' now lay in a heap under my hands; the whole floating capital of the gambling-house was waiting to pour into my pockets!

'Tie up the money in your pocket-handkerchief, my worthy sir,' said the old soldier, as I wildly plunged my hands into my heap of gold. 'Tie it up, as we used to tie up a bit of dinner in the Grand Army; your winnings are too heavy for any breeches pockets that ever were sewed. There, that's it! Shovel them in, notes and all! And now, as an ancient grenadier, as an ex-brave of the French Army, what remains for me to do! I ask what? Simply this: to entreat my valued English friend to drink a bottle of champagne with me, and toast the goddess fortune in foaming goblets before we part!'

'Excellent ex-brave! Convivial ancient grenadier! Champagne by all means! An English cheer for an old soldier!'

'Bravo! the Englishman; the amiable, gracious Englishman, in whose veins circulates the vivacious blood of France! Another glass? Ah,— the bottle is empty! Never mind! *Vive le vin!* I, the old soldier, order another bottle!'

'No, no, ex-brave; never—ancient grenadier! *Your* bottle last time, *my* bottle this. Behold it! Toast away! The French Army!—The great Napoleon!—The present company! The croupier! The honest croupier's wife and daughters—if he has any! The ladies generally! Everybody in the world!'

By this time the second bottle of champagne was emptied. I felt as if I had been drinking liquid fire—my brain seemed all aflame. No excess in wine had ever had this effect on me before in my life. Was it the result of a stimulant acting upon my system when I was in a highly excited state? Was my stomach in a particularly disordered condition? Or was the champagne amazingly strong?

'Ex-brave of the French Army!' cried I, in a mad state of exhilaration, '*I* am on fire! how are *you*? You have set me on fire! Do you hear, my hero of Austerlitz? Let us have a third bottle to put the flame out!'

The old soldier wagged his head, rolled his goggle eyes, until I expected to see them slip out of their sockets; placed his dirty forefinger by the side of his broken nose, solemnly ejaculated, 'Coffee!' and immediately ran off into an inner room.

The word pronounced by the eccentric veteran seemed to have a magical effect on the rest of the company present. With one accord they all rose to depart. Probably they had expected to profit by my intoxication; but finding that my new friend was benevolently bent on preventing me from getting dead drunk, had now abandoned all hope of thriving pleasantly on my winnings. Whatever their motive might be, at any rate they went away in a body. When the old soldier returned and sat down again opposite to me at the table, we had the room to ourselves. I could see the croupier, in a sort of vestibule which opened out of it, eating his supper in solitude. The silence was now deeper than ever.

A sudden change, too, had come over the 'ex-brave'. He assumed a portentously solemn look, and when he spoke to me again his speech was ornamented by no oaths, enforced by no finger-snapping, enlivened by no apostrophes or exclamations.

'Listen, my dear sir,' said he, in mysteriously confidential tones, 'listen to an old soldier's advice. I have been to the mistress of the house—a very charming woman, with a genius for cookery!—to impress on her the necessity of making us some particularly strong and good coffee. You must drink this coffee in order to get rid of your little amiable exaltation of spirits before you think of going home—you *must*, my good and gracious friend! With all that money to take home tonight, it is a sacred duty to yourself to have your wits about you. You are known to be a winner to an enormous extent by several gentlemen present tonight, who, in a certain point of view, are very worthy and excellent fellows; but they are mortal men, my dear, sir, and they have their amiable weaknesses! Need I say more? Ah, no, no! you understand me! Now, this is what you must do. Send for a cabriolet when you feel quite well again, draw up all the windows when you get into it, and tell the driver to take you home only through the large and well-lit thoroughfares. Do this, and you and your money will be safe. Do this, and tomorrow you will thank an old soldier for giving you a word of honest advice.'

Just as the ex-brave ended his oration in very lagubrious tones, the coffee came in, ready poured out in two cups. My attentive friend handed me one of the cups with a bow. I was parched with thirst, and drank it off at a draught. Almost instantly afterwards I was seized with a fit of giddiness, and felt more completely intoxicated than ever. The room whirled round and round furiously; the old soldier seemed to be regularly bobbing up and down before me like the piston of a steam-engine. I was half deafened by a violent singing in my ears; a feeling of utter bewilderment, helplessness, idiocy overcame me. I rose from my chair, holding on by the table to keep my balance, and stammered out that I felt dreadfully unwell, so unwell that I did not know how I was to get home.

'My dear friend,' answered the old soldier—and even his voice seemed to be bobbing up and down as he spoke—'my dear friend, it would be madness to go home in *your* state; you would be sure to lose your money; you might be robbed and murdered with the greatest ease. *I* am going to sleep here: *you* sleep here, too—they make up capital beds in this house—take one; sleep off the effects of the wine, and go home safely with your winnings tomorrow—tomorrow, in broad daylight.'

I had but two ideas left: one, that I must never let go hold of my handkerchief full of money; the other, that I must lie down somewhere immediately and fall off into a comfortable sleep. So I agreed to the proposal about the bed, and took the offered arm of the old soldier, carrying my money with my disengaged hand. Preceded by the croupier, we passed along some passages and up a flight of stairs into the bedroom which I was to occupy. The ex-brave shook me warmly by the hand, proposed that we should breakfast together, and then, followed by the croupier, left me for the night.

I ran to the wash-stand, drank some of the water in my jug, poured the rest out, and plunged my face into it, then sat down in a chair and tried to compose myself. I soon felt better. The change for my lungs from the stinking atmosphere of the gambling-room to the cool air of the apartment I now occupied; the almost equally refreshing change for my eyes from the glaring gaslights of the salon to the dim, quiet flicker of one bedroom candle, aided wonderfully the restorative effects of cold water. The giddiness left me, and I began to feel a little like a reasonable being again. My first thought was of the risk of sleeping all night in a gambling-house; my second, of the still greater risk of trying to get out after the house was closed, and of going home alone at night, through the streets of Paris, with a large sum of money about me. I had slept in worse places than this on my travels; so I determined to lock, bolt, and barricade my door, and take my chance till the next morning.

Accordingly, I secured myself against all intrusion, looked under the bed and into the cupboard, tried the fastening of the window, and then, satisfied that I had taken every proper precaution, pulled off my upper clothing, put my light, which was a dim one, on the hearth among a feathery litter of wood ashes, and got into bed, with the handkerchief full of money under my pillow.

I soon felt not only that I could not go to sleep, but that I could not even close my eyes. I was wide awake, and in a high fever. Every nerve in my body trembled—every one of my senses seemed to be preternaturally sharpened.

What could I do? I had no book to read. I raised myself on my elbow, and looked about the room, which was brightened by a lovely moonlight pouring straight through the window—to see if it contained any pictures or ornaments that I could at all clearly distinguish.

There was, first, the bed I was lying in; a four-post bed, of all things in the world to meet with in Paris!—yes, a thorough clumsy British four-poster, with the regular top lined with chintz—the regular fringed valance all round—the regular stifling unwholesome curtains, which I remembered having mechanically drawn back againt the posts without particularly noticing the bed when I first got into the room. Then there was the marble-topped wash-stand, from which the water I had spilt, in my hurry to pour it out, was still dripping, slowly and more slowly, on to the brick floor. Then two small chairs.

Then the window—an unusually large window. Then a dark old picture, which the feeble candle dimly showed me. It was the picture of a fellow in a high Spanish hat, crowned with a plume of towering feathers. A swarthy, sinister ruffian, looking upward, shading his eyes with his hand, and looking intently upward—it might be at some tall gallows at which he was going to be hanged. At any rate, he had the appearance of thoroughly deserving it.

This picture put a kind of constraint upon me to look upward too—

at the top of the bed. It was a gloomy and not an interesting object, and I looked back at the picture. I counted the feathers in the man's hat—they stood out in relief—three white, two green. I observed the crown of his hat, which was of a conical shape, according to the fashion supposed to have been favoured by Guy Fawkes. I counted the feathers again—three white, two green.

While I still lingered over this very improving and intellectual employment, my thoughts insensibly began to wander. The moonlight shining into the room reminded me of a certain moonlight night in England—the night after a picnic party in a Welsh valley. Every incident of the drive homeward, through lovely scenery, which the moonlight made lovelier than ever, came back to me, though I had never given the picnic a thought for years; though, if I had *tried* to recollect it, I could certainly have recalled little or nothing of that scene long past.

I was still thinking of the picnic—of our merriment on the drive home—of the sentimental young lady who *would* quote *Childe Harold* because it was moonlight. I was absorbed by these past scenes and past amusements, when, in an instant, the thread on which my memories hung snapped asunder: my attention immediately came back to present things more vividly than ever, and I found myself, I neither knew why nor wherefore, looking hard at the picture again.

Looking for what?

Good God! the man had pulled his hat down on his brows!—No! the hat itself was gone! Where was the conical crown? Where the feathers—three white, two green? Not there! In place of the hat and feathers, what dusky object was it that now hid his forehead, his eyes, his shading hand?

Was the bed moving?

I turned on my back and looked up. Was I mad? Drunk? Dreaming? Giddy again? Or was the top of the bed really moving down—sinking slowly, regularly, silently, horribly, right down throughout the whole of its length and breadth—right down upon me as I lay underneath?

My blood seemed to stand still. A deadly paralysing coldness stole all over me as I turned my head round on the pillow and determined to test whether the bed-top was really moving or not by keeping my eye on the man in the picture.

The next look in that direction was enough. The dull, black, frowsy outline of the valance above me was within an inch of being parallel with his waist. I still looked breathlessly. And steadily, and slowly—very slowly—I saw the figure, and the line of frame below the figure, vanish as the valance moved down before it.

I am, constitutionally, anything but timid. I have been on more than one occasion in peril of my life, and have not lost my self-possession for an instant; but when the conviction first settled on my mind that the bed-top was really moving, was steadily and continuously sinking down upon me, I looked up shuddering, helpless, panic-stricken, beneath the hideous machinery for murder, which was advancing closer and closer to suffocate me where I lay.

I looked up, motionless, speechless, breathless. The candle, fully spent, went out; but the moonlight still brightened the room. Down and down, without pausing and without sounding, came the bed-top, and still my panic-terror seemed to bind me faster and faster to the mattress on which I lay—down and down it sank, till the dusty odour from the lining of the canopy came stealing into my nostrils.

At that final moment the instinct of self-preservation startled me out of my trance and I moved at last. There was just room for me to roll myself sideways off the bed. As I dropped noiselessly to the floor the edge of the murderous canopy touched me on the shoulder.

Without stopping to draw my breath, without wiping the cold sweat from my face, I rose instantly on my knees to watch the bed-top. I was literally spellbound by it. If I had heard footsteps behind me, I could not have turned round; if a means of escape had been miraculously provided for me, I could not have moved to take advantage of it. The whole life in me was, at that moment, concentrated in my eyes.

It descended—the whole canopy, with the fringe round it, came down—down—close down, so close that there was not room now to squeeze my finger between the bed-top and the bed. I felt at the sides, and discovered that what had appeared to me from beneath to be the ordinary light canopy of a four-post bed was in reality a thick, broad mattress, the substance of which was concealed by the valance and its fringe. I looked up and saw the four posts rising hideously bare. In the middle of the bed-top was a huge wooden screw that had evidently worked it down through a hole in the ceiling, just as ordinary presses are worked down on the substance selected for compression.

I looked up beneath the hideous machinery for murder, which was advancing closer and closer to suffocate me where I lay.

The frightful apparatus moved without making the faintest noise. There had been no creaking as it came down; there was now not the faintest sound from the room above. Amid a dead and awful silence I beheld before me—in the nineteenth century, and in the civilized capital of France—such a machine for secret murder by suffocation as might have existed in the worst days of the Inquisition, in the lonely inns among the Hartz Mountains, in the mysterious tribunals of Westphalia! Still, as I looked on it I could not move, I could hardly breathe, but I began to recover the power of thinking, and in a moment I discovered the murderous conspiracy framed against me in all its horror. My cup of coffee had been drugged, and drugged too strongly. I had been saved from being smothered by having taken an overdose of some narcotic. How I had chafed and fretted at the fever-fit which had preserved my life by keeping me awake! How recklessly I had confided myself to the two wretches who had led me into this room, determined, for the sake of my winnings, to kill me in my sleep by the surest and most horrible contrivance for secretly accomplishing my destruction! How many men, winners like me, had slept, as I had proposed to sleep, in that bed and had never been seen or heard of more! I shuddered at the bare idea of it.

But ere long all thought was again suspended by the sight of the murderous canopy moving once more. After it had remained on the bed—as nearly as I could guess—about ten minutes, it began to move up again. The villains who worked it from above evidently believed that their purpose was now accomplished. Slowly and silently, as it had descended, that horrible bed-top rose towards its former place. When it reached the upper extremities of the four posts, it reached the ceiling too. Neither hole nor screw could be seen; the bed became in appearance an ordinary bed again—the canopy an ordinary canopy—even to the most suspicious eyes.

Now, for the first time, I was able to move—to rise from my knees—to dress myself in my upper clothing—and to consider of how I should escape. If I betrayed, by the smallest noise, that the attempt to suffocate me had failed, I was certain to be murdered. Had I made any noise already? I listened intently, looking towards the door.

No! No footsteps in the passage outside—no sound of a tread, light or heavy, in the room above—absolute silence everywhere. Besides locking and bolting my door I had moved an old wooden chest against it, which I had found under the bed. To remove this chest (my blood ran cold as I thought of what its contents might be!) without making some disturbance was impossible; and, moreover, to think of escaping through the house, now barred up for the night, was sheer insanity. Only one chance was left me—the window. I stole to it on tiptoe.

My bedroom was on the first floor, above an *entresol*, and looked into the back street. I raised my hand to open the window, knowing that on that action hung, by the merest hair's-breadth, my chance of safety. They keep vigilant watch in a house of murder. If any part of the frame cracked, if the hinge creaked, I was a lost man! It must have occupied me at least five minutes, reckoning by time—five *hours*, reckoning by suspense—to open that window. I succeeded in doing it silently—in doing it with all the dexterity of a house-breaker—and then looked down into the street. To leap the distance beneath me would be almost certain destruction! Next, I looked round at the sides of the house. Down the left side ran the thick water-pipe—it passed close by the outer edge of the window. The moment I saw the pipe I knew I was saved. My breath came and went freely for the first time since I had seen the canopy of the bed moving down upon me!

To some men the means of escape which I had discovered might have seemed difficult and dangerous enough—to *me* the prospect of slipping down the pipe into the street did not suggest even a thought of peril. I had always been accustomed, by the practice of gymnastics, to keep up my schoolboy powers as a daring and expert climber, and knew that my head, hands, and feet would serve me faithfully in any hazards of ascent or descent. I had already got one leg over the window-sill when I remembered the handkerchief filled with money under my pillow. I could well have afforded to leave it behind me, but I was revengefully determined that the miscreants of the gambling-house should miss their plunder as well as their victim.

So I went back to the bed and tied the heavy handkerchief at my back by my cravat. Just as I had made it tight and fixed it in a comfortable place, I thought I heard a sound of breathing outside the door. The chill feeling of horror ran through me again as I listened. No! dead silence still in the passage—I had heard the night air blowing softly into the room. The next moment I was on the window-sill—and the next I had a firm grip on the water-pipe with my hands and knees.

I slid down into the street easily and quietly, as I thought I should, and immediately set off at the top of my speed to a branch Prefecture of Police, which I knew was situated in the immediate neighbourhood. A Sub-prefect and several picked men among his subordinates happened to be up, maturing, I believe, some scheme for discovering the perpetrator of a mysterious murder which all Paris was talking of just then. When I began my story, in a breathless hurry and in very bad French, I could see that the Sub-prefect suspected me of being a drunken Englishman who had robbed somebody; but he soon altered his opinion as I went on, and before I had anything like concluded, he shoved all the papers before him into a drawer, put on his hat, supplied me with another (for I was bare-headed), ordered a file of soldiers, desired his expert followers to get ready all sorts of tools for breaking open doors and ripping up brick-flooring, and took my arm in the most friendly and familiar manner possible to lead me with him out of the house. I will venture to say that when the Sub-prèfect was a little boy, and was taken for the first time to the play, he was not half as much pleased as he was now at the job in prospect for him at the gambling-house!

Away we went through the streets, the Sub-prefect cross-examining and congratulating me in the same breath as we marched at the head of our formidable posse. Sentinels were placed at the back and front of the house the moment we got to it; a tremendous battery of knocks was directed against the door; a light appeared at a window; I was told to conceal myself behind the police—then came more knocks, and a cry of 'Open in the name of the law!' At that terrible summons bolts and locks gave way before an invisible hand, and the moment after the Sub-prefect was in the passage, confronting a waiter half-dressed and ghastly pale. This was the short dialogue which immediately took place:

'We want to see the Englishman who is sleeping in this house.'

'He went away hours ago.'

'He did no such thing. His friend went away; *he* remained. Show us to his bedroom!'

'I swear to you, Monsieur le Sous-prefect, he is not here! He——'

'I swear to you, Monsieur le Garçon, he is. He slept here—he didn't find your bed comfortable—he came to us to complain of it—here he is among my men—and here am I ready to look for a flea or two in his bedstead. Renaudin! (calling to one of the subordinates and pointing to the waiter) collar that man and tie his hands behind him. Now, then, gentlemen, let us walk upstairs!'

Every man and woman in the house was secured—the 'old soldier' the first. Then I identified the bed in which I had slept, and then we went into the room above.

No object that was at all extraordinary appeared in any part of it. The Sub-prefect looked round the place, commanded everybody to be silent, stamped twice on the floor, called for a candle, looked attentively at the spot he had stamped on, and ordered the flooring there to be carefully taken up. This was done in no time. Lights were produced, and we saw a deep raftered cavity between the floor of this room and the ceiling of the room beneath. Through this cavity there ran perpendicularly a sort of case of iron thickly greased, and inside the case appeared the screw which communicated with the bed-top below. Extra lengths of screw, freshly oiled; levers covered with felt; all the complete upper works of a heavy press—constructed with infernal ingenuity so as to join the fixtures below, and when taken to pieces again to go into the smallest possible compass—were next discovered and pulled out on the floor. After some little difficulty the Sub-prefect succeeded in putting the machinery together, and, leaving his men to work it, descended with me to the bedroom. The smothering canopy was then lowered, but not so noiselessly as I had seen it lowered. When I mentioned this to the Sub-prefect, his answer, simple as it was, had a terrible significance. 'My men,' said he, 'are working down the bed-top for the first time—the men whose money you won were in better practice.'

We left the house in the sole possession of two police agents—every one of the inmates being removed to prison on the spot. The Sub-prefect, after taking down my statement in his office, returned with me to my hotel to get my passport. 'Do you think,' I asked as I gave it to him, 'that any men have really been smothered in that bed as they tried to smother *me*?'

'I have seen dozens of drowned men laid out at the morgue,' answered the Sub-prefect, 'in whose pocket-books were found letters stating that they had committed suicide in the Seine, because they had lost everything at the gaming-table. Do I know how many of those men entered the same gambling-house that *you* entered, won as *you* won, took that bed as *you* took it, slept in it, were smothered in it, and were privately thrown into the river with a letter of explanation written by the murderers and placed in their pocket-books? No man can say how many or how few have suffered the fate from which you have escaped. The people of the gambling-house kept their bedstead machinery a secret from *us*—even from the police! The dead kept the rest of the secret for them. Good-night, or rather good-morning, Monsieur.'

One good result was produced by my adventure: it cured me of ever again trying *rouge-et-noir* as an amusement. The sight of a green cloth, with packs of cards and heaps of money on it, will henceforth be forever associated in my mind with the sight of a bed-canopy descending to suffocate me in the silence and darkness of the night.

BETTER LET BLAME' WELL ALONE

Mark Twain

Huckleberry Finn is living with the Widow Douglas, who has custody of him, and is slowly adapting to a life of schoolwork and regular habits. However, his drunken father reappears and is granted custody of the boy by a new judge. Huck makes his escape, and stages it so that it seems he has been murdered. On Jackson Island in the Mississippi he meets Jim, the Widow Douglas's Negro, who has run away because he thinks the widow's sister is about to sell him. They link their fortunes, and continue together down the Mississippi.

It must 'a' been close on to one o'clock when we got below the island at last, and the raft did seem to go mighty slowly. If a boat was to come along we was going to take to the canoe and break for the Illinois shore; and it was well a boat didn't come, for we hadn't ever thought to put the gun in the canoe, or a fishing line, or anything to eat. We was in ruther too much of a sweat to think of so many things. It warn't good judgment to put *everything* on the raft.

If the men went to the island I just expect they found the campfire I built, and watched it all night for Jim to come. Anyways, they stayed away from us, and if my building the fire never fooled them it warn't no fault of mine. I played it as low-down on them as I could.

When the first streak of day began to show we tied up to a towhead in a bend on the Illinois side, and hacked off cottonwood branches with the hatchet, and covered up the raft with them so she looked like there had been a cave-in in the bank there. A towhead is a sand-bar that has cottonwoods on it as thick as harrow teeth.

We had mountains on the Missouri shore and heavy timber on the Illinois side, and the channel was down the Missouri shore at that place, so we warn't afraid of anybody running across us. We laid there all day, and watched the rafts and steamboats spin down the Missouri shore, and up-bound steamboats fight the big river in the middle. I told Jim all about the time I had jabbering with that woman; and Jim said she was a smart one, and if she was to start after us herself *she* wouldn't set down and watch a campfire—no, sir, she'd fetch a dog. Well, I said, why couldn't she tell her husband to fetch a dog? Jim said he bet she did think of it by the time the men was ready to start, and he believed they must 'a' gone uptown to get a dog and so they lost all that time, or else we wouldn't be here on a towhead sixteen or seventeen mile below the village—no, indeedy, we would be in that same town again. So I said I didn't care what was the reason they didn't get us as long as they didn't.

When it was beginning to come on dark we poked our heads out of the cottonwood thicket, and looked up and down and across; nothing in sight; so Jim took up some of the top planks of the raft and built a snug wigwam to get under in blazing weather and rainy, and to keep the things dry. Jim made a floor for the wigwam, and raised it a foot or more above the level of the raft, so now the blankets and all the traps was out of reach of steamboat waves. Right in the middle of the wigwam we made a layer of dirt about five or six inches deep with a frame around it for to hold it to its place; this was to build a fire on in sloppy weather or chilly; the wigwam would keep it from being seen. We made an extra steering oar, too, because one of the others might get broke on a snag or something. We fixed up a short forked stick to hang the old lantern on, because we must always light the lantern whenever we see a steamboat coming downstream, to keep from getting run over; but we wouldn't have to light it for upstream boats unless we see we was in what they call a 'crossing'; for the river was pretty high yet, very low banks being still a little under water; so upbound boats didn't always run the channel, but hunted easy water.

This second night we run between seven and eight hours, with a current that was making over four mile an hour. We catched fish and talked, and we took a swim now and then to keep off sleepiness. It was kind of solemn, drifting down the big, still river, laying on our backs looking up at the stars, and we didn't ever feel like talking loud, and it warn't often that we laughed—only a little kind of a low chuckle.

We had mighty good weather as a general thing, and nothing ever happened to us at all—that night, nor the next, nor the next.

Every night we passed towns, some of them away up on black hill-sides nothing but just a shiny bed of lights; not a house could you see. The fifth night we passed St Louis, and it was like the whole world lit up. In St Petersburg they used to say there was twenty or thirty thousand people in St Louis, but I never believed it till I see that wonderful spread of lights at two o'clock that still night. There warn't a sound there; everybody was asleep.

Every night now I used to slip ashore toward ten o'clock at some little village, and buy ten or fifteen cents' worth of meal or bacon or other stuff to eat; and sometimes I lifted a chicken that warn't roosting comfortable, and took him along. Pap always said take a chicken when you get a chance, because if you don't want him yourself you can easy find somebody that does, and a good deed ain't ever forgot. I never see Pap when he didn't want the chicken himself, but that is what he used to say, anyway.

Mornings before daylight I slipped into cornfields and borrowed a watermelon, or a mushmelon, or a punkin, or some new corn, or things of that kind. Pap always said it warn't no harm to borrow things if you was meaning to pay them back sometime; but the widow said it warn't anything but a soft name for stealing, and no decent body would do it. Jim said he reckoned the widow was partly right and Pap was partly right; so the best way would be for us to pick out two or three things from the list and say we wouldn't borrow them any more—then he reckoned it wouldn't be no harm to borrow the others. So we talked it over all one night, drifting along down the river, trying to make up our minds whether to drop the water-melons, or the cantaloups, or the musk-melons, or what. But toward daylight we got it all settled satisfactory, and concluded to drop crab-apples and p'simmons. We warn't feeling just right before that, but it was all comfortable now. I was glad the way it come out, too, because crab-apples ain't ever good and the p'simmons wouldn't be ripe for two or three months yet.

We shot a waterfowl now and then that got up too early in the morning or didn't go to bed early enough in the evening. Take it all round, we lived pretty high.

The fifth night below St Louis we had a big storm after midnight, with a power of thunder and lightning, and the rain poured down in a solid sheet. We stayed in the wigwam and let the raft take care of itself. When the lightning glared out we could see a big straight river ahead, and high, rocky bluffs on both sides. By and by says I, 'Hel-*lo*, Jim, looky yonder!' It was a steamboat that had killed herself on a rock. We was drifting straight down for her. The lightning showed her very distinct. She was leaning over, with part of her upper deck above water, and you could see every little chimbly guy clean and clear, and a chair by the big bell, with an old slouch hat hanging on the back of it, when the flashes come.

Well, it being away in the night and stormy, and all so mysterious-like, I felt just the way any other boy would 'a' felt when I seen that wreck laying there so mournful and lonesome in the middle of the river. I wanted to get aboard of her and slink around a little, and see what there was there. So I says:

'Le's land on her, Jim.'

But Jim was dead against it at first. He says:

'I doan' want to go fool'n' 'long er no wrack. We's doin' blame' well, en we better let blame' well alone, as de good book says. Like as not dey's a watchman on dat wrack.'

'Watchman your grandmother,' I says; 'there ain't nothing to watch but the texas and the pilothouse; and do you reckon anybody's going to resk his life for a texas and a pilothouse such a night as this, when it's likely to break up and wash off down the river any minute?' Jim couldn't say nothing to that, so he didn't try. 'And besides,' I says, 'we might borrow something worth having out of the captain's stateroom. See-gars, *I* bet you—and cost five cents apiece, solid cash. Steamboat captains is always rich, and get sixty dollars a month, and *they* don't care a cent what a thing costs, you know, long as they want it. Stick a candle in your pocket; I can't rest, Jim, till we give her a rummaging. Do you reckon Tom Sawyer would ever go by this thing? Not for pie, he wouldn't. He'd call it an adventure—that's what he'd call it; and he'd land on that wreck if it was his last act. And wouldn't he throw style into it?—wouldn't he spread himself, nor nothing? Why, you'd think it was Christopher C'lumbus discovering Kingdom Come. I wish Tom Sawyer *was* here.'

Jim he grumbled a little, but give in. He said we mustn't talk any more than we could help, and then talk mighty low. The lightning showed us the wreck again just in time, and we fetched the starboard derrick, and made fast there.

The deck was high out here. We went sneaking down the slope of it to labboard, in the dark, towards the texas, feeling our way slow with our feet, and spreading our hands out to fend off the guys, for it was so dark we couldn't see no sign of them. Pretty soon we struck the forward end of the skylight, and clumb on to it; and the next step fetched us in front of the captain's door, which was open, and by Jimminy, away down through the texas hall we see a light! and all in the same second we seem to hear low voices in yonder!

Jim whispered and said he was feeling powerful sick, and told me to come along. I says, all right, and was going to start for the raft; but just then I heard a voice wail out and say:

'Oh, please don't, boys; I swear I won't ever tell!'

Another voice said, pretty loud:

'It's a lie, Jim Turner. You've acted this way before. You always want more'n your share of the truck, and you've always got it, too, because you've swore 't if you didn't you'd tell. But this time you've said it jest one time too many. You're the meanest, treacherousest hound in this country.'

By this time Jim was gone for the raft. I was just a-biling with curiosity; and I says to myself, Tom Sawyer wouldn't back out now, and so I won't either; I'm a-going to see what's going on here. So I dropped on my hands and knees in the little passage, and crept aft in the dark till there warn't but one stateroom betwixt me and the cross hall of the texas. Then in there I see a man stretched on the floor and tied hand and foot, and two men standing over him, and one of them had a dim lantern in his hand, and the other one had a pistol. This one kept pointing the pistol at the man's head on the floor, and saying:

'I'd *like* to! And I orter, too—a mean skunk!'

The man on the floor would shrivel up and say, 'Oh, please don't, Bill; I hain't ever goin' to tell.'

And every time he said that the man with the lantern would laugh and say:

''Deed you *ain't!* You never said no truer thing 'n that, you bet you.' And once he said: 'Hear him beg! and yit if we hadn't got the best of

'In there I see a man stretched on the floor tied, hand and foot, and two men standing over him.'

him and tied him he'd 'a' killed us both. And what *for?* Jist for noth'n'. Jist because we stood on our *rights*—that's what for. But I lay you ain't a-goin' to threaten nobody any more, Jim Turner. Put *up* that pistol, Bill.'

Bill says:

'I don't want to, Jake Packard. I'm for killin' him—and didn't he kill old Hatfield jist the same way—and don't he deserve it?'

'But I don't *want* him killed, and I've got my reasons for it.'

'Bless yo' heart for them words, Jake Packard! I'll never forgit you long's I live!' says the man on the floor, sort of blubbering.

Packard didn't take no notice of that, but hung up his lantern on a nail and started toward where I was, there in the dark, and motioned Bill to come. I crawfished as fast as I could about two yards, but the boat slanted so that I couldn't make very good time; so to keep from getting run over and catched I crawled into a stateroom on the upper side. The man came a-pawing along in the dark, and when Packard got to my stateroom, he says:

'Here—come in here.'

And in he come, and Bill after him. But before they got in I was up in the upper berth, cornered, and sorry I come. Then they stood there, with their hands on the ledge of the berth, and talked. I couldn't see them, but I could tell where they was by the whisky they'd been having. I was glad I didn't drink whisky; but it would't made much difference anyway, because most of the time they couldn't 'a' treed me because I didn't breathe. I was too scared. And, besides, a body *couldn't* breathe and hear such talk. They talked low and earnest. Bill wanted to kill Turner. He says:

'He's said he'll tell, and he will. If we was to give both our shares to him *now* it wouldn't make no difference after the row and the way we've served him. Shore's you're born, he'll turn state's evidence; now you hear *me*. I'm for putting him out of his troubles.'

'So'm I,' says Packard, very quiet.

'Blame it, I'd sorter begun to think you wasn't. Well, then, that's all right. Le's go and do it.'

'Hold on a minute; I hain't had my say yit. You listen to me. Shooting's good, but there's quieter ways if the things *got* to be done. But what *I* say is this: it ain't good sense to go court'n' around after a halter if you can git at what you're up to in some way that's jist as good and at the same time don't bring you into no resks. Ain't that so?'

'You bet it is. But how you goin' to manage it this time?'

'Well, my idea is this: we'll rustle around and gather up whatever pickin's we've overlooked in the staterooms, and shove for shore and hide the truck. Then we'll wait. Now I say it ain't a-goin' to be more'n two hours befo' this wrack breaks up and washes off down the river. See? He'll be drownded, and won't have nobody to blame for it but his own self. I reckon that's a considerable sight better 'n killin' of him. I'm unfavourable to killin'a man as long as you can git aroun' it; it ain't good sense, it ain't good morals. Ain't I right?'

'Yes, I reck'n you are. But s'pose she *don't* break up and wash off?'

'Well, we can wait the two hours anyway and see, can't we?'

'All right, then; come along.'

So they started, and I lit out, all in a cold sweat, and scrambled forward. It was dark as pitch there; but I said, in a kind of a coarse whisper, 'Jim!' and he answered up, right at my elbow, with a sort of a moan, and I says:

'Quick, Jim, it ain't no time for fooling around and moaning; there's a gang of murderers in yonder, and if we don't hunt up their boat and set her drifting down the river so these fellows can't get away from the wreck there's one of 'em going to be in a bad fix. But if we find their boat we can put *all* of 'em in a bad fix—for the sheriff'll get 'em. Quick—hurry! I'll hunt the labboard side, you hunt the stabboard. You start at the raft, and——'

'Oh, my lordy, lordy! *Raf'?* Dey ain' no raf' no mo'; she done broke loose en gone!—en here we is!'

Well, I catched my breath and 'most fainted. Shut up on a wreck with such a gang as that! But it warn't no time to be sentimentering. We'd *got* to find that boat now—had to have it for ourselves. So we went a-quaking and shaking down the stabboard side, and slow work it was, too—seemed a week before we got to the stern. No sign of a boat. Jim said he didn't believe he could go any farther—so scared he hadn't hardly any strength left, he said. But I said, come on, if we get left on this wreck we are in a fix, sure. So on we prowled again. We struck for the stern of the texas, and found it, and then scrabbled along forwards on the skylight, hanging on from shutter to shutter, for the edge of the skylight was in the water. When we got pretty close to the cross-hall door there was the skiff, sure enough! I could just barely see her. I felt ever so thankful. In another second I would 'a' been aboard of her, but just then the door opened. One of the men stuck his head out only about a couple of foot from me, and I thought I was gone; but he jerked it in again, and says:

'Heave that blame lantern out o' sight, Bill!'

He flung a bag of something into the boat, and then got in himself and set down. It was Packard. Then Bill *he* come out and got in. Packard says, in a low voice:

'All ready—shove off!'

I couldn't hardly hang on to the shutters, I was so weak. But Bill says:

'Hold on—'d you go through him?'

'No. Didn't you?'

'No. So he's got his share o' the cash yet.'

'Well, then, come along; no use to take truck and leave money.'

'Say, won't he suspicion what we're up to?'

'Maybe he won't. But we got to have it anyway. Come along.'

So they got out and went in.

The door slammed to because it was on the careened side; and in a half second I was in the boat, and Jim come tumbling after me. I out with my knife and cut the rope, and away we went!

We didn't touch an oar, and we didn't speak nor whisper, nor hardly even breathe. We went gliding swift along, dead silent, past the tip of the paddlebox, and past the sterm; then in a second or two more we was a hundred yards below the wreck, and the darkness soaked her up, every last sign of her, and we was safe, and knowed it.

When we was three or four hundred yards downstream we see the lantern show like a little spark at the texas door for a second, and we knowed by that that the rascals had missed their boat, and was beginning to understand that they was in just as much trouble now as Jim Turner was.

Then Jim manned the oars, and we took out after our raft. Now was the first time that I begun to worry about the men—I reckon I hadn't had time to before. I begun to think how dreadful it was, even for murderers, to be in such a fix. I says to myself, there ain't no telling but I might come to be a murderer myself yet, and then how would I like it? So says I to Jim:

'The first light we see we'll land a hundred yards below it or above it, in a place where it's a good hiding place for you and the skiff, and then I'll go and fix up some kind of a yarn, and get somebody to go for that gang and get them out of their scrape, so they can be hung when their time comes.'

Acknowledgements

The Publishers would like to thank the following authors, publishers and others for kindly granting them permission to reproduce the copyrighted extracts and stories included in this anthology.

JOURNEY TO DRUID'S BOTTOM from *Carrie's War* by Nina Bawden. © copyright 1973 Nina Bawden. Reprinted by permission of Victor Gollancz Ltd.

THE FIRST LADY OF FLYING from *Air adventures* by Graeme Cook. Reprinted by permission of Macdonald and Jane's Publishers Ltd.

THE COMPUTER SUSPECTS from *The Computer Nut* by Betsy Byars. © copyright 1984 Betsy Byars. Reprinted by permission of The Bodley Head.

HARRIET'S HAIRLOOM from *A Small Pinch of Weather* by Joan Aiken. Reprinted by permission of Jonathan Cape Ltd.

THE TAMING OF PERCY from *Three Singles to Adventure* by Gerald Durrell. Reprinted by permission of Granada Publishing Ltd.

MIRACLE NEEDED from *The Hundred and One Dalmatians* by Dodie Smith. Reprinted by permission of William Heinemann Ltd.

THE ESCAPE OF PRINCESS CLEMENTINA from *A Book of Escapes and Hurried Journeys* by John Buchan. Reprinted by permission of Thomas Nelson & Sons Ltd.

HIS FIRST FLIGHT from *The Short Stories of Liam O'Flaherty*. Reprinted by permission of Jonathan Cape Ltd.

THE MAN WHO COULD WORK MIRACLES from *The Short Stories of H.G. Wells*. Reprinted by permission of The Estate of the late H.G. Wells.

ARRIETTY'S FIRST ENCOUNTER from *The Borrowers* by Mary Norton. Reprinted by permission of J.M. Dent & Sons Ltd.

Every effort has been made to clear copyrights and the publishers trust that their apologies will be accepted for any errors or omissions.